Met Her on the Mountain

ALSO BY MARK I. PINSKY

The Gospel According to the Simpsons:
  The Spiritual Life of the World's Most Animated Family

The Gospel According to Disney: Faith, Trust, and Pixie Dust

A Jew among the Evangelicals: A Guide for the Perplexed

Amazing Gifts: Stories of Faith, Disability, and Inclusion

Mark I. Pinsky

Met
Her
on the
Mountain

A Forty-Year Quest to Solve
the Appalachian Cold-Case
Murder of Nancy Morgan

JOHN F. BLAIR, PUBLISHER *Winston-Salem, North Carolina*

JOHN F. BLAIR,
PUBLISHER
1406 Plaza Drive
Winston-Salem, North Carolina 27103
www.blairpub.com

By agreement, some names and identifying details in this book
have been changed to protect the privacy of individuals.

Library of Congress Cataloging-in-Publication Data

Pinsky, Mark I., 1947-
  Met her on the mountain : a forty-year quest to solve the Appalachian cold-case murder of Nancy Morgan / by Mark Pinsky.
       pages   cm
  Includes bibliographical references and index.
  ISBN 978-0-89587-611-9 (alk. paper) — ISBN 978-0-89587-612-6 (ebook)
  1. Morgan, Nancy Dean. 2. Volunteers in Service to America—Employees. 3. Murder—North Carolina—Madison County—Case studies. 4. Murder investigation—Appachian Region—Case studies. 5. Volunteer workers in social service—Crimes against—Appalachian Region—Case studies. I. Title.
  HV6533.N8P56 2013
  364.152'3092—dc23

                          2013013542

10 9 8 7 6 5 4 3 2 1

For Elmer Hall and Joe Huff—
and of course,
for Nancy Dean Morgan

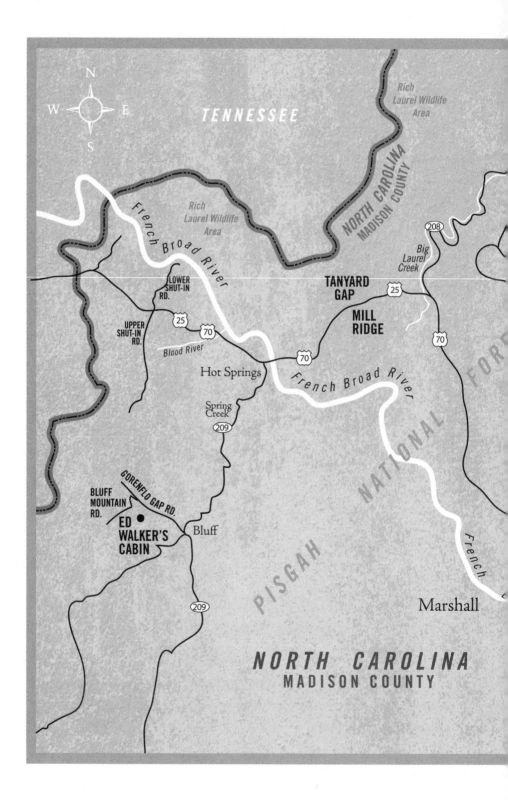

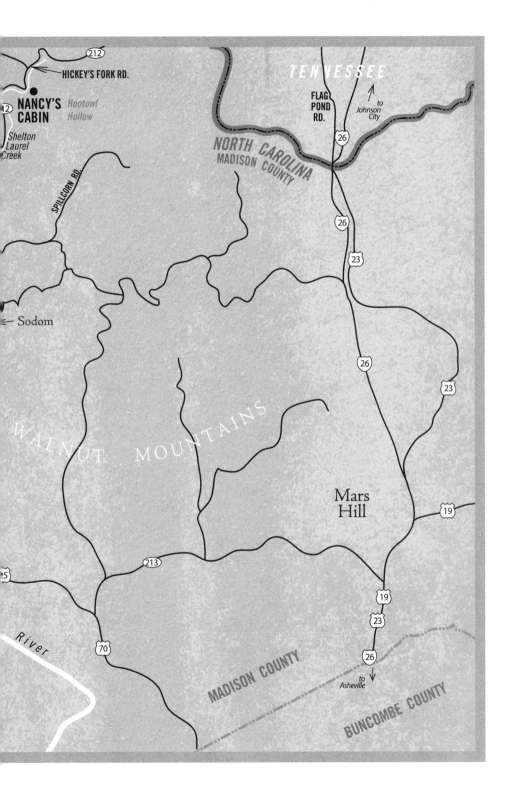

Contents

I met her on the mountain,
There I took her life.

"Tom Dooley," traditional lyrics

Prologue

The first reports of the murder were vague. A young antipoverty worker had been kidnapped, raped, and murdered in the mountains of North Carolina, her body discovered almost within sight of the Appalachian Trail. Although the brutal and sexually charged details were downplayed, they would come out soon enough.

The woman's college yearbook photo, her life and work, and the circumstances of her death were sketched out across the front page of the *Durham Sun* on June 18, 1970. And authorities had no suspects.

I read the article sitting at a pitted wooden desk in an office of the Duke student newspaper, where I had spent—some might say squandered—much of my five years as an undergraduate. Paint peeled in patches on the room's gabled eaves; the desktop veneer was coming loose at the corners. Across from the desk sat a worn red sofa where exhausted staffers found sleep—or solace.

Much of my writing for the *Chronicle*, including a column called "The Readable Radical," was typical of the time—alternately blazing with justified indignation and self-righteous moralizing. I was a Jew from the Jersey suburbs, swept up in the era's unfolding history. Duke was the place my political life formed in the late 1960s, when, like many others of my generation, I marched, demonstrated, made speeches on the quad, and drove to anti–Vietnam War protests in Washington, where I once got arrested. Since finishing my classwork the previous January, I had vague thoughts of a future journalism career of some kind.

By mid-June, the campus was finally quiet after days of rancorous upheaval. Protests in the wake of the National Guard killings of students at Kent State University, the invasion of Cambodia six weeks earlier, and the shooting of African-American students at Jackson State University in Mississippi had ended the school year. With classes and exams canceled and the semester abruptly over, most of the students trickled home.

I learned from the *Durham Sun* that the murder victim was Nancy Dean Morgan, just twenty-four, a recent graduate of Southern Illinois University at Edwardsville, where she had majored in social welfare. A community organizer for the Volunteers in Service to America, she worked with children and helped set up a thrift shop that sold used clothing. Her service was to have lasted only a few more weeks, as she had planned to attend nursing school in New York in the fall. She'd be back, she had promised her friends—back with even more skills, to help and maybe to stay.

She had lived, though briefly, and died in Madison County, in the western mountains of the state. Madison was widely known by travelers for its beauty and less widely by historians for its Civil War violence.

I took Nancy Morgan's death personally, feeling a palpable kinship. In "Ohio," Neil Young's song about the Kent State killings, Crosby, Stills, Nash & Young asked what each of us would have done had we found one of the shooting victims. I didn't know Nancy, and I didn't find her in that mountain glade, but I remember feeling as though I had. Politics and idealism ignited both of us. A gifted generational avatar shaped and transformed by the civil-rights and antiwar movements, feminism, and the fight against poverty, she had been drawn by, and killed in, my adopted state. I had friends serving elsewhere in VISTA, so maybe my connection to the killing was a throwback to the old Wobblies slogan, "An injury to one is an injury to all."

I reached across the desk, picked up a metal ruler, and used its edge to tear out the article. Grabbing a manila folder, I marked it "Morgan" and dropped the clipping into it. I wasn't sure what I would do with the file, but I held on to it.

That file grew—and reproduced—for more than forty years. When I had a spare weekend, I often visited friends in Madison County. I spent days in the library and the government records offices. I sought out anyone who might have known Nancy or who lived in the county at the time. I asked questions that many people did not want to hear. What unfolded was a tangled tale of rural noir.

But it wasn't all work. I hiked the county's trails and mountaintop "balds" and rafted the French Broad River. I stayed in the historic inns, ate the food, listened to the bluegrass and traditional musicians, even entered a turkey shoot, and just watched the stars come out at night.

And I learned to work as a journalist—a true-crime journalist. I covered the case of Joan (pronounced Jo-Ann) Little, a young black woman accused of murdering her white jailer in a small eastern North Carolina town. Supposedly, she had lured him into her cell with a promise of sex. Eventually, a racially integrated jury acquitted Little in less than ninety minutes. That led to other stories, none quite so dramatic, though many of them raised similar issues of race, class, and gender.

During the years that followed, I bounced around the Southeast from courthouse to courthouse, often reporting on capital cases, spending more time in courtrooms than most lawyers. My specialty was investigating and writing about criminal cases that evolved into political causes. Many of the defendants became better known by city and number than by name: the Wilmington Ten, the Charlotte Three, and, in Georgia, the Dawson Five. These were crimes of a sort often called "Southern justice," an ironic, jaundiced shorthand for lingering racial injustice and the political outrage the trials provoked. In a larger sense, my focus was on *justice*, or the lack of it, across the spectrum— racial, economic, political, and criminal. Sometimes, my reporting was credited with helping derail defendants on the fast track to death row.

However, as my proficiency in investigative and courtroom reporting skills developed, my subjects shifted from defendants who were poor, black, and often innocent to those who were more likely to be middle class, white, and guilty. In the spring of 1979, I found myself covering two sensational murder cases. The first involved cross-country serial killer Ted Bundy and the second Jeffrey MacDonald, the Green Beret doctor accused of murdering his wife and two young daughters at their Fort Bragg home. I had the disconcerting experience of conducting the first exclusive, face-to-face interview with Bundy since he was arrested for killing a twelve-year-old and two Florida State University sorority sisters.

One case had a personal connection. Beginning in November 1979, I reported on the Greensboro, North Carolina, shooting, funerals, and (the following year) trials growing out of a clash of antiracist communists versus Nazis and Klansmen from the mountains of western North Carolina. It was a clear breach of journalistic objectivity and detachment, since some of the five dead leftists and others gravely wounded in the shooting were friends and classmates from Duke.

In the process of all this freelance reporting, I got an ad hoc legal education. I learned how to sit for tedious hours reading through depositions and autopsy reports. I learned how to interview family members for overlooked details and how to examine crime scenes long after the yellow tape came down. At one point, I took a week-long course in blood-spatter and death-scene analysis with homicide detectives and coroner's investigators. The quest was always for the one piece of scientific evidence that might set an innocent person free.

Still, I always knew that nothing beat face-to-face interviews, even when, or maybe especially when, they were with individuals I'd never want to socialize with, in places I'd never take my family.

True-crime and thriller writers tend to make dogged detectives—sworn officers and private investigators—their heroes, or at least their protagonists. But that's not how I began as a reporter, nor is it how I've ended up as a writer.

Often—but less frequently—journalists, too, solve murders in mystery novels, in movies, and on television. Yet as reporters who have covered cops and courts for any length of time will tell you, apart from DNA-related exonerations like those documented by Project Innocence, it rarely happens in real life.

Fiction and *CSI*-type shows notwithstanding, murders typically get solved when a guilt-stricken family member confesses or slips up before the lawyer arrives, or when someone snitches while trying to cut a deal. Police usually catch a murderer within forty-eight hours or not at all. The defendant makes a plea bargain or is convicted by a jury in a few hours, in a trial that lasts less than a week. A precious few cold cases are resolved with deathbed revelations that only family members may hear.

Glamour is as scarce as drama, unless the victim or the accused is an attractive young white woman and the case becomes a cable-television sensation. Most killers are stupid, banal, closely linked to their victims, and obviously guilty. Unlike on the screen or page, few in real life are masterminds. And they are rarely handsome, beautiful, or charming (Bundy and MacDonald being exceptions). Reporters rarely play a part in the process.

Eventually, my professional focus took an unlikely turn from crime to religion (and a better class of felon, I used to joke) and from North Carolina to California and then Florida. But murder was always in the background. Nancy Morgan's murder. My files and clippings grew exponentially in the 1990s when my editors at the *Los Angeles Times* dragged me back to courts and cops—the crime beat.

And when in the upheaval of twenty-first-century journalism I found myself unemployed, I returned to Madison County to finally figure out who killed Nancy Morgan, and why.

Part One
The Murder

1

At age twenty-four, federal antipoverty worker Nancy Dean Morgan was nearing the end of a one-year stint with Volunteers in Service to America—VISTA. Some of the people she worked with found her plain, others pretty. She had lively brown eyes, reddish brown hair, and a faint band of freckles running from cheek to cheek across the bridge of her nose. All who knew her agreed she had a quick, infectious smile, a love of puns, and an effervescent laugh.

On Friday, June 12, 1970, Nancy threw on jeans and a white button-down shirt, headed out of her two-bedroom, hundred-year-old cabin in the community of Shelton Laurel in Madison County, North Carolina, and hopped into her silver-gray 1965 Plymouth. The words stenciled on the door—"Government Service Administration—Interagency Motor Pool"—advertised her role in the county. She wheeled the four-door Belvedere out the gravel driveway and past Cutshall's Grocery, turning onto Highway 208, with its canopy of tall, leafy trees and its knee-high grass on the shoulder.

The season had turned everything a vibrant green, speckled with buds and blossoms, pink quinces and yellow forsythias. On her left rushed the Laurel River. Together with the rugged mountains, it was fast-flowing streams and the roadways along them that defined Madison County.

Everywhere in this terrain, cold drops trickled from high rockfaces, timelessly cut by nature or blasted by men for switchback roads. They collected in creases large and small, forming waterways that birthed the homes and settlements below. Wooden shacks, cabins, and white-painted churches—some just feet from the pavement or accessible only by rickety cross-creek bridges or narrow foot logs—lined the twisting country byways. Along the more robust tributaries, farmhouses and barns perched on stilts and pilings to allow them to survive when the water overflowed its banks. Footpaths, gravel and packed-earth roads, and two-lane blacktops intersected many of these veins of tumbling water.

In the towns and along the main thoroughfares, brown and gray fieldstone buildings—schools, stores, even motels—were mortared together like small forts and blockhouses, giving Madison County a feeling of substance and history. Along and above the waterways stood signs of transience—the ruins of missions and clinics built by outsiders who came to help the Appalachian people, gave up, and left. To Nancy Morgan, they might have seemed cautionary reminders of the limits of good intentions.

Hard by the Tennessee border, the county was five hundred square miles of ear-popping drives and breathtaking views. Distant vistas of ridges and ranges, of forested peaks carpeted with laurel thickets, conjured up the fog-shrouded swells of an inland ocean. Closer, in spring and summer, the rich green mountainsides looked like vegetable bins packed tight with ripe broccoli tops. In fall and winter, the slopes turned into patchwork quilts of brown, yellow, red, and faded green.

Madison County was a land with its own soundtrack, performed by traditional musicians and singers. Nearly every crossroads was a fiddlers'—or, as likely, a banjo and guitar pickers'—grove. Wherever two or three gathered—under a tree at a school-board picnic, in a judge's chambers—mountain music was often heard. The songs were about the pain and hardships of life, about deadly encounters along the creeks, the coves, and the narrow valleys called hollows or "hollers." Madison County was, wrote Bascom Lamar Lunsford, the county's balladeer bard, "the last stand of the natural people," where music provided the chords that bound tradition.

For many years, the French Broad River and the road and rail line that grew up along its banks served collectively as the main artery through Madison, tracing the trails of early Cherokee warriors. Unfortunately for residents in earlier decades, the county's waterways—despite their loveliness—were neither commercially navigable nor sufficient to generate electrical power for industry. The countless tributaries and creeks, stony and mostly unpolluted, were shallow and prone to flooding. When too much rain fell, the rivers turned from clear blue to brown and roiling white, covering boulders and in places creeping up the steep rock walls. One nineteenth-century writer marveled at the "wild beauty of the gorge ... fringed with ferns and mosses" and towering walnut and chestnut trees, some nearly a dozen feet in diameter.

Some newcomers to Madison County felt claustrophobic when driving the mountain crests in the azure haze that old-timers called "bluejon." Then, suddenly, the mist would give way to sunny valleys, especially along the French Broad, which meandered across Madison County like an undulating tattoo.

The very names of the crossroads communities reflected their origins and hard times: Spillcorn, Upper and Lower Shut-In, Blood River,

Sodom, Faust, Devil's Fork Gap, Troublesome Gap.

Nancy Morgan's first stop that Friday morning was Marshall, the county seat, a town hemmed in by the French Broad and steep mountainsides. Marshall was once described in "Ripley's Believe It or Not" as "a block wide, a mile long, sky high, and hell deep." The movie-set town had been quietly dying since a highway bypass and a new interstate had routed traffic away from the county. As a result, Marshall's early-twentieth-century ambience was preserved in amber.

Nancy's first order of business was to have her hair done, reviving her medium-length bouffant.

Her favorite stop, however, was next door at Penland and Son Grocery and General Store. The worn tongue-and-groove floor there creaked as customers walked down the center aisle, over the dark rectangle at the center with the name of the store's founder, and between rows of wicker baskets full of produce flanking the doorway. The rack behind the checkout counter featured jars of homemade jam, honey, preserves, and pickled fruits and vegetables. Display tables, racks, and shelves along the walls were stacked with blue jeans, underwear, overalls, flannel shirts, boots, guns, hats, sport coats, and jackets. Sitting on his stool by the vintage cash register, proprietor George Penland liked to tell visitors about the 1950s, when customers jammed the place every day. The storekeeper with the full head of ink-black, slicked-back hair recalled how he had to push and shove to wait on them. Out front, Marshall bustled with crowds so thick "you couldn't walk down the sidewalk without getting knocked off the curb, there'd be so many people walking, coming and going."

That day, Nancy was looking for old-fashioned bib overalls for her upcoming vacation, and she asked clerk Clarine Rector for help. "I went in the dressing room with her, and she got her a red bandana and put it in her pocket," said Rector, who remembered her as "a jolly little thing. She was real excited about her overalls."

Back in Shelton Laurel later that day, Nancy made her customary stop at Cutshall's Grocery, owned by Glendora and Clarence Cutshall, who were also her landlords. The thriving store sold hunting and fishing licenses as well as food, packaged and prepared. It was also an informal community center, which enabled Nancy to make invaluable organizing contacts, thanks to her association with the Cutshalls.

The previous autumn, Clarence and Glendora had taken Nancy and her VISTA roommate, Diana Buzzard, under their wing like surrogate parents. They drove the two women to Asheville several times—a ride of about forty-five minutes—to go bowling and for a Loretta Lynn concert. They also took the VISTAs on trips to mountain tourist attractions like Frontier Land and Ghost Town in the Sky. Glendora felt especially close to Nancy, probably because the younger woman was such an extrovert. "She never knew a stranger," Glendora often said. Nancy "was always friendly to anyone, and had confidence even in strangers." Still, Glendora was troubled that Nancy insisted on driving people home from evening meetings, regardless of how remote their houses were. Many friends and family members worried that she was the kind of person likely to pick up hitchhikers. "I often asked her whether she wasn't afraid driving around so much, late at night," Glendora said, but Nancy just brushed aside the older woman's concern.

That Friday evening at the store, Nancy ran into her friend Ruth Hensley, a German native married to a local serviceman. When they first met, the two women had bonded almost immediately. Nancy was an air force brat and had once lived in Germany, where Ruth's husband was then stationed. Although Ruth was several years older than Nancy, married with two young sons, both were Madison County outsiders living on their own. According to mountain culture, young women without men at home were considered implicit threats to local wives. This was particularly true of Nancy, given her habit of joking with men of all ages. But Ruth was impressed with Nancy's sensitivity. Nancy recognized the poverty of those around her but never put herself above them. She recruited Ruth as a chaperone for many of the outings she organized for local children.

At the store, Ruth mentioned that she had received orders to report with her children to South Carolina so they could join her husband in Germany. The bus to Charleston was leaving Marshall early Sunday morning.

Nancy reacted instinctively: "Ruth, I'm going to take you to the bus." To save time, Nancy invited the Hensleys to dinner and to stay over Saturday night.

"I sure do appreciate that," Ruth said.

Nancy returned to Marshall around noon on Saturday just as an acquaintance, Harold Reed, was quitting work at French Broad Chevrolet, where the VISTA cars were serviced. He later remembered that, at a red light, Nancy "asked me about my back, which I had hurt."

Nancy picked up a county van, collected some young people, and headed to the town of Mars Hill. At the pool on the campus of Mars Hill College, she ran into Ed Walker, another VISTA worker, who had brought a group of young people from the Spring Creek community, where he was based. The volunteers decided that the next day, Walker would buy a watermelon and invite some kids over to his house. "I said to Nancy, 'Why don't you come over on Sunday evening if you're not doing anything? Just come by in the afternoon and stay.'" The two wanted to talk about their respective VISTA projects because of Nancy's imminent departure for nursing school in New York. "It was very casual. If she showed, fine. If she hadn't showed up, it wouldn't have been a big deal."

On Saturday night at her cabin, Nancy cooked the Hensleys dinner, including a homemade lemon meringue pie. Afterward, the small group had plenty of room to spread out, because Nancy's roommate had left three months earlier. Nancy asked for photos of Ruth and the kids.

The two women stayed up late and rose early the next morning. To Ruth, Nancy seemed restless. After breakfast, they swung by Glendora's to say goodbye before driving to Marshall, where Nancy insisted on waiting until the bus stopped at the Rock Café, next to the courthouse.

Then she picked up a package in town and headed home. Returning to the cabin, she showered, called her parents, and strolled over to Cutshall's store to chat with Glendora and some of the customers. As she often did, Nancy did her ironing in the store, pressing a pair of maroon cutoff shorts and a ribbed blue top. She told the storekeeper she planned to have dinner that evening with Ed Walker in the Bluff community. It was only about ten miles away, but almost an hour's drive on winding mountain roads. "She kept on ironing, and we told her she ought not to be out at night by herself," Glendora recalled, "that someone might harm her in some way."

"Who would harm me?" Nancy asked. "Nobody would harm me."

As she left the store around one-thirty that afternoon, Nancy grabbed a sweatshirt and told her friends she was going to stop first in the neighboring community of Sodom to see Myrtle Ray, another Madison County VISTA worker, a native of the area. She needed to drop off some notes she had transcribed from a recent meeting and had to pick up a skillet, two umbrellas, and a book she had left.

By four-thirty, she was again driving along the Laurel River, then along Spring Creek to Bluff. Nancy arrived at Walker's house before dark, around five-thirty. His was also a hundred-year-old cabin, its logs concealed behind white clapboard siding. It had four rooms, a sleeping loft, and no telephone. Walker's roommate, a student at Mars Hill College, was away for the weekend. Nancy had visited a number of times, including once when she and another VISTA came with a group of kids to throw Walker a birthday party.

When Nancy arrived, the two strolled the property. Walker showed her the barn, the well, the spring, and the woods. She praised the view. "I showed her the garden. Dempsey Woody's garden was right next to my house, and we picked some lettuce and onions."

Nancy, who took pride in her cooking skills, made an omelet and a side dish of lettuce wilted with bacon grease, but she ate only a few bites. After dinner, two of Walker's neighbor boys stopped by, and the four watched the comedy movie *It's a Mad, Mad, Mad, Mad World* on television. "I remember after the movie, there was the news, and the guys left right after the news or after the movie," Walker recalled.

After that, the two, along with a wandering dog, adjourned to the boxy wooden couch on the porch, lingering on its lumpy cushions for hours. Walker's dog lay nearby. The night was still hot, but they benefited from an evening breeze. They talked shop about the difficulties of community organizing in Madison County. Each had connected in small but significant ways with people in their respective communities, although Nancy had recently run into problems with one local woman. They smoked cigarettes. Walker retrieved Nancy's cream sherry from the refrigerator but refrained from drinking any because he still expected some other kids to visit, and he didn't want them to smell alcohol on his breath. He was always cautious about neighborhood sensibilities. Once when Nancy, her friend Alanna Paulson, and her then-roommate wanted to spend the night at his cabin, he took care to get his landlady's permission.

Over dinner and afterward on the porch, they reflected on their time in that beautiful, hardscrabble place, how it had marked them and helped them grow, how it might influence the rest of their lives. Walker wanted to know what Nancy was going to do after VISTA. She expected to travel a bit, visiting friends, then start nursing school in New York. Her cap and uniform had already arrived, and she had modeled them for her friends. She had promised some of the people she worked with that, after her studies, she would return to Madison County armed with skills that could benefit the area, where poor health care was commonplace.

Her mood was upbeat; she seemed excited over the new turn her life was about to take. "She was happy, everyday normal, not overjoyed, not depressed," Walker recalled. He thought his coworker was glad to be moving forward. She felt as if she had been in limbo, living in Shelton Laurel by herself since her roommate left, not knowing whether her supervisor would allow her to stay there alone.

The two discussed the future of VISTA and what Walker planned to do when he finished his obligation, whether or not Mars Hill College would continue to sponsor the project, and whether or not their supervisor would be rehired.

Walker went inside for another cigarette and noticed how late it was—about three-thirty in the morning. Because the road to his house was steep and narrow, he turned Nancy's car around for her. Walker watched until he was sure she had made it through a small creek that flowed over the road. "It was possible to get stuck or get off at the side," he said. "I remember standing there and watching the headlights go until she got out to the hard road." Once he saw the car lights turn and disappear, he returned to the house and went to bed.

He would never again see her alive.

2

Nancy Morgan had come to VISTA by way of a white, middle-class adolescence in a military family. Born on January 6, 1946, she was the second of three children and the only daughter of Earl and Abigail Morgan, at that time stationed at Barksdale Air Force Base in Louisiana. Earl and Abigail had met when he was a World War II flight instructor and she an air corps nurse at the same San Antonio base.

Like other military brats, Nancy moved with her family from base to base around the country and abroad as her father rose in rank. She spent her middle- and high-school years, from the late 1950s through the early 1960s, in Wiesbaden, West Germany, where her father was director of international law for the United States Air Force in Europe. Nancy's father was assigned some high-level national security cases. CIA officers were sometimes dinner guests.

At school, Nancy found she had a gift for languages, studying enough German to speak it. She was too self-conscious, though, to use it in front of her father, who was fluent in both French and German.

She would bellow at the sight of a spider but scream even louder if her brother George tried to kill it, insisting he catch it and take it outside.

Like most twelve- or thirteen-year-old girls of the time, Nancy experimented with hairstyles and wore bobby socks and saddle shoes. She danced with her girlfriends to Jerry Lee Lewis, Frankie Avalon, Paul Anka, and Elvis Presley. The best known of her fellow high-school students was Priscilla Beaulieu, stepdaughter of another air force officer, who was famously dating Elvis.

In 1962, Colonel Morgan was transferred to Washington, D.C., where he divided his time between the Pentagon, where he had a top-secret security clearance, and Bolling Air Force Base. The family settled in Northern Virginia. Nancy attended Mount Vernon High School in Alexandria, a typical suburban public school of the time—honor code, short hair, loafers, crew-neck sweaters. Students' earnest, serious faces—all white—looking out from the yearbook pages could have come from the 1940s as easily as the 1960s.

One year, Donn Garvey Jr. was in the first and last classes of the day with Nancy. She made an indelible impression on him. "I recall a slim, pretty girl with auburn hair and clear, fair skin," friendly but modest, he recalled. She liked to sit by the door and was "serious but quick to laugh." Both she and Garvey were singled out for special attention by one speech teacher. When Garvey won a regional American Legion speech contest their senior year, Nancy was the only student to congratulate him.

Life in Virginia seemed uncomplicated, at least until President Kennedy's assassination in 1963 and the looming specter of Vietnam. When Kennedy was shot, Nancy and a friend wept while Abigail Morgan tried to comfort them. Later, a group of family members waited in line at the Capitol to view JFK's casket. Nancy was becoming drawn to social issues, her brother George recalled. "She was very interested in the civil-rights movement. She was liberal on the subject of race and thought the civil-rights movement was a great thing." Around that time, she began a spiritual search as well, trying out the Methodist and Presbyterian churches near her home, finally landing with the Unitarians.

After graduating from Mount Vernon High in the spring of 1964, Nancy enrolled at Radford College in the Blue Ridge Mountains of southwestern Virginia, then a state college for women that specialized in turning out teachers. She excelled in German and earned Bs in health, English, and psychology. She dated young men from Virginia Tech and, at home in the D.C. area, air force men. One young lieutenant turned out to have a wife and children. Nancy, in love for the first time, was so upset when the relationship began to dissolve that she dropped out of Radford and worked for a time at a Virginia ski resort.

Soon, she started over. When her father was assigned to Scott Air Force Base in Belleville, Illinois, fifteen miles east of St. Louis, Nancy transferred to a new branch of Southern Illinois University at Edwardsville, in another county named Madison. The student body there was a heterogeneous mix of recently returned Vietnam veterans, antiwar hippies, serious older students, stoners, binge drinkers, urban African-Americans from East St. Louis, rural whites from nearby farms, people from steel-mill and coal-mining towns. She began attending classes in the summer of 1966 and graduated in June 1969, choosing social work as her major. A friend recalled that Nancy "wanted to make the world a better place, but quietly."

No serious upheavals erupted at Southern Illinois–Edwardsville (SIUE) after the 1968 assassination of Martin Luther King Jr., but King's death, like JFK's, deepened Nancy's thinking about race. "She was a big fan of Martin Luther King Jr.," George said, recalling favorable comments his sister made while the family watched television coverage of the civil-rights movement. "She always had a social conscience and wanted to help people," remembered the wife of a professor.

Another faculty member was not surprised she would later join

VISTA, calling her "an idealist and a young lady who was trying to do good in the world."

Still, it was romance that dominated Nancy's personal life. Almost as soon as the family moved to Illinois, she literally met the boy next door, the son of another air force officer and a senior at the Citadel in Charleston, South Carolina. For two weeks, the pair spent nearly every summer evening together. An engagement followed, but no wedding. Around that time, according to George Morgan, his sister began a romance with an SIUE professor many years her senior, a man with a reputation for such relationships. The professor was single and wanted to marry Nancy, yet this relationship, too, ended with Nancy alone and in pain.

After graduation, she seemed to drift. She decided she wanted to go to nursing school, "but probably not for a year and a half," she wrote in a 1968 Christmas card. Living in Washington, D.C., she briefly took clerical jobs at the Kennedy Foundation, the Interior Department, and the American Pharmaceutical Association, searching for something meaningful to do before graduate school.

By September 1969, she decided to make a one-year commitment to VISTA.

Nancy's decision might have been influenced by the recently published novel *Christy*, by Catherine Marshall. When she arrived in the mountains, she brought with her a copy of the book, which was made into a CBS television series in 1994. Set in 1912, *Christy* is the inspirational tale of a young woman who moves to the mountains of East Tennessee to teach children for a year at a Quaker mission school. The fictional heroine, based on Marshall's mother, hears an evangelist's call: "Beyond the great mountains, outstretched hands and beseeching voices cry, 'Come over and help us.' These highlanders are your countrymen, your neighbors. Will you hear and help, or will you leave them to their distress and ignorance?"

Despite her father's misgivings, Christy, only nineteen, takes a train to Tennessee and settles in a house without indoor plumbing or running water. In the mountains, she finds fulfillment, folk music, and ultimately true love. However, in ways foreshadowing Nancy Morgan's experience, she encounters a culture she finds mystifying, a place where murder is not uncommon and often goes unpunished. "In the eyes of the mountaineers, the courts are always unfair, slanted toward one side or another," a local doctor explains to Christy. "It isn't as silly as you think, not when families plot for years to get one of their clan elected a judge, a sheriff or county squire. If the case comes before a jury, the jurors put family loyalty ahead of everything else, too. So do all the witnesses."

On several occasions, the young woman finds herself in situations in which she feels menaced by groups of drunken men. "Looking back," says Christy, "I can see that the young walk unabashedly into many a situation which the more experienced would avoid at all costs."

In October 1969, Nancy Morgan arrived for VISTA training in Atlanta. Later that fall, she was living in Madison County, described by one writer as "probably the least known [and] . . . most misunderstood and interesting of all the counties in North Carolina."

3

Ed Walker was awakened Monday morning much earlier than he wished by his neighbor Johnny Waldroup, but neither he nor anyone knew something was wrong. However, that afternoon, Richard Haimes, who was in charge of the Madison County VISTAs, started to worry that he couldn't reach Nancy. He wanted to let her know that two new tires had arrived for the Plymouth, which was registered in his name. Haimes, a large, affable man with a mustache who lived in the Walnut community, had last seen Nancy the previous Thursday at a staff meeting at his house.

Haimes called Clarence Cutshall at the grocery store on Tuesday morning, trying to locate Nancy, but Clarence hadn't seen her. Fearing something had happened to her, Haimes said he contacted the sheriff's department. Sheriff Roy Roberts would later claim he had not been notified the young woman was missing, so no official search was launched.

By Tuesday, Nancy's friends in the Shelton Laurel and Sodom communities heard she was missing and took action. Their first stop was Haimes's house in Walnut, where the other VISTAs already had gathered. Some of the locals sensed the VISTAs were uneasy with them. For their part, the locals viewed the federal antipoverty workers with amused tolerance, doubting their value in any nighttime search of the county roads. Still, they divided into teams, piled into their cars, and began searching areas where they believed Nancy might have wrecked. They covered and re-covered the route between Cutshall's Grocery and Walker's house in Bluff, paying particular attention to turns and drop-offs along the road, especially around Hot Springs Mountain.

On Tuesday evening, concern turned to alarm. Nancy had been working with some teens in Shelton Laurel and had gotten an old shack cleaned up so they could sell hot dogs to make money for a recreation area. She was expected at a meeting to plan a fundraiser for the project but never showed up. The number of community volunteers in the search grew, a testament to their affection for Nancy. "I wouldn't have gone walking up Hot Springs Mountain at night looking for most people," said Ellen Banks.

On Tuesday, Ed Walker received several phone messages from Richard Haimes, relayed by a neighbor, asking if he knew where Nancy was. Walker's initial thought was that she had been in a car wreck. That night, he joined the search. Walker and two other Madison County VISTAs drove over Hot Springs Mountain and back again, one of the men holding a flashlight out the window, looking for any evidence of Nancy's car. "We were looking for tire tracks primarily, just driving real slowly across the mountain along the edge, looking for any evidence of a car going off the edge," Walker said. The roadway was so steep and narrow that they couldn't pull off or get out of the car and walk.

The combined search of locals and VISTAs lasted until four o'clock Wednesday morning. A few hours later, Haimes phoned the VISTA supervisor for North Carolina, Jeffrey Hammer, to let him know Nancy was missing. In bed at his home in Atlanta when he got the call,

Hammer was concerned, although not overly so. He knew Nancy had plans to leave for a ten-day vacation that would take her around the country to see friends, including an old boyfriend, and to make a speech in West Virginia to idealistic young people like herself about what she had learned in the mountains.

For his part, Haimes also worried that Nancy's government-issued vehicle was missing. He feared she might have had an accident on one of the twisting roads or hairpin switchbacks. Still, Haimes thought it likely she might have been in a last-minute rush and simply left the car parked at the airport.

Hammer decided that Nancy's apparent disappearance was a good opportunity to make a site visit to Madison County. He flew to Asheville later on Wednesday. He didn't go with a sense of panic. Rather, it was an opportunity to be supportive of the project, which seemed to be going well.

As soon as he landed, Hammer searched the airport parking lot for Nancy's car, fully expecting to solve the mystery. When he didn't find it, he rented a car and drove to Haimes's house in Walnut.

≡≡

On Wednesday morning, Jimmy Lewis was driving from his home in Sodom, not far from Shelton Laurel, with a load of empty soda bottles from his family's store. He was going to redeem them in Hot Springs, six miles away, and shoot pool. About nine, halfway down the mountain, he had to pee. Lewis pulled onto an old, unpaved logging road on his right, in an area known as Tanyard Gap, and drove far enough to ensure some privacy. He stumbled around, avoiding the thickets, looking for a level spot.

After accomplishing his task, Lewis noticed something on what was once a wagon trail. In a glade of towering poplar and oak trees, he saw a gray car parked in dappled sunlight. The wheels were sunk to the hubcaps in the moist earth where the vehicle had come to rest after knocking over several saplings. Its doors were closed, and the hood was pointed uphill, to the west. At night, the road sometimes served as a lovers' lane, so Lewis carefully walked up and peered through the closed windows. He saw Nancy Morgan on the backseat, obviously dead.

The musical tradition of young women meeting tragic ends along the creeks and in the hollers runs deep in mountain culture. From "Pretty Polly" to "Matty Groves" to "Down in the Willow Garden," lily-white female bodies lie nestled in the laurel. "I don't know what it is about American folk songs," Pete Seeger once said. "They all end up with the girl getting killed." Yet the hellish scene that morning on Hot Springs Mountain was anything but lyrical. There was no silver dagger this time. Nancy's body was naked, hogtied from behind in a kneeling position.

Lewis was extremely shaken. He didn't recognize the body, though he later recalled he had seen Nancy several times in Marshall. Frantic, he drove to Sheriff Roy Roberts's home, two miles away, but the sheriff wasn't there. He told the sheriff's brother what he had seen. Bert Roberts called his sibling at his office at the jail, but he wasn't there either.

Roy Roberts was finally located in court at Marshall. Told what Jimmy Lewis had found, he bolted the courtroom for the site. Roberts knew the area well—the wooded section on both sides of Highway 25-70 had until recently been the sheriff's own property. Four months earlier, he had sold the two-hundred-acre tract, where he once had a farm, to the United States Forest Service for thirty-five thousand dollars. It was now part of Pisgah National Forest and included a section of the Appalachian Trail. Roberts was certain the location of the body on federal land would complicate the investigation.

News of the grim discovery spread quickly through the county via police scanners and drew a large number of law-enforcement officers. Soon, the crime scene was a case study in confusion and barely controlled jurisdictional chaos. As a member of VISTA, Nancy was considered a federal employee and drove a United States government–owned vehicle. That could have made it a case for the FBI. The area where the car was found was the responsibility of the United States Forest Service, but that agency rarely handled serious crimes. Ordinarily, any murder in the county would be the sheriff's case, though frequently when murders took place, agents of the more highly trained North Carolina State Bureau of Investigation (SBI) were called in.

In small jurisdictions like Madison County, a serious crime can quickly become an occasion for various overlapping law-enforcement agencies to jockey for turf and primacy. Absent clear lines of authority, damage can be done. The greater the number of investigators, the greater the likelihood of a contaminated scene. At stake is credit for solving a newsworthy case, the coin of the realm for law-enforcement personnel, both those who have to run for office and those who have to go to the state legislature or Congress each year for appropriations. The downside to such scrums, as experienced investigators (and even regular viewers of TV courtroom dramas) know, is that a chaotic crime scene is sure to be the centerpiece of a defense attorney's argument to the jury, the preferred constructions being "like a herd of elephants" and "like Keystone Cops."

Charlie Chambers, the resident SBI agent in Asheville, was home on vacation in the nearby town of Enka when his supervisor called from Raleigh and told him to get to Hot Springs as soon as possible. Harold Elliot, the SBI agent in Haywood County, to the southwest, received a similar call at his office in Waynesville and arrived at the scene about the same time as Chambers. Both agents realized that jurisdiction and control of the scene would be a touchy issue, so they deferred to Sheriff Roberts and two FBI agents, although the SBI men's experience with homicide investigations ran much deeper than that of their local and federal colleagues. The state agents stayed discreetly close to the sheriff and the FBI agents and were careful to provide advice only when asked.

"They were receptive," said Elliot, a former FBI fingerprint special-ist, choosing his words diplomatically. "No friction between us and the FBI. We both wanted the same thing—to find the guilty party." For ex-ample, Elliot advised the FBI agents to shorten the chain of custody for any of the evidence they found, to ensure against a defense attorney's effort to discredit it. "You find evidence and secure the site and maintain the security of the evidence."

For much of the morning and afternoon, local, county, state, and federal law-enforcement agents, officers, and deputies milled around the gray car. Investigators at the scene wore short-sleeved, button-down white shirts and knit polos. Some sported straw porkpie hats pushed back on their sweaty brows as they made notes on clipboards, joked and chatted, and smoked cigarettes. The police photographer and the local coroner worked the scene, still carpeted with leaves from the previous fall and winter.

After the first set of crime-scene photos was shot, Nancy's maroon shorts, which covered her face—the crotch had been ripped—were re-moved from her head. Her knees rested on the floor of the backseat. One buttock was on the edge of the seat directly behind the driver. Her body, face up, lay sprawled across the seat on her right side, her head turned at an odd angle against the back cushion. Her pierced earrings were still in place. A watch on her left wrist had stopped at twelve-thirty. The fingers of both hands were curled. She had been tied with multi-strand blue and olive nylon cord and trussed in such a way that, as she tried to free herself or even straighten up, she would have choked. Dr. Page Hudson, the state's highly regarded chief medical examiner, said later, "There was so much tension in that rope that it would have strangled her." A state fish-and-game officer on the scene lent an FBI agent a hawkbill knife to cut the cord.

A road map and two umbrellas sat on the floor nearby, along with a pile of Nancy's clothes, including a bra with a torn strap and one of her sandals. "They didn't take her clothes off," a sheriff's deputy said. "They tore them off." Investigators found a copy of the *Asheville Citizen-Times* on the passenger side of the front seat and a pair of women's sunglasses on the cluttered dashboard. Scattered around the vehicle were a skillet and several books, as well as a bloodstained piece of clothing. Nancy's other white sandal turned up outside the rear passenger door. Some distance away on a carpet of pink and white trillium lay her handbag, containing her identification.

The car's windows were closed and its doors unlocked. The exterior was wet from a recent rain, but the leaves beneath the wheels and chassis were dry. Keys dangled from the ignition. In the trunk was the woman's multicolored jacket, which investigators described in their report as "psychedelic."

The sheriff called Clarence Cutshall at the grocery, and he sped over in his pickup for the sorrowful task of identifying Nancy Morgan. The body was removed from the scene and taken to Memorial Mission Hospital in Asheville for autopsy.

Sheriff Roberts was the distinctly junior partner of the trio leading the investigation at the site. In 1966, he had been prevailed upon by county Republicans to be the sacrificial candidate against the longtime incumbent sheriff. The lingering animosity from a Democratic scandal propelled Roberts—extremely well liked throughout the county, beloved as a Sunday-school teacher, and thought of as a moral man—to a narrow and unexpected victory. "He wasn't interested in sheriffing much," recalled Dedrick Brown, his chief deputy. Instead, Roberts liked to play checkers at the jail. Tall, bald, and lean, he preferred a dress shirt and pants to a uniform, adding a tie and jacket for court appearances. Most of his income came from farming, a pulp operation, and some rental property. He was known for his hobby of de-scenting skunks and for hunting squirrels with a musket, because it seemed more sporting than picking them off with a modern rifle. As the days passed, he would quietly cede his role in the investigation to Dedrick Brown.

One of SBI agent Charlie Chambers's first tasks was crowd control. Although the crime scene was roped off, "you had to have a stick to keep people away," he recalled. County residents who had been involved in the search for the missing woman, as well as a growing number of curiosity seekers, parked their cars and trucks nearby. People gathered along the shoulder, leaning against the vehicles, sitting on hoods and trunks. Shirtless boys, adolescents in T-shirts, women with folded arms, and at least one woman holding a toddler stared at the goings-on. Some of those who would figure prominently as the murder case unfolded—including former Madison County sheriff E. Y. Ponder—chanced on the scene that day.

Hot Springs police chief Leroy Johnson, his troublemaking son, Richard, and one of Richard's buddies had been in court in Marshall, a result of an earlier altercation between the two young men and some VISTAs working in Hot Springs. Leroy Johnson had witnessed Sheriff Roberts running from the courtroom but had thought nothing of it until he saw the collection of law-enforcement vehicles at the crime scene. He pulled in and told Richard and his friend to stay put while he went to find out what had happened.

Ed Walker and his roommate were driving back to Walnut from Bluff, over Hot Springs Mountain. As they rounded a curve, still searching for Nancy, "there's a bunch of cars parked, and of course police cars and a couple of cars I recognize," Walker recalled. He pulled off the road and quickly realized the scene had something to do with Nancy's disappearance. Walker's friend and neighbor Rochelle Parker came over and told him Nancy's car had been found. He and Richard Haimes, the VISTA supervisor, then sat for a while in the bed of Parker's pickup. Walker had his head in his hands, weeping.

Sometime later, the authorities dusted Nancy's Plymouth inside and out for fingerprints, then inspected Walker's trunk and that of another VISTA worker. Haimes and Walker were taken aside for a brief interview. While the antipoverty workers weren't exactly suspects, it is standard procedure in homicide investigations to interview those closest to the deceased, since killers usually know their victims. All of the VISTAs at the scene were fingerprinted.

4

Suspicion of well-intentioned do-gooders originated hundreds of years before the VISTA workers moved into Madison County. More than two centuries earlier, people looked warily at Francis Asbury, the circuit-riding Methodist missionary who traveled on horseback along the French Broad River, toting Christian temperance in one saddlebag and disdain for fiddle music in the other. Generations of proponents of the social gospel followed, from northern Presbyterians to New Dealers, all trying to wean mountain people from violence and the debilitating use of alcohol, while bringing education and raising the standard of living.

Over the years, Protestant and a few Catholic missionaries constructed dozens of small churches throughout western North Carolina. But few of the denominations' larger schemes, from building schools and medical clinics to attracting a railroad through the southern Appalachians—not to mention their attempts to curb alcohol consumption—won enduring victories. "A million Americans in the Southern Appalachians live today in conditions of squalor, ignorance and ill health," wrote Harry Caudill in his 1962 classic, *Night Comes to the Cumberlands: A Biography of a Depressed Area.* "The highlander is a challenge to all Americans everywhere. His sorrowful history has deposited him as a material and spiritual orphan on the nation's doorstep. He will not go away, and, unless he is helped, his situation will not improve. In his mute suffering, he appeals to the mind and conscience of his country."

Secular missionaries followed religious ones during the Great Depression. Franklin Roosevelt's New Dealers set up three Civilian Conservation Corps (CCC) camps in Madison County and shipped in hundreds of young men to work there. Most of them received jobs in Pisgah National Forest, maintaining roads, planting trees, stringing telephone lines, cutting fire trails, and building observation towers. Federally funded Works Progress Administration (WPA) projects employed local men to labor on Madison County roads and public buildings, and an infusion of cash arrived through the new Social Security system. In a local effort, the Farmer's Federation of Western North Carolina organized a cooperative to sell the hooked rugs that mountain women made with fabric scraps and sock tops from area textile mills. The co-op's success, selling even to major retail outlets in New York and Chicago, briefly brought a mild prosperity in tough economic times, just when much of the old-growth timber that had earlier survived the chestnut blight and fueled the county's logging industry had been clearcut or taken by the federal government for new national parks and forests.

Eventually, as the United States' entry into World War II demanded military enlistments, the CCC camps closed and the WPA projects wound down. Ironically, the New Deal's wage and hour regulations, implemented in the early 1940s to protect industrial workers, killed

Madison County's homegrown rug industry. The secular do-gooders achieved as little long-term success as their religious predecessors.

The reason so many missionaries of both sorts failed to leave a lasting imprint "is that they were imported people who came with the idea of sort of looking down their nose at the people," explained Mars Hill College history professor Evelyn Underwood. Mountain people "can smell a superior attitude ten miles away. You won't get anything from them if you come with that attitude."

Natives of Appalachia know that the American public has long embraced a stereotype of their mountain land as a benighted place, home to backward, ignorant, hard-drinking, poor people of dubious morals and fundamentalist faith. Paradoxically, the stereotype has a flipside that can induce its own brand of condescension: the simple, hardworking citizens of Appalachia also carry in their cultural history, if not in their DNA, a love of singing and banjo picking that makes them natural musicians.

Perhaps it is no coincidence that one of the few universally well-received outsiders in western North Carolina was the English folklorist Cecil Sharp, who in 1916 scoured Madison County on horseback, mule, and foot as he collected ballads that had crossed the Atlantic from the British Isles and evolved in mountain isolation. Madison County, the Englishman wrote, was "the richest pocket of culture in America."

In the 1960s, little industry existed in Madison County. The primary legal means of earning a living were subsistence farming, schoolteaching, and other government jobs, which some people supplemented by manufacturing and selling illegal whiskey. Those not on welfare had to commute to jobs in Asheville or Tennessee.

But the 1960s also brought Lyndon Johnson's Great Society and his War on Poverty, with its huge outpouring of public spending. Observing the infusion of cash in Madison County, Mars Hill native Harold Bailey recalled "Showers of Blessings," an old hymn sung in Baptist churches. At the time, Bailey recalled, "Madison County wasn't getting showers. They were getting downpours of federal money, the likes of which they'd never beheld before."

A central part of the War on Poverty was the federally funded Office of Economic Opportunity. The OEO, in turn, brought VISTA to Madison County—and to a reception of legendary Appalachian hospitality, along with equally legendary mistrust.

＝＝

In his 1963 State of the Union address, President John F. Kennedy, who had been deeply affected by what he saw during his 1960 West Virginia primary campaign, suggested a national service program "to help provide urgently needed services in urban and rural poverty areas."

Although the idea found no traction in Congress before JFK's assassination, Lyndon Johnson incorporated the concept into his 1964 War on Poverty legislation. LBJ held a White House reception for the first twenty VISTA workers, telling them their mission would be "to guide the young, to comfort the sick, to encourage the downtrodden, to teach the skills which may lead to a more satisfying and rewarding life." He warned them that their pay would be low and their working conditions often difficult. "But you will have the satisfaction of leading a great national effort, and you will have the ultimate reward which comes to those who serve their fellow man."

As soon as that first group completed a six-week training course, its members marched off to assignments aiding migrant workers in California, the urban poor in Connecticut, and Appalachian communities in eastern Kentucky. By the end of 1966, the number of VISTAs reached thirty-six hundred. Those idealistic young people were instrumental in implementing programs such as Head Start and the Job Corps, as well as independent community projects. Although VISTA was dubbed "the domestic Peace Corps," VISTAs served for only a year, rather than the two-year Peace Corps terms. They earned a stipend of just fifty dollars a month, plus expenses and educational benefits, but that only after completing their service. Many VISTAs, joining in the middle and late 1960s, when students' political consciousness had begun to shift to the left, considered themselves more activist and radical, and their projects grittier, than those of the starry-eyed Peace Corps liberals. The program's best-known participant was Jay Rockefeller, a scion of one of America's wealthiest families, who was posted to West Virginia, a state he fell in love with and later represented in the United States Senate.

It was an amiable political scientist at Mars Hill College, Richard Hoffman, who spearheaded the idea of bringing VISTA to Madison County. After graduating from the University of North Carolina, Hoffman arrived to teach at Mars Hill in 1959. He went back to Chapel Hill for graduate school and returned to Madison County toting a briefcase full of liberal ideas for change, both at the college and in the county.

Wielding his new Ph.D. in community organizing—his dissertation was titled "Community Action: Innovative and Coordinative Strategies in the War on Poverty"—Hoffman hoped to mobilize both insiders and outsiders to help improve the lives of Madison County residents. According to his protégé George Peery, Hoffman was enthusiastic about Johnson's Great Society and saw it as an opportunity to break down barriers between the college and the community. It was also a way "to give our students many more opportunities to do tutoring, to do community organizing, to get out into the county in ways that they hadn't before," Peery said.

One aspect of Hoffman's ambitious plan was to invite VISTA workers to Madison County. Like their Peace Corps counterparts, VISTAs had to be requested by local groups for specific projects.

From the beginning, some VISTA officials voiced doubts about the Madison County project. Jeffrey Hammer, who would direct all North

Carolina programs, believed colleges made poor project sponsors because few of their staff members were native to the area or part of the local establishment, and they tended to overestimate the value of applying academic theories to concrete community problems. "I would have worked months with the local community to ensure local ownership of the project," he said. All too often, he thought, volunteers "were simply parachuted into communities and left on their own to fail."

Nonetheless, the Madison County project was approved. In October 1969, a total of 120 VISTA recruits—Nancy Morgan among them—gathered in Atlanta for ten days of preliminary training for programs around the Southeast. The classroom training was intense, volunteer Peggy Breckenridge recalled. "They were absolutely pouring stuff in. It seemed like ten weeks. It was excellent training, with a focus on bringing the people together and helping organize them so that they could create more power in their lives," after which the VISTAs "would disappear." The curriculum was essentially Saul Alinsky's "Community Organizing 101." The guiding principles were, first, to live where you organized; second, to survey your target area before choosing your project, and to work on what people in the neighborhood, not you yourself, thought was most important; and third, to build a base before acting and to make certain local people led.

One instructional text the VISTAs were not offered but would have benefited from was Horace Kephart's *Our Southern Highlanders*, in particular a few pages from the chapter entitled "The Outlander and the Native." In it, Presbyterian minister Warren H. Wilson advised any missionaries, secular or religious, with ambitions to uplift the Appalachian mountaineers to proceed with caution. A mountaineer, Wilson cautioned, would "refuse even what he sorely needs if he detects in the accents or the demeanor of the giver any indication of an air of superiority." Known by some as "the Bishop of the Mountains," Wilson advised, "Those who would help them must do so in a perfectly frank and kindly way, showing always a genuine interest in them, but never a trace of patronizing condescension."

Perhaps instinctively, Nancy Morgan would understand and adopt this approach to organizing in Madison County.

⇒⇐

Volunteers selected for Appalachian projects received additional instruction in how to adapt to the local culture. It involved "admonitions about what not to do more than what to do," Ed Walker recalled. The VISTAs were warned to be careful about getting politically involved in the community and to be aware of "attitudes about outsiders going into communities, demeanor, dress." They heard the same ironclad strictures that had applied for the previous two hundred years to outsiders determined to administer "uplift" to locals: Don't drink with them, don't sleep with them (unless you marry them first), don't try to change them, and watch your language in mixed company.

Richard Haimes, an ex-volunteer from Pennsylvania who would head the Madison County contingent, selected seven former college students from around the country. Ed Walker, who came from a small town in central Florida, was the only Southerner among them. The eighth choice, completing the project, was Myrtle Ray, an older local woman from Madison County. Even in training, Nancy Morgan made an impression. "Nancy was beautiful and intelligent and a natural leader," said one on-site trainer who worked with the Madison County VISTAs. "The others looked up to her."

The Madison County contingent headed for North Carolina and five weeks of on-the-job orientation at Mars Hill College before being dispatched to their communities with the broadest of mandates. "Just getting to be known and trusted in the community—that was our whole focus. No real activities," said Walker. Dismissing a modest brick apartment as too luxurious, he found a log cabin in the Bluff community that he rented from a local family for eight dollars a month. Like most visitors to Madison County over the centuries, Walker was impressed by the area's splendor. "The geography was just incredible. Rugged, beautiful mountains. I don't think any of us wasn't awed."

Walker was soon comfortable, working informally with young people, taking them swimming in Mars Hill, playing basketball with them, giving adults rides to the doctor and the store. "I really had very little trouble getting into the community because I was from a rural background. I understood a little about agriculture. I came from a Southern Baptist upbringing, so I knew about religion. It wasn't as big a cultural shock to me as it was to these volunteers coming from the Northeast."

Richard Haimes tried to get things off on the right foot in his comments to the Madison County *News-Record* in a story announcing the VISTAs' arrival. "We are set up not to do things for people but to help people do things for themselves," he said, reciting from the community organizers' handbook. The county program was to be loosely structured in order to allow each volunteer to respond to local needs. "It isn't as if an outside group is trying to ram something down the community's throat."

The volunteers were pretty much on their own to identify needs and launch projects in their communities. Peggy and Frank Breckenridge, going door to door, learned that what people in Hot Springs wanted was better medical care, so Peggy began by organizing a women's health support group in town. "All of a sudden, they not only had something to say," she recalled, "they needed to do it." Peggy provided leadership and direction, but Hot Springs residents did much of the legwork. "The empowerment happened, and that was a real treat," she recalled. "We hit on the idea of a drug co-op because Hot Springs had no drugstore." Her next project concentrated on trying to get a retired doctor from Asheville to hold office hours in Hot Springs. Ultimately, after the Breckenridges' departure, the Hot Springs Health Program won federal funding and hired a physician and other staff, who saw patients three days a week.

Frank Breckenridge, meanwhile, wanted to work with young people. When some teens complained that an old movie theater had been shut down, Frank began talking to the people who owned the building, and "lo and behold, we developed a way in which the kids could renovate the theater," he recalled. Breckenridge and the teens cleaned it, painted it inside and out, and then hired someone to run the projector. The young people did everything else, before long even ordering the films. On weekends, Hot Springs again had a movie theater. "As soon as the parents saw that I was working for the kids and that it might bring them some extra money and get them out of the pool hall, there was enormous support."

Nancy Morgan, too, had some early success in her community organizing—once people in Shelton Laurel decided she wasn't a federal snoop checking out welfare fraud or moonshiners. She concentrated on nutrition education and recreational activities for young people and provided transportation for those needing medical care. By December 1969, Nancy seemed happy with her assignment, as she reported to her junior-high friend Kristin Johnson (née Peterson) from her cabin next to Cutshall's Grocery.

"Dear Kristin," she wrote, "I am in the Blue Ridge Mountains of North Carolina working as a VISTA volunteer. I am in a rural area—Madison County. It is very poor. Only about 25% of the people in my community, Shelton Laurel, even have indoor plumbing. Jobs are generally seasonal with tobacco farming being the prime source of income. Health facilities are practically non-existent in this county and education is also very poor (despite the grandiose words of the county superintendent)."

Just after Christmas, Nancy's two brothers, John and George, visited her in North Carolina. Her cabin, George said, "was like where the Beverly Hillbillies came from, out in the sticks among old, run-down houses." Nancy seemed in good spirits, though. The siblings talked about family matters but also about Nancy's work.

"She was trying to educate the locals on proper nutrition, because that was a problem she felt she could address," George said. "She told me that many of the natives there were simultaneously morbidly obese and malnourished. Their main meal might consist of corn or rice, potatoes, and bread."

John had a similar take on his sister's sense of mission. "She conveyed a satisfaction and a contentment with what she was doing. Nancy cared about people. She would listen."

In addition to her work with young people, Nancy had spontaneous minor successes like the time she and fellow VISTA Diana Buzzard ran into two traveling musicians from the West Coast on the Mars Hill campus. On the spur of the moment, and with the help of local musician Peter Gott, they organized an evening concert at the grocery store, bringing together newcomers and old-timers around Glendora's wood stove.

Around the time of her brothers' visit, Nancy reported in her letter to Kristen Petersen about the cabin where she and Diana Buzzard were living. "My roommate and I," she wrote, "were first living in a two room log cabin dating back to 1820—outhouse, only cold running water (which froze over the third night there so we had to haul in buckets of water), a coal oil stove for heat and two coal oil lamps for lights. Very rustic and I actually enjoyed the challenge, but a couple of male mountainfolk paid us a visit desiring our company to drink, etc. Diana was scared pea-green and our trainers feared they might come back drunk so we moved in with a community family. We'll be moving again soon, but won't be so secluded even though we will be by ourselves. We will have a phone and government car. I'm not worried."

After signing off, she added, "P.S. My love life is nil so let me hear yours!"

Diana Buzzard was more than scared pea-green by the incident. A shy, religious redhead from Pennsylvania, Buzzard called one of her VISTA trainers, upset and crying. She explained that on the night Nancy mentioned in her letter, there was a loud knock at their door. Two men were outside, drunk. Diana didn't want her roommate to open the door. Nancy thought she could handle the situation—and she did, talking the men into leaving. But Diana was still petrified, she told the trainer, and wanted a transfer. The two attended a staff meeting about the incident to hash out their differences. Diana agreed to stay with Nancy and to try to keep in closer touch, but it was also decided that the women would move to a less isolated location. That turned out to be the cabin just below Cutshall's Grocery, which had been built for Glendora's grandparents in 1889.

Diana's high-spirited roommate drove her crazy. She considered Nancy a spoiled brat, she later wrote, and didn't like that Nancy drank so much. What really divided the two women was their attitudes toward sex, which became a flashpoint. No evidence came to light that Nancy was promiscuous while living in Madison County; she was more of a romantic, yearning for love with the right man. Although she was not shy about acknowledging that her previous experiences had been less than ideal, she believed that sex was right when it felt right.

Nancy enjoyed teasing Diana about her commitment to wait until she married. "She had no morals and even less common sense," Diana later wrote. "I was a virgin and that cramped her style. One of her top goals was to correct that. God protected me through a number of her schemes."

Before long, Diana Buzzard quit VISTA and headed back to Pennsylvania. "I knew if I didn't [leave], something bad would happen to me," she recalled in a letter.

≡≡

Even among the small number of volunteers, ideological differences materialized almost immediately, first during the weeks of training at Mars Hill College and then in monthly meetings over the next year. Some of the sessions almost erupted into confrontational "encounter groups," phenomena of a time when many insisted that "the personal is political."

Considered strange, aloof, and uncomfortable by the other VISTAs, Diana Buzzard was probably the least political and the least suited to community organizing of all the volunteers. "She was not one of the liberal thinkers," recalled Walker.

The affluent Breckenridges were the pragmatists, the reformers, comfortable operating within the limits of what seemed possible. When some of the local people they surveyed complained about exploitation and corruption at a tomato-packing plant, the couple declined to become involved, sticking with health care and the movie theater.

At the other end of the spectrum was hot-tempered Ed Walker, rooted in his class and cultural background, radical in his approach to community organizing. He wanted the VISTAs to confront local politicians and merchants for charging high prices to customers who had no other places to shop. He criticized the Breckenridges as indulgent because they had a small portable television and because Frank, an amateur geologist, displayed his modest rock collection.

Nancy Morgan usually found herself in the middle in these battles. She was often a peacemaker, more politically conscious than the Breckenridges but less confrontational than Walker.

The VISTAs had been trained to work, if possible, through existing institutions. So Nancy—much like Christy in the novel she brought with her—tried to base her efforts in what was effectively a women's group, the Shelton Laurel Community Club, which met on weekdays. One project she proposed the club undertake was to open a secondhand clothing store, using garments donated by more affluent outsiders, including Morgan's own parents; again, this echoed Christy's efforts. Trying to get men to attend the club's community improvement meetings, Nancy arranged a special night meeting. It was "the first evening meeting since I've been here," she wrote her parents, "and the first one at which men were present—much more representative of the community than afternoon gossip sessions."

But in working with the community club, she ran afoul of a local woman who had been sent to Atlanta for VISTA training in the same group with Nancy but was rejected after eight days for health reasons, possibly because she was overweight. At a club meeting, Virginia Stirling charged that Nancy had made derogatory remarks about her, including the claim that Stirling had taken some of the donated clothing and sold it herself. Stirling accused Nancy of dividing the club, then said loudly to anyone within earshot that if she ever caught up with Nancy, she would "whup" her.

Richard Haimes remembered Nancy as neither shy nor reserved but as someone who made people feel, even on first meeting her, that she was their friend. Being accepted in the mountain communities was difficult, he said, "but the acceptance Nancy got from the people was fantastic."

Their initial successes notwithstanding, the VISTAs soon encountered serious problems, both internal and external. They had joined VISTA thinking they would make a difference—perhaps they would launch a cooperative enterprise on an Indian reservation or work on civil rights in an African-American community. "Those were the glamorous parts," said Ed Walker, "and here we were in this little Appalachian community with no real focus, no organization." To the VISTAs, *community organizing* sometimes seemed a nebulous phrase, and putting it into practice was proving difficult. As they saw it, mountain culture didn't lend itself to organization. The locals were rugged individualists who found the whole concept of organizing themselves into groups alien. "I think we were all frustrated," Walker said.

≥≤

Just as the VISTAs struggled with mixed feelings about their local experiences, so did Madison County residents have mixed reactions to the VISTAs. Jerry Plemmons, a lifelong resident and an acute observer of the mountain way of life, said, "Some people were pleased there were national volunteers here, while others felt like it was another indication that people outside the area saw all mountain people as dumb and lazy and not able to make their own decisions." The unfamiliar ways in which the VISTAs dressed, talked, and behaved made some locals feel uncomfortable, he thought, although "others were very accepting."

Harold Bailey was one of the VISTAs' supporters. "They were able to teach people how to improve their living conditions," he said, "either in food preparation or personal hygiene or other things of that nature."

Anthony James, who lived outside Marshall and who later became embroiled in the aftermath of the Nancy Morgan murder, had the same feeling. "Everybody around seemed to really like them and get along good with them."

Even Jeffrey Hammer, despite his initial misgivings, was impressed with the volunteers' dedication. "It was obvious to me that the Madison County VISTAs were well integrated into the community and quite well liked," he said. "I had the sense they'd worked out very well, that they'd made a number of local friends and had local supporters." Despite the program's national reputation, these VISTAs "weren't hippies." They weren't protesting the war, fighting segregation, or rallying the poor white masses against mine and factory owners. In short, he saw nothing to make him think "the local power structure would view the VISTAs as a threat."

Madison County's young people proved to be the most receptive to the volunteers, according to Sheila Kay Adams, who was a high-school senior when the VISTAs arrived. The local teenagers, she recalled, spent little time with the VISTA workers but took an interest in them because they were "new faces and not much older than we were." The VISTAs seemed exotic simply because they were from "away," as Adams and her friends put it. They had different life experiences and seemed part of a larger world, one "where a lot of the civil rights was going on."

"I remember folks referring to the VISTA workers as hippies," said Adams, who later became a nationally renowned singer, musician, novelist, and folklorist. They wore blue jeans and talked differently from the way Madison County natives did, but she remembered that rather than feeling animosity toward them, people reacted with a "benign curiosity" and amused acceptance. "Kind of, 'Oh, Lord, here we go again,'" at least from the older generation, she said.

Not everyone was so accepting. Some residents of Madison County resisted VISTA's presence from the beginning. Clyde Parks, a civic-minded Republican, was vice president of a local community development club when the VISTA program was proposed. He almost resigned, he said, because he didn't want VISTA included in the club's projects. Earlier, while stationed in South Dakota during a career in the air force, he had met a few VISTAs. "They were from all over the United States instead of the area they're concerned with," he said. He thought local people could do a better job of helping with OEO projects because "outsiders don't have in their head what we do. . . . They wouldn't meld in with the people."

"Folks who didn't like it were using rhetoric about outsiders coming in. 'They don't know what we're about, they're creating too much trouble,'" said George Peery, the Mars Hill professor. People feared that VISTA was one more wave of well-meaning but obtuse people arriving in Madison County with the same attitudes held by previous missionaries, secular and religious.

"We're resistant to change," said Jerry Adams, a pharmacist in Marshall, born and raised in Madison County and a cousin of Sheila Adams's. "I can't see where people who are sent in to change us are any better off than we are, and I think that's pretty much the attitude."

As young people shaped by the liberal college culture of the 1960s, the VISTAs tried to the best of their ability to restrain their behavior and take precautions in deference to local sensibilities. When they got together socially, remembered Peggy Breckenridge, "we brought wine and took it home with us. I remember being scared somebody would stop us and discover our stash of wine bottles." The volunteers agreed on their own to leave drugs behind while they were in Madison County.

But one party in particular damaged their reputation. It was a Thanksgiving potluck at Richard Haimes's house in the Walnut community, held at the end of the VISTAs' training. "We all sort of pooled our family recipes," said Peggy Breckenridge, "and tried to make do in Richard's kitchen with whatever pots were there and whatever turkey we came up with."

The gathering produced one discordant note, although few of the VISTAs realized it at the time. "There was drinking going on and a lot of foul language, which to us, the national volunteers, was just ordinary college dormitory talk," said Ed Walker. But to the local guests, "we were what was considered a wild party. . . . We may have said 'goddamn' several times. . . .

"We did get loud. We had music playing, and somebody nearby came out and yelled something. Some neighbor, which would have probably been a quarter-mile away, yelled something about shutting up, and I think somebody said, 'Go fuck yourself.'"

5

On Wednesday afternoon, Nancy Morgan's body was taken by ambulance to Asheville, to the south entrance of Memorial Mission Hospital, and wheeled through the double doors and into the ground-floor morgue just inside. The body was lifted into one of the three drawers of the small cooler, awaiting Richard Haimes's formal identification.

Several hours later, Dr. Page Hudson, North Carolina's renowned chief medical examiner, arrived. The morgue, lined with tiny, pale green ceramic tiles, was nearly bare, nothing like Hudson's own sophisticated facility on the campus of the University of North Carolina at Chapel Hill. Hudson thought it looked like something out of the 1920s.

Hudson, a tall, courtly man with a Tidewater accent, usually conducted autopsies in his lab. But his facility was jammed with corpses, and he thought a trip to Asheville might save a few days in preparing his final report for investigators. The case was producing headlines from Charlotte to Raleigh, which meant law-enforcement officials would feel pressure to solve it quickly. At the same time, it might give him an opportunity to show the flag for the statewide medical-examiner system he was building.

Normally, autopsies at Mission took place during the day, which enabled doctors to make use of the sunlight streaming through the bank of frosted windows on the morgue's south wall. However, the hurried procedure for Nancy Morgan began at nine that night, so Hudson and the others had to rely on the fluorescent lights.

The victim's nude body, five feet two inches tall, one hundred pounds, was laid out on the stainless-steel autopsy table when Hudson approached his work area. With Hudson at the start of the procedure were Dr. George Lacy, Mission's senior pathologist; another doctor; two North Carolina State Bureau of Investigation agents; and an investigator from Hudson's office.

The autopsy got off to a bad start. The FBI agents were late, to Hudson's annoyance. The medical examiner was also put out by the bureau's performance, including the handling of crucial evidence. "None of the ties or ropes that I heard so much about, that had been described to me over the telephone, were present. As it turned out, they were in the automobile trunk of an FBI agent who showed up about halfway through the autopsy. This is not quite the way it's done, even back in 1970."

Hudson described the FBI's participation as "Mickey Mouse. That's supposed to have been the nation's top-flight law-enforcement organization, and the agents involved didn't seem to know better than to remove the evidence—remove the ties that had been associated with the body and presumably had caused the death. It just reminded me of dealing with some of the most inexperienced of law-enforcement officers, which occasionally happened in North Carolina. By and large, they all seemed to know better than to remove potential evidence from the body at the site of the murder."

Nancy's body was so slight and the mechanics of the task so uncomplicated that progress was fairly swift. Hudson quickly identified the cause of death as strangulation. "It is impossible to determine whether she had been strangled and then bound or whether she died after being trussed up," he wrote. The death certificate read, "This was a murder, by party or parties unknown," the standard terminology in such cases. Hudson recorded that Nancy had been dead at least forty-eight hours before the time of the autopsy, which put her death sometime before about nine o'clock Monday night. He found sperm in Nancy's vaginal and anal cavities but took no swabs from her mouth. He observed no semen stains on her clothing and no residue under her fingernails. Hudson wrote that the sperm could have been deposited no more than twenty-four hours before her death. The samples were transferred to four glass slides, preserved in paraffin.

Besides the deep groove made in Nancy's neck about an inch and a half below her chin, Hudson noted abrasions on each elbow, consistent with her having been dragged. Although her blood type was O, type A stains appeared on one piece of unidentified white cloth. Her stomach contained "a considerable amount of partly masticated food material. There was a relatively large quantity of what appeared to have been salad greens or possibly lettuce. Many carrot fragments were also recognized." Her blood alcohol content measured .02 percent. Contrary to what investigators had said at the scene, Hudson found that the front of Nancy's blouse was cut open with a sharp instrument, rather than ripped.

After less than three hours, Hudson was finished.

⇒⇐

In the days that followed Nancy's killing, reporters from the wire services and newspapers across North Carolina—Asheville, Charlotte,

Raleigh—tried to leverage the information dribbled out by Sheriff Roberts. The reporters attempted to construct a meaningful, if hurried, sense of who Nancy Morgan was, as well as a timeline of her last days. The results, as might be expected under the circumstances, were sketchy and imperfect.

Myrtle Ray, the local VISTA worker, described Nancy to Kerry Gruson of the Raleigh *News & Observer* as "overfriendly. Mountain folks are suspicious of strangers, especially if they are too friendly."

"Nancy had the sweetest personality I've ever seen," said Glendora Cutshall, her landlady and friend. "Everybody here loved her. All the teenagers and adults here are saying they would love to get hold of the person that did it, and do the same to them." Still, Cutshall acknowledged some hostility toward the VISTA workers in the county, especially among teenage boys. They resented the male volunteers, who tended to wear their hair longer than the local fashion and, it was rumored, had access to the free-thinking VISTA women.

People offered contradictory reports about Nancy's state of mind, sometimes in the same conversation. Cutshall told another reporter that, in recent days, the young woman had seemed "deeply depressed," although Nancy also had told Cutshall she had met a man she liked named Mike, a fellow VISTA in the town of Brevard, North Carolina. But the young woman was deeply insecure about her looks and her prospects for a successful romantic relationship. "Who would have me?" she once asked.

A good friend of Nancy's, Alanna Paulson, another military kid then living in Miami, said that Nancy had written her a letter several weeks earlier in which she reported that "half the community wanted her evicted and the other half was behind her."

According to the Asheville newspaper, some people in Shelton Laurel believed Nancy "had a premonition" that something might happen. She gradually had changed from being a buoyant, outgoing girl into a subdued and quieter person, they told the reporter.

Kerry Gruson's was the best of the out-of-town newspaper ac-counts, dramatically different in depth and tone—notwithstanding that it was reported on the fly, written in her car, dictated by phone to the newsroom's city desk on the way back to Raleigh, and published less than a week after Nancy's body was found. The front-page article in the *News & Observer* bore the headline, "Slaying Brings Fear to Madison County." Gruson, the daughter of *New York Times* power couple Syd-ney Gruson and Flora Lewis, was already a veteran of covering gothic violence, having previously worked for the *Southern Courier*, a publica-tion that chronicled the civil-rights movement in the Deep South.

This mountain county of Madison, she wrote, was one "where dis-putes are sometimes settled with a bullet and electoral politics are some-times as crooked as the roads, [and] the seemingly motiveless murder of an attractive young anti-poverty worker last week has brought fear" among her fellow volunteers and even some locals, given its gruesome nature. The circumstances of the killing were out of character for that part of the country, according to a state trooper she quoted: "Usually it's a clean straightforward knifing or shooting. They get stomped or run over by an automobile, but in the sixteen years I've been here we've never had a strangulation. People here don't know that kind of killing."

In Gruson's account, a more nuanced picture of Nancy Morgan emerged than some local residents might have imagined. Glendora Cutshall said she had offered to modernize the four-room frame cabin she rented to Nancy but was turned down: "She said she wanted to do things the hard way; she wanted to live here because it was so old." When Nancy's pipes froze, requiring the young woman to store water in the cabin next to a coal stove, "she got a kick out of getting the water from outside and keeping it in the tub. . . . She said living the hard way and doing things for herself was fun after being in comfort all her life."

Gruson was clearly troubled by Nancy's death. The antipoverty worker, she wrote, "was by all accounts a very likable person and seemed to have no enemies. Her program had aroused no more than the usual amount of controversy. Indeed, before her death, many Madison people had never heard of VISTA. So many questions and so few answers, one N.C. State Bureau of Investigation agent said. But Sheriff Roy Roberts is hopeful. 'The whole community is eager to help and that makes it a lot easier. This is a murder we cannot let go unsolved. It's a horrible thing to have hanging over our community.'"

Nancy's friend Harold Reed took a darker view. Years later, he remembered thinking that "due to politics, it wasn't going to be solved, and it never will be solved."

A sloppy investigation with political undertones would soon bear him out.

6

As Richard Haimes formally identified Nancy Morgan's body at the Asheville hospital, Colonel Earl Morgan in Baton Rouge received the phone call all parents dread. It came from Jeffrey Hammer. Morgan later told a reporter that his daughter's death was "just too much to comprehend. She always had as her goal to help the underprivileged."

The family had moved to Louisiana on Christmas Eve 1969, after Earl Morgan retired from the judge advocate general's office. He took a job as head of the law library at Louisiana State University, where he had earned three degrees.

Nancy's younger brother, George, then a teenager, worked at the law library part-time and was there when the phone rang. George was called into his father's office, where he learned the news. Within seconds, George was in his car driving home "like a maniac" to console his mother, who he thought had been informed first.

Others received word of the killing in equally shattering ways. The mother of one of Nancy's friends in Northern Virginia was on her way to the Washington, D.C., airport to pick up Nancy for the start of her vacation when she heard the murder reported on the car radio.

≡≡

The VISTAs migrated from the site where the body was found to Haimes's house in Walnut, and then to the sheriff's department in Marshall. They were both providing and gathering information about the killing. Walker recalled little questioning by Sheriff Roberts or his deputies, "just a little bit of conversation."

The volunteers agreed to meet later that evening back at Haimes's house, where they heard Walter Cronkite announce Nancy's death on the six o'clock news. The item was brief, having to compete with the ongoing United States military action in Cambodia, the Charles Manson trial, rioting in the black section of Miami, and several unfolding Washington scandals. Some of the volunteers were so shaken they forgot to call their parents to let them know they were okay.

Jeffrey Hammer had received the news as he got out of his car at Haimes's house, after checking for Nancy's car at the Asheville airport. With Haimes's and Hammer's help, VISTA officials then shared Nancy's death with the media, writing a news release and sending it to the Associated Press. The one-page account said who she was, that she served as a volunteer, and that she'd been found strangled in a federal park.

Naturally, the conversation that evening among the VISTA workers and their friends centered on who might have been responsible for the killing. "We were scared, very afraid, once we found out the details—as much as they would tell us," said Walker. The workers thought the killing might have had something to do with Nancy's recent feud with Virginia Stirling. "Maybe it was more than we thought it was at first, and maybe there was somebody out to get VISTA," Walker said. A passing thought flashed through his mind: If the authorities didn't arrest someone soon, he would be the prime suspect, as the last person who admitted seeing Nancy alive.

It might have been irrational, but some of the VISTA workers began to fear their neighbors. The killing conjured up the worst stereotype of the mountains—Appalachian people's reputation for violence and brutality. The timing couldn't have been worse. Memories of the killings of civil-rights workers in the Deep South were still fresh and raw. James Dickey's chilling novel *Deliverance*, set in the mountains of northern Georgia, not far from Madison County, was published that summer. The book, and later the movie, told the story of four men from the Atlanta suburbs who were attacked—and one of them raped—by hillbillies along a raging river. From those first nights onward, Walker never stayed alone in the house in Bluff. He was scared.

The next night, the volunteers regrouped at the apartment of George Peery, the Mars Hill College professor, in nearby Weaverville to continue the discussion. Peery, a tall, slender political scientist, was so upset that, after having given up smoking several years earlier, he lit up in the pressure of the moment. It took him another year to quit again. The VISTAs were still trying to make sense of the murder in a gathering that first had the feeling of an informal wake.

The VISTAs discussed what to do next, wondering whether they would—or should—remain in their Madison County communities. Peggy and Frank Breckenridge had quit the program early and returned home to Cincinnati not long before the murder. Frank had been especially concerned that Nancy was living alone after her roommate, Diana Buzzard, also quit. Buzzard said she had no clue who killed Nancy. But much like the Breckenridges, she felt that, had she stayed, she might have been murdered as well. Nearly forty years after Nancy's death, Buzzard said she still prayed for her roommate's soul and for her family.

Frank Breckenridge had written a letter to Richard Haimes urging him to move Nancy to safer quarters. Breckenridge recalled that when he heard the news of Nancy's death, "I thought, *Richard, why didn't you get someone to live with her like I had asked you to over and over again?*" At the very least, if Nancy had been living with a local family or another VISTA, her disappearance would have been noticed by Monday morning.

Everett Gill, a VISTA trainer who had accompanied the group to Madison County, was not surprised by the local reaction. Earlier, he had been active in the civil-rights movement in South Carolina, where VISTAs were run out of town. What did surprise him was the morbid interest residents had in the murder. "Even the grannies were talking casually about the most awful details. It struck me that this must be the way those old, gory mountain ballads got started centuries ago in England or Scotland and then passed down generation to generation."

Many residents seemed to feel that however well-intentioned the VISTAs might have been, they were outsiders not entirely welcome in the county, and must in some way have brought on their own catastrophe. Chief among those taking this position were supporters of longtime political power holders Zeno Ponder, the county Democratic Party chairman, and his brother E. Y. Ponder, the former sheriff. "That's what they preached," recalled Joe Huff, a Mars Hill attorney and Ponder foe. "The VISTAs had no business here. They ought not to have been here, and they brought it on themselves. That was the position they took."

Jeffrey Hammer perceived "a sense that VISTA had shamed the county. That seemed to me to be the prevailing attitude in the newspapers. I remember thinking how odd it was that the victim was seen as the perpetrator, a dog that had chosen to crawl into their home and die." Reading the local weekly newspaper, Hammer said he noted an attitude that "an outsider came here, somehow got herself killed, and brought shame to the county. So, therefore, it was her fault." When he attended a community meeting, "they came out at the end of it and said, 'Best if [the VISTAs] left the county.'"

In an editorial entitled "Justice—Mountain Style," the *Western Carolina Tribune*, a quirky alternative weekly, wrote,

> At the risk of being "blasphemed" once again we say: The murder of Nancy Morgan, VISTA government worker of Shelton Laurel, N.C., is yet another example of "mountain justice" at work. Many, many people of all walks and stations believe in "mountain justice," a 200-year-old and more code that preaches: Adhere, believe, do, act, conduct yourself, follow, lead, say and otherwise exhibit, to wit: the straight-and-narrow, biblical, sex-concealing, low-toned, reverent, undemonstrative, Sunday-go-to-meeting way is the only way; be it, get with it brother or sister or reap "mountain justice."
>
> Take a young, impressionable, brilliant, rebellious, outgoing and healthy young lady of 24, project her into Madison County backwoods culture with all its archback conviction, have her wear shorts at any hour, ride with bearded hippies through the countryside, make broad and bold statements, exhibit herself unduly, more out of bubbling, young and healthful femininity than overt sex, and you have the denizens of "mountain justice" watching closely, very closely, as they did during the last, tragic months of Nancy's life.
>
> "Mountain justice" has, once again, taken its toll. And countless drones, would-be witches, pitchfork wielders and preachers of the "straight-and-narrow" now nod their heads, ever so slightly, around Shelton Laurel and Marshall and thereabouts, indicating, once again, "them outlanders'll some day learn how we live in these mountains."

Nancy's North Carolina friends and coworkers who were unable to attend her funeral in Louisiana held a memorial service for her in Asheville. Already, they felt a sense of foreboding about the reaction in

Madison County. Their anxiety was not misplaced. Anger arose during a town gathering at the Walnut Community Center.

"There was a meeting to that effect," said Harold Reed. "There was a lot of people thought it would bring bad publicity to Madison County, which we've got a bad name as it is." After Nancy's murder, locals thought, *Oh, no, "Bloody Madison" again.* An infamous massacre of civilians during the Civil War had bequeathed the lingering moniker.

Longtime resident Jerry Plemmons had the same recollection. "I do remember there was some strong feeling that [the murder] was an internal issue with the VISTAs and that there was not local involvement. So a lot of folk felt like that was unfairly presenting the area in a very bad light." In part, Plemmons shared this view. The killing, he said, was "atypical of anything that I ever heard about in the mountains."

The VISTA national office in Washington, with Haimes's concurrence, decided to pull the remaining volunteers from Madison County right away. They each received a week's leave and a plane ticket home and were told to clear out as soon as practicable. If they wanted to terminate their VISTA service, they could, or they could try to find another project.

When Walker came back a week later, he packed up his clothes at his house and began spending his nights with Haimes in Walnut and another volunteer in Mars Hill, returning to Bluff during the days to continue his community work. Within days, the remaining three volunteers and supervisor were gone from Madison County.

In July, the Madison-Buncombe Rural Development Council, organizational sponsor of the VISTA program, voted almost unanimously to end VISTA in the county and replace it with a program staffed by people "born and reared in western North Carolina and Madison County." The council's development officer told a reporter that "the root of the problems with VISTA arose from differences in outlook between the often young volunteers and the people they were trying to help."

7

For Jeffrey Hammer, the Eastern Airlines flight that ended late at night on the Baton Rouge tarmac was the longest and saddest he had ever taken.

As the father of a daughter himself, Hammer was aware of the tragic implications of his role. He had been advised by a government psychologist to expect an outwardly detached reaction from Colonel Morgan to his daughter's death, and so it was at the airport. Military men, Hammer was told, were trained to handle death in a professional, unemotional manner. Earl Morgan and his weeping wife, Abigail, thanked Hammer and left him as they accompanied Nancy's body to the Welsh Funeral Home in Baton Rouge.

Hammer's journey had begun about forty-eight hours earlier, when VISTA officials drafted him to bring Nancy home. Her body remained at the hospital until it was released to a funeral home to be prepared for its flight to Louisiana. The VISTA director visited Penland and Sons Funeral Home on the outskirts of Asheville to discuss details with the director and receive the papers required by law to transport a corpse between states. At the Asheville airport, Hammer again met with the funeral director to verify that the coffin was sealed and to pick up additional documents.

Like most flights passing through the Southeast at that time, the one from Asheville to Baton Rouge stopped in Atlanta, where Hammer lived. He needed a clean white shirt and a suit for the funeral, so his wife met him at the terminal and handed them off. Once on the ground in Baton Rouge, Hammer was shepherded toward the rear of the plane to wait for Nancy's remains to be removed. While standing on the poorly lit tarmac, the thought occurred to him that an American flag draped over the box would have been appropriate. In a sense, Nancy had died in the service of her country. Hammer prayed that he was sufficiently dignified for the occasion.

He handed the papers to the Baton Rouge funeral director, briefly expressed his condolences to Colonel Morgan, and accepted the colonel's expression of gratitude for having accompanied his daughter. The local VISTA supervisor appeared and drove Hammer into town, where he would stay with members of a Baton Rouge project. Someone asked if he was hungry, and he replied that what he needed most was a strong drink.

At two o'clock the next morning, the fragile peace at the Morgan home was shattered by a phone call from a reporter, who was bluntly dismissed.

The Morgans were relatively recent returnees to Baton Rouge, after the colonel's career in the military, and had no church affiliation. So they relied on the Welsh Funeral Home to arrange services for Nancy. Just a month before, most of the same family members—some wearing the same mourning clothes—had gathered at the same place for the funeral of George Green Morgan, Nancy's grandfather. The patriarch died peacefully at the family's home within weeks of his ninety-fourth birthday. That service was as much a celebration of a life well and fully lived as a funeral, as though a page had inevitably turned.

For Nancy's brief funeral, on Saturday afternoon, June 20, the contrast was stark. This was a sober gathering, different in spirit and demeanor. George Morgan, Nancy's younger brother, later reflected that his grandfather's death was a reminder that "life is long but will certainly end for all of us in time. Nancy's death seemed to render futile all attempts at making plans for the future that for her would never come."

George couldn't let go of the hope that this was somehow all a mistake—until he looked into the open casket. Hammer grimly observed that the marks around Nancy's neck were barely concealed. Someone must have communicated the condition of the body to Abigail Morgan, a slender, brown-eyed woman who resembled her daughter. She chose not to join the line of people proceeding past Nancy's casket. Mattie Jo Ratcliffe, Nancy's second cousin, recalled "the somber and dark feelings that permeated those in attendance. I personally felt violated and helpless against the evil that exists in this world."

Some Madison County VISTAs had driven through the night from Mars Hill. Hammer was relieved to see them seated in the hall. The intensity of the past few days made him feel as though they were family. Dressed in their rumpled Sunday best, long hair slicked back, they looked too young to be part of this dark drama and too out of place for the southern setting. This was especially true of Ed Walker, with his long sideburns and bushy hair that tumbled over his collar. Joined by the Baton Rouge VISTA contingent, they sat together during the service, heads bowed, moods hovering between gloom and despair. Mars Hill College professor George Peery listed his feelings on the occasion: "Shock. Stunned. Emotional exhaustion. Fear. A sense of loss."

VISTA and its parent, the Office of Economic Opportunity, sent only a mid-level official to represent Washington, which offended Hammer.

The Reverend Harold Price, of St. John's Methodist Church in Baton Rouge, stood at a wooden podium and read the Twenty-third Psalm, then delivered short, generic remarks about Nancy. He had never met the young woman in the casket. The talk was standard mainline Protestant fare—her young life meant more than her death, etc. But one section of the pastor's talk was quite relevant to what had brought people to the service.

"As we live and come to maturity, we discover that life has many mysteries," Price said. "Not simple mysteries that are dark corners unknown and unexplored, but real mysteries—areas that cannot be known. Death is the foremost mystery. Men have pondered it as long as there have been men. And the death of one so young only serves to compound the mystery. It poses questions that must forever remain unanswered."

Almost unconsciously, more than one person in the pews substituted *murder* for the preacher's word *death*, giving the thought a distinctly less theological resonance.

Earl Morgan rose to the podium and shared Jeffrey Hammer's thoughts at the airport, calling his daughter "a soldier in another war," who had given her life for her country.

After the service, about a third of those at the funeral home left in a cortege to Roseland Cemetery several miles away, in the town where Earl Morgan was born. Nancy's mother was still so upset she remained in the limousine, rather than walking to the grave site. An early-afternoon thunderstorm drove the mourners off before the casket could be lowered into the ground. Only Colonel Morgan remained to see his daughter laid to rest near his father's fresh grave.

The atmosphere was hushed back at the family's new white-brick home. There was the usual post-funeral mix of emotions. Those present shared memories of Nancy, some sad, some funny. Friends, relatives, and neighbors brought food: casseroles, a ham, potato salad, and cakes.

At first, the VISTAs stuck together at the house. But then, not wanting to seem standoffish, they circulated and socialized among the Morgans and Nancy's friends. Spontaneously, Abigail hugged Ed Walker, which caused him to burst into tears.

As the crowd at the house thinned, Colonel Morgan quietly indicated to the Madison County VISTAs and Jeffrey Hammer that he would like to speak with them privately. He ushered them through a set of wooden double doors into the living room, just off the house's main entrance. The antipoverty workers arranged themselves on a sofa and in a chair next to it. Unpacked boxes from the recent move stood stacked on the beige carpet, and temporary curtains hung at the window to provide some privacy. George Morgan entered the room, but his father asked him to leave before he began speaking.

Colonel Morgan closed the doors and addressed the group, alternately standing and sitting on a wicker chair, which he moved closer to face them. Throughout the day, Hammer had found the colonel, a pipe-smoking six-footer with glasses and close-cropped black hair, just as the psychologist had predicted: impersonal and almost devoid of emotion. So he was not unprepared for the way the colonel began to question those in the room. Morgan was solicitous of the VISTAs and seemed genuinely empathetic to the feelings of his daughter's friends. He skillfully created an opening for them to express what had been until then bottled up within their own heads. This was the volunteers' first opportunity to talk directly and privately with one of Nancy's parents.

The colonel had already begun his own investigation, probing in a dispassionate, professional way. What had happened the day before Nancy disappeared? Where had she been, and when? Did she have enemies?

Ed Walker was especially impressed that he was able to talk to Nancy's father without thinking he was a suspect. Oddly, even when the colonel asked Walker if he had engaged in sex with his daughter—

Walker said he hadn't—he felt neither threatened nor offended by the question.

Walker and the others began to wonder why they hadn't already been asked these questions over the past few days by the sheriff or the North Carolina SBI agents. For the first time, they felt they were part of a real investigation. *Here's a guy who's going to push to get this case solved,* Walker thought.

"The only thing that keeps me going is the determination to find out who did this thing, and see that person brought to justice—legal justice," Earl Morgan explained to a reporter after the meeting. The colonel was already formulating a theory of who may have been responsible: "I cannot escape the thought that it may turn out to be some bitter, twisted product of the very kind of environment Nancy was trying to help eliminate."

Later in the day, as furniture movers, electricians, and plumbers incongruously came and went through the new house, the Morgan parents talked about their daughter to a reporter for the *Baton Rouge Advocate.* "Nancy really found herself in VISTA," Abigail told him. "She was completely dedicated and was always selling the importance of VISTA's work. The other day she sent us a poster saying, 'If you're not part of the solution, you're part of the problem.' She enjoyed needling us."

Colonel Morgan added, "She never let me forget that I tried to talk her out of joining VISTA when she was still in college." Nancy was one of those kids who needed a purpose in life. During her college years, she searched for that purpose and began to talk about VISTA. Her father convinced her to finish school. "Then she was on her way. She decided she wanted to do what she could to help the poor and the underprivileged, and the only thing to do was to go find out more about their problems before she went on with any more education."

The family, including Nancy's older brother, John, a recent Air Force Academy graduate stationed in Texas, also wanted to talk about

Nancy's post-VISTA plans to become a nurse and her deep, undiminished commitment to help those in need. Abigail Morgan said, "She always was interested in nursing, and she decided to take time out from VISTA to get her master's degree in nursing. From what she had seen, she felt she could do the most good trying to solve the health problems of the underprivileged."

Some of the Madison County VISTAs joined the newspaper interview. "She wanted to come back to Appalachia. She fell in love with Appalachia," said Peter McDermott of Paramus, New Jersey.

"The thing that's hard to explain to people who didn't know Nancy," her father told the reporter, "was her complete dedication. . . . I still find it hard to believe myself."

Days later, two FBI agents met with Earl and George Morgan in the same room where the father had talked with the VISTAs. The men all sat "pretty close together," George recalled, "so that our speech could be quiet and still understandable." One of the agents described how Nancy had been hogtied. "He created a visual image that has cost me many hours of sleep over the years," George acknowledged later. They also conveyed chilling details of what they said was a postmortem sexual assault, and they described what the FBI intended to do to bring those responsible to account.

What the agents did not know was how a high-level bureaucratic battle among government officials would cripple the investigation.

8

Although FBI agents had shared control at the crime scene, the agency effectively withdrew from the case—without explanation—as early as June 21, the day after Nancy's funeral. Page Hudson, the state medical examiner, remembered "one of the State Bureau of Investigation agents chuckling and [saying] that the FBI had it long enough to see if they could come up with a quick solution, and when they couldn't, they gave the jurisdiction back to the state bureau."

That left Madison County sheriff Roy Roberts to take the lead in the case, along with agents from the SBI. Ed Walker voiced nothing but scorn for both parties, dismissing them as incompetent.

The North Carolina State Bureau of Investigation was founded in 1937. At the time of the Nancy Morgan killing, it had seventy-six investigators and local field offices in Asheville and Waynesville, south and southwest of Madison County.

During the 1950s and 1960s, states in the South and sparsely populated areas of the Midwest and West established similar statewide investigative units. Some were outgrowths of the highway patrol or the state police. These units often included primitive crime labs, along with plain-clothes investigators trained by the FBI. However, behind their backs, the state investigators were frequently disparaged by their FBI instructors as arrogant "Junior G-Men."

By Friday of the week of the killing, a spokesman for the SBI said that although investigators had found no concrete clues, they expected some favorable developments in the case soon. "We're just fitting the pieces together now," Sheriff Roberts told reporters. North Carolina governor Robert Scott offered a six-thousand-dollar reward for information leading to the arrest and conviction of the killer or killers. Pressure to solve the case grew. Even Charles Dunn, head of the SBI, soon recognized that the investigation would require resources beyond those available in North Carolina. On July 8, he formally requested assistance from the FBI for out-of-state interviews. Political forces were at work behind the scenes, too, building momentum for J. Edgar Hoover's FBI, under the United States Department of Justice, to take control of the investigation.

Within two days of the discovery of the body, Richard P. Doyle, the assistant general counsel for the Office of Economic Opportunity, began pressing the Justice Department to become involved in the case. In part, this was because some people at the upper reaches of the OEO did not trust local law enforcement.

For more than a month, in letters and telephone calls, Doyle argued strenuously for federal jurisdiction, saying it was his "personal opinion" that the FBI should take over or at least become actively involved. The three possible grounds on which the Justice Department could intervene were that Nancy Morgan's murder might have been a federal civil-rights violation; that the body was found on a United States government reservation, Pisgah National Forest; and that Nancy's death fell under the "Assaulting a Federal Officer" statute.

For a time, the local United States attorney in Asheville, Keith Snyder, urged the Justice Department to reject each of these arguments. There was, he said, no indication that Nancy had been killed for advocating civil rights; the federal government, although it had proprietary rights, did not customarily exercise law-enforcement authority in the national forest; and the VISTA worker was not considered a federal officer. An assistant United States attorney general for civil rights agreed. In a July 24 letter to Snyder, the OEO's Doyle admitted that "it would be difficult to determine whether there was a [civil rights] violation . . . unless and until the person or persons responsible for this murder are apprehended and a determination made as to whether any part of their motivation amounted to a violation."

Before long, politics outside the law-enforcement bureaucracy intervened and settled the matter. Earl Morgan had gone to law school at LSU with United States senator Russell Long of Louisiana. The colonel, as he had shown Ed Walker and the other VISTAs after Nancy's funeral, distrusted the motives and abilities of North Carolina law enforcement. After his daughter's death, the distraught father sent a telegram to Long, saying diplomatically, "Despite sincere efforts of very fine North Carolina investigators, full participation of the Federal Bureau of Investigation is urgently needed. . . . Request your assistance in obtaining full FBI participation at ground level."

Long's office contacted Doyle at the OEO and also forwarded Morgan's wire directly to Hoover. In reply, Hoover suggested that any further communication on the subject go through Jerris Leonard, assistant United States attorney general for civil rights. Still, someone copied the director's letter to Long to the FBI's other top officials, together with details of the case and Hoover's handwritten notation—the implication of which could not be missed—that the "Bureau has enjoyed cordial relations with Senator Long in the past."

Putting the FBI's Charlotte office in charge of the Nancy Morgan case for the bureau, Hoover's deputies dispatched or contacted agents to conduct interviews in nearly a dozen cities outside the state, including Atlanta, Baton Rouge, Cincinnati, Cleveland, Columbus, Miami, Pittsburgh, St. Louis, and Washington, D.C.—all places where Nancy had family, friends, or colleagues.

Jurisdictional issues went out the window as FBI agents moved back into Madison County to interview and reinterview people involved in the case. Hoover ordered copies of all field reports sent to him as they came in. However, some bureaucratic maneuvering still went on. Although VISTA's counsel received permission to review the FBI files, the bureau withheld some material, including Ed Walker's SBI polygraph tests. One bureau official wrote in a memo to his superiors, "We cannot control what Doyle of OEO would do with this information."

The conservative career staff at the FBI simply did not trust the OEO—considered a holdover bastion of liberal political appointees—with everything it learned. This included material that might reflect negatively on any of its volunteers or supervisors. The feeling was widespread in Washington that the Nixon administration was looking for any excuse to kill the VISTA program, as well as the entire War on Poverty. Having a volunteer turn out to be a murderer could provide lethal ammunition in that effort.

Earl Morgan continued to monitor the investigation. The father of one of Nancy's friends, also an air force career officer, left the service to become a special agent at the FBI. As a personal favor to the colonel, the man kept informal tabs on the bureau's involvement.

≥≡

After Nancy's death, details of her life emerged that challenged the notion of the girl so many thought they knew. Landlady Glendora

Cutshall found Kentucky bourbon and white lightning in Nancy's spice rack and enough beer cans under her bed to fill several trash bags. Glendora's husband, Clarence, took them to the dump before the SBI agents could find them. A paperback book discovered in Nancy's car turned out to be titled *Sexual Deviance*. Under her pillow was a book about breast development. Glendora found only one pair of panties—black with red lace—and one bra. From doing Nancy's laundry, the landlady knew that her late tenant had at least a dozen panties and four bras, but they were nowhere to be found.

Late in Nancy's college career, she had become romantically involved with an older professor, gotten pregnant, and had an abortion. She was open in telling her friends about the episode, and word had traveled around Madison Country. Years later, Sheila Kay Adams, Nancy's teenage acquaintance at the time of the murder, said, "I remember the community just being absolutely appalled, because . . . abortion was just something that was unheard of and a crime and a sin and an abomination."

Adams remembered thinking at the time that people in the community seemed to be trying to justify what had happened. "It was almost like, since she had an abortion and had an affair with this older man and got pregnant and everything, well, it almost serves her right. Now, that was never voiced, but I know that that story went around and was talked about pretty openly."

Despite a strict VISTA rule about not dating local residents, Nancy had gone out with an area man who, she later learned, was married. Even some of her defenders acknowledged that her behavior might easily have been misunderstood, in view of local mores. Ed Walker admitted that Nancy's flirtatiousness made her seem like "a teaser who gave all males the impression of a good come-on."

Alanna Paulson, Nancy's college friend, told the FBI that, in retrospect, she thought her friend's "easygoing and friendly attitude has sometimes been mistaken by young men as an expression of personal liking. Her approach is sometimes naïve and open to misinterpretation."

One former VISTA trainer told the FBI that gossip had circulated that Nancy was too quick to form friendships, but that there was no question about her morality or any suggestion she was promiscuous. "She was flirty with men, but I don't think she realized that she was playing with fire there," said longtime friend Kristin Johnson. The consensus was that Nancy was in search of a serious romantic relationship.

Locals took note of an incident during a square dance at the old roller-skating rink in Marshall. The early-June gathering drew a crowd of about fifty. The smattering of newcomers included some of the VISTAs. Peter Gott, a Northerner who had arrived with his family in 1961 and was embraced by the community for his love of music (and was later featured in a *National Geographic* article), called the dances. When the four-piece band wanted to take a break, it retreated and let the dancers strap on skates and circle the hardwood floor beneath a haze of cigarette smoke.

Nancy Morgan was there and had been drinking beer. Gott recalled that she wore cutoff jeans and sang along when the band gave the square dancers a rest and played a raucous rendition of "I Know You're Married (But I Love You Still)." Nancy came over to where Sheila Adams was sitting with some cousins and other family members, some of them from Sodom. As Adams remembered it, Nancy sat in the lap of one of the young men in the group. He was not one of her relatives and "not of sterling character." The move left Adams almost speechless. "I remember thinking that that was just not quite right. She sat there for a long time and was kind of flirtatious." Adams recalled the incident two weeks later, when Nancy's body was discovered. She wondered if the two events were related, a view shared by others in the county.

In Madison County, VISTA workers like Nancy, whom Ed Walker described as "a liberated woman of the sixties," found a sexual culture of which they had little understanding. It was a highly repressed culture with a rigid moral code, at least on the surface. Infidelity not infrequently ended in violence. Unattached single women—especially those who smoked and drank in public, used rough language in mixed company, and lived alone—were considered vulnerable and available.

Nancy once joked to Alanna Paulson that a thirteen-year-old Shelton Laurel boy had tried to seduce her. She probably didn't understand that the incident spoke to the cultural assumption about the accessibility of a young woman living alone—particularly an outsider, and even to an adolescent. Given the national atmosphere of the late 1960s, it was perhaps natural that local people projected onto the longhaired outsiders a belief in sexual freedom and moral laxity.

≡≡

Ed Walker—a slender, volatile twenty-two-year-old Florida native with curly hair and a pitted complexion—quickly became a suspect.

Immediately after Nancy's body was found, state and federal investigators conducted a series of interviews with Walker at his home and at the Madison County Courthouse. Walker, who did not think it necessary to consult a lawyer, told them he had enjoyed a friendly, casual relationship with his coworker. The two had met during VISTA training in Atlanta in October 1969 and saw each other about five times a month in connection with their work. They had gone out on one double date, to watch professional wrestling and have pizza in Asheville, a night that ended with a kiss. Walker insisted the two had never had sex. He gave investigators his account of the evening Nancy spent at his house before she disappeared—the dinner, the young neighbors who dropped by, the TV watching on the couch, the conversation on the porch.

"The agent informed him that as the last person to see Morgan alive he was a prime suspect," according to an FBI document. "He then became sullen and cried," voicing fear that when the FBI turned the investigation over to local authorities, he would be arrested. The FBI agent advised Walker that he had the right to remain silent, and to have a lawyer present. At that point, Walker broke off the interview because he needed to drive fifteen hours to Nancy's funeral in Baton Rouge.

Later, after their home leaves, all the VISTAs met at Richard Haimes's house and voluntarily traveled to Asheville to take SBI-administered polygraph tests. Walker's turned into a series of increasingly adversarial examinations. In the first, the examiner stalked around the room, grabbed a pack of cigarettes from Walker's shirt pocket, and told him the results indicated he had killed Nancy. When Walker demanded to see the results himself, the SBI agent refused. Walker demanded to take the test again, which he did. But then the examiner asked him to take a third test, which Walker refused to do. The next day, Walker packed a U-Haul trailer and left Madison County for Atlanta, to arrange for a new VISTA assignment.

The results of the polygraph tests, according to FBI files, showed "textbook signs of deception" when Walker was asked if he killed Nancy Morgan—information not shared with the OEO in Washington.

Meanwhile, local and state law-enforcement officials developed a theory of the case that involved a sharply different version of what happened that night at Walker's house. What Walker described as a quiet dinner with periodic interruptions by a few neighbors was, in their scenario, a raucous party fueled by alcohol and involving rough group sex that ended fatally for Nancy, perhaps unintentionally. In addition to the teenage boys present, investigators believed several other VISTAs, including Richard Haimes, had joined the bash, and that Nancy had allowed herself to be tied up.

The theories that found currency among the deputies and SBI investigators included one in which Nancy died during a sexual climax, part of an act in which she was a willing participant. Another was that she strangled accidentally when two men, one of them Walker, were distracted during a fight. Investigators thought the second man might have been a neighbor or perhaps Haimes. Then, the theories went, Walker and the second (and possibly a third) man drove Nancy's car and at least one other vehicle nine miles to Tanyard Gap, where the body was discovered, and drove home.

Other scenarios also insisted Nancy was a willing participant. "We feel like she went along with it, from everything we know," said one of Roy Roberts's deputies. "There's no signs of any kind of foul play, bruises or anything." The deputy claimed investigators had learned from some of Nancy's women friends that for several months she had been "experimenting with being whipped and tied up when she had sex to stimulate her sexual relations." None of Nancy's friends could later confirm any such behavior on her part.

In any event, the story of an out-of-control party took firm hold in Madison County lore in the years after Nancy's death. "Supposedly, they were having a party and she was tied up, apparently from some sexual thing that was going on," remembered Dal Peek, a longtime sheriff's deputy. People said "that a fight broke out between two guys, and everybody was watching the fight or something, and that she choked to death . . . that there was a lot of drinking." Peek was unsure if the fight was over Nancy. By the time the partygoers got things calmed down, they realized she was dead.

"There were a hundred opinions about how it happened," said local resident Richard Dillingham, who was building an outdoor church amphitheater nearby at the time Nancy's body was found. Some people thought she had "instigated it and caused it herself. They're saying that surely outsiders did this horrible deed," he recalled decades later. "If it were an outsider who committed that crime . . . they would be hunted down and prosecuted. But if it were local folks that were responsible for that, then it possibly should be ignored."

Nancy's conduct and demeanor continued to dominate speculation about the murder. Law-enforcement personnel and many Madison County residents preferred to believe the victim had brought the crime on herself and that she must have been killed by an outsider.

But some potential local suspects turned up, too. FBI investigators stumbled onto what seemed a promising path when they looked into the relationship between Nancy and her most recent prospective boy-friend, the VISTA worker identified only as Mike, who had just returned home to Ohio. Mike—whose last name none of Nancy's friends knew and the SBI kept confidential—had read about her death in the newspaper and contacted the FBI. He told agents that he and Nancy had met at a VISTA meeting at the beginning of May 1970 and hit it off. On May 17, Mike drove over to Madison County to visit her. They had lunch and drove around the countryside, sightseeing and taking pictures.

On their return to Shelton Laurel about eight-fifteen that evening, Mike told the FBI, they noticed they were being followed by a 1957 or 1958 Ford sedan, green and white. Inside were three large, short-haired white men in their late thirties or early forties. One of them, whom Nancy recognized and called Ben, spoke to her in what seemed to Mike an antagonistic manner. "Who you shacking up with?" the Ford's driver asked as the two cars pulled into the space between Glendora Cutshall's grocery and Nancy's cabin. Pointing to Mike, he then asked, "When's he going to get a haircut? Do you want a drink?"

Mike told the agents he was frightened by the encounter, but that Nancy showed no fear and answered the men's questions evasively. Finally, the men left. Nancy told Mike that when she had lived in another cabin after first coming to Madison County in October 1969, the same Ben had come around asking if she wanted some company. She had brushed him off. Mike recounted "that he was very frightened when he left and was afraid these individuals might try to run him off the road or do him some physical harm," according to the FBI.

In an interview with the FBI, Earl Morgan said "he had a 'feeling' that the Klan or a Klan-type group could be responsible for his daughter's death." The beatings and murders of civil-rights workers across the South in the 1960s were no doubt fresh in the colonel's mind. But although the KKK had been active in Madison in the years following the Civil War, the group was practically nonexistent in the county in the modern era, for there were few local African-Americans and no significant civil-rights movement.

It is unclear how many of these leads the SBI or FBI pursued. Nearly a month after the murder, J. Edgar Hoover apparently believed, rightly or wrongly, that the SBI had failed to follow them adequately. Hoover circulated throughout the bureau a July 14, 1970, memo from Jerris Leonard, the assistant United States attorney general, with the FBI director's pointed notations in the margin. Leonard directed the bureau to take fingerprints from Nancy's car, to identify them, and to interview those to whom they belonged. Next to the sentence, Hoover wrote, "Why wasn't this done originally?"

Leonard also referred to the FBI's interview with Nancy's former roommate, and her account of her and Nancy's being "bothered" by a pair of men. Leonard urged that the men be identified and interviewed "to determine if they have any knowledge of the victim's death." Next to that, Hoover wrote, "Same question as above."

The same notation accompanied a report of Nancy's clash with Virginia Stirling.

Similarly, Leonard referred to the account by Nancy's friend Mike about being harassed by three men on May 17. Again, Hoover jotted, "Same question as above."

Leonard asked for copies of all Madison County and North Carolina state police reports regarding the killing. At the bottom, the FBI director added, "The things asked for in this memo were certainly elemental to any limited investigation."

As sometimes happens in murder investigations—especially those that go disastrously awry—local, state, and federal investigators settled on a likely suspect and scenario early on and would not be dissuaded or distracted by any evidence to the contrary. Their target was Ed Walker. But even from Hoover's office in Washington, the possibility seemed obvious that locals might have been involved in Nancy Morgan's death.

Frustrated by the case and other matters, Madison County sheriff Roy Roberts, a Republican, announced he would not run for reelection in November 1970, and resigned before his term was up. Dedrick Brown, his young chief deputy, ran for the office but was defeated by the former longtime sheriff, Democrat E. Y. Ponder, who used the killing in his campaign. "He made it an issue," recalled Brown. "He said with what all he knew about this murder, with all the information he had on the case, that he could solve it within three weeks."

The SBI's district supervisor, P. R. Kitchen, told reporters on March 4, 1971, that the investigation had branched out into several states, Puerto Rico, and Germany—where Nancy had lived while her father served in the air force—but without much success. "We track down leads every week, sometimes two or three a week, but we still don't have anything concrete," he said.

On March 22, 1971, nine months after the murder, the FBI agent in charge of the Charlotte office sent a memo to Hoover, copied to the SBI's Charles Dunn, saying that as far as the FBI was concerned, "this case is being closed." The SBI, having conducted 150 to 200 interviews, reduced the number of its own agents working on the case from four to two.

For more than a decade, the investigation would lie dormant.

9

Although Roy Roberts officially headed the investigation of Nancy Morgan's murder for the Madison County sheriff's office, many people in the county considered E. Y. Ponder, then out of office for a term, the sheriff-in-exile. Ponder had lost the previous election when a coalition of Republicans and reform Democrats backed Roberts. Together with his brother Zeno, chairman of the county Democratic Party, E.Y. led a potent, hard-knuckled political machine. Thus, when people had information about a crime—including the VISTA killing—they often took it to E. Y., who sometimes passed it along to Roberts and sometimes didn't.

Ponder ran a pervasive network of informants throughout the county. As sheriff, he had dispensed justice selectively, targeting outsiders with no local political ties but going light on "local boys" who could be counted on to vote Democratic. His peculiar subscription to the tenets of mountain justice would have serious repercussions in the Nancy Morgan case.

If machine politics writ large in American history was New York's Tammany Hall, then writ small it was Madison County. There, in contrast to the big-city bosses' grand department stores of graft, the Ponder brothers constructed a thriving convenience store no less efficient for its scale. One North Carolina reporter said that in comparison to Madison County's Democratic boss, Zeno Ponder, Chicago mayor Richard M. Daley was Bambi. Others suggested Zeno's resemblance to an amiable, charming Stalin—without the executions.

Until recently, politics in these thinly populated mountains, with their scant industry and mostly subsistence farming, was a mixture of fundamentalist faith, blood sport, and war. It was deadly serious, affecting financial well-being, if not survival itself, during cold winters and hard times. State and local governments, particularly the school system, were the county's largest and most reliable employers. In return for their jobs, teachers knew to kick back part of their salaries to the "Pondercrat" wing of the Democratic Party and to support it at the polls. Even the sixty-four dollars a month a school-bus driver earned in the 1960s was enough to deliver one or two families' votes. The Ponders, through local government agencies, administered federal aid programs as well.

In Madison County, whoever controlled the politics also controlled the economy.

≡≡

The politics that pitted Ponders against Republicans was just one more way in which Madison County, like so much of the South, continued to relive the Civil War, especially the events that spawned the nickname "Bloody Madison."

But Appalachia's reputation for bloodshed stretched back even farther than that. The first white immigrants to the southern Appalachians were yeoman farmers with roots in Ulster and Scotland, especially the Highlands—a people "born fighting," in the words of Virginia senator

James Webb. Scottish history abounds with ill-fated insurrections and bloody internecine warfare. Many of those who emigrated to the southern Appalachians had survived the Duke of Cumberland's genocidal 1745 campaign of retribution in the Highlands. Earlier, in 1646, after a battle in the English Civil War, the leader of Clan Campbell accepted the surrender of more than three hundred members of Clan Lamont—supporters of the royalist Stuarts—and guaranteed their safety and property. Instead, Campbell's men plundered the Lamont strongholds, slaughtering women and leaving their bodies for wild animals. Thirty-six Lamont leaders were then hanged from an ash tree in a churchyard and another 250 captives killed at the foot of the tree. Over time, legend has it, the hanging tree withered, its roots oozing blood, until the Campbells hacked it to pieces.

The early Scots-Irish immigrants to North America brought with them this tradition of explosive anger. "A paradox of violence and gentleness, their crimes are not as a rule the impersonal cold-blooded robberies and murders of the big cities and the gangs," observed Wilma Dykeman in *The French Broad*. "They are crimes of emotion, sudden as the spring freshets, sweeping all before them, over as soon as they begin, and with no gain, or thought of it, to anyone. And almost always they are personal."

Thomas Wolfe wrote in *The Web and the Rock*, "The hill men . . . kill about a fence, a dog, the dispute of a boundary line. They kill in drunkenness or in the red smear of the murder lust."

In *Christy*, the novel Nancy Morgan brought with her to Shelton Laurel in 1969, the fictional character noted the dark quality of local ballads. In the songs, Christy observed, "there seemed to be plenty of blood flowing and . . . men being hanged. But then the ballads were honest about that too, for life in seventeenth- and eighteenth-century Britain and on the American frontier later on must always have had its gory side."

The blood and the killing ran through the roots of Madison County history, and they were not as easily hacked from the soil as the ancient Scottish ash tree.

＝＝

Madison County was evenly split between Union and Confederate supporters. Some families sent one son to fight with the Union and another to serve with the Confederacy, much as their Scots ancestors had done during rebellions and civil wars. Regardless of the war's outcome, they would preserve their farms. Slavery wasn't much of an issue, as the 1860 census counted only 46 slaveholders and 213 slaves among Madison County's population of 5,678.

But the brutality of the war brought out the old Scots-Irish blood lust.

"Acre for acre, there was probably more gunfighting and gratuitous cold-blooded murder in Appalachian North Carolina during the Civil War than there was in any comparable chunk of the Wild West during any four-year period," wrote William R. Trotter in *Bushwhackers: The Civil War in North Carolina, The Mountains.* "The coming of war merely added the respectability of a national cause to a long-standing pattern of personal vengeance."

When the citizens of Madison County gathered in Marshall to vote for delegates to a state secession convention, a gunfight broke out in the streets. A Union man killed the county sheriff, a secession supporter. The vote was 28 for secession delegates and 144 for Union delegates. But that certainly didn't mean the county was united. Men marched off from Madison County to join both armies. Many of those left behind gravitated to units like the Confederate Home Guard. Later, joined by renegades and deserters (North Carolina had the highest rate of desertion in the Confederacy), they formed even more informal units and became known as "outliers" and "bushwhackers." Their raids and skirmishing frequently crisscrossed the fine lines among partisan warfare, family vendetta, and simple banditry.

The residents of Shelton Laurel, where Nancy Morgan would live more than a century later, called themselves "Laurelites" and were strong for the Union. Shelton Laurel provided a haven for some of the region's most notorious Union raiders, who used the community as a base for guerrilla strikes across the border into Tennessee. It also served as a recruiting area for Union resistance, especially in the wake of the April 16, 1862, Confederate Draft Act. Despite their loyalty to the Union, men from the community were conscripted—some at gunpoint—into the Sixty-fourth North Carolina Infantry, commanded by James A. Keith. Often, they deserted at the first opportunity and returned home. A third of the company disappeared by the winter of 1864–65.

In order to punish Shelton Laurel for its Unionist actions, Confederate authorities and merchants in Marshall cut the community off from its stock of salt, a critical, life-sustaining commodity necessary for curing meat in cold months. The custom of the time was to slaughter hogs at the first frost and salt the meat in order to feed people through the winter, as well as to preserve the hides for use in harnesses and mess kits.

According to one account, the Union raider John Kirk, wearing his Federal uniform, gathered more than fifty local men, some of them deserters from the Sixty-fourth, to raid the undefended county seat and seize enough salt to get Shelton Laurel families through the winter. On January 8, 1863, the raiders shot up the town and then ransacked and pillaged the homes of wealthy Confederates, particularly those of Colonel Keith and his cousin, Colonel Lawrence Allen, who had helped organize and lead the Sixty-fourth.

When word of the raid reached Keith and Allen in Tennessee, they were outraged. They asked their commander for permission to return immediately to Marshall and Shelton Laurel. General Henry Heth, Keith's commanding officer, instructed him, "I want no reports from you about your course at Laurel." According to an account from Keith after the incident, substantiated by two witnesses, Heth said, "I do not want to be troubled with any prisoners and the last one of them should be killed."

Keith and Allen, with the Sixty-fourth and several other units—including two hundred Cherokee Indians—approached Shelton Laurel from different directions in cold, snowy weather. As one of the columns made its way along the Laurel River, the Confederates were tormented by witheringly accurate sniper fire from the wooded hillsides. The first group to reach the community killed twelve men and took twenty prisoners. A cavalry charge by Allen's men broke a clash with about fifty defenders and left another six Shelton Laurel men dead on the field. The combined columns proceeded farther into the valley, stopping to arrest and interrogate people who had not heard the warnings of residents' hunting horns. Some men fled, or tried to, but fifteen men and boys were picked up, most of them without resistance. Relatives of the suspects were beaten, robbed, whipped, and hanged until nearly strangled in order to find out where the suspected raiders were. Those treated this way included old men, children, and women. "These women," Keith later wrote, "as well as a large majority of the females in that section are base prostitutes and devoid of moral worth."

Among those taken prisoner were Aronnate Shelton, fourteen, and David Shelton, who was either twelve or thirteen. The two boys were captured along with their father, James Shelton. Keith and Allen held the prisoners in Shelton Laurel over a weekend while they decided what to do with them. Before the officers could resolve the matter, two of the men, one of them a sharpshooter and Shelton in-law named Peat McCoy, overpowered their guards and slipped away.

On the morning of January 18, the senior officers told the remaining prisoners they were to be marched to Knoxville for trial. Later investigations found that only five of the thirteen who began the march might have been involved in the Marshall raid. Seven were part of the extended Shelton family.

After just a few miles, the column halted in an open field near a creek. The captives were separated into three groups, and the first group of five was ordered to kneel in a line. Keith assembled a firing squad ten paces in front of the prisoners.

"For God's sake, men, you are not going to shoot us? If you are going to murder us at least give us some time to pray," said one sixty-four-year-old man.

When some members of the firing squad balked, an officer shouted, "Fire or you will take their place!"

All thirteen prisoners died, including young David Shelton, who begged to be spared after being wounded in both arms. The boy was pulled back into line and shot because, a member of the firing squad explained, "a nit becomes a louse."

The executions aroused indignation around the state. North Carolina governor Zebulon Vance, a native of neighboring Buncombe County, had wanted the homegrown Unionists crushed, yet he called the act "barbaric conduct" and "a scene of horror." He damned Keith as "a disgrace to the service and to North Carolina." The *Raleigh Standard* denounced the massacre as "a cowardly and wicked act," "cold-blooded murder," and "butchery." But in a familiar outcome in such cases, then as now, military investigators dragged their feet, relieved four low-ranking officers of duty, and scrambled to evade any taint of responsibility. In the end, Keith and Allen were allowed to resign from the army. Although Keith served two years in jail in Marshall awaiting criminal trial, the two men eventually escaped Madison County and settled in Arkansas.

"Shelton Laurel has never gotten over the Shelton Laurel Massacre," said Ellen Banks, who was raised in neighboring Revere, also known as Sodom. "That's a community where there's been a lot of pain and anger. . . . That community has never healed from that event, and I think it shows in some of the violence that the community's noted for."

The massacre inflamed the guerrilla warfare between Unionists and Confederates in Madison County. Partisans on both sides continued to ambush each other. Even the formal end of hostilities in 1865 failed to halt the bloodshed. Retribution killings shook the mountain communities. Among many other incidents, sharpshooter Peat McCoy came home with a taste for vengeance and learned that one of the men in the Shelton Laurel firing squad was living in Buncombe County. "He walked by night and slept by day until he found where the man lived," according to an unpublished Shelton family history. McCoy lay in wait in front of the enemy's house. "He told afterwards how the man ate his breakfast, walked out on the front porch, picking his teeth with a splinter. Peat McCoy took dead aim from a rail fence that run around a small clearing where the man's house stood. At the crack of the rifle he said the man pitched headfirst into the yard and lay still."

For years, this kind of unofficial civil war raged in Madison County. The schism followed the old political loyalties—Democrats dedicated to the Confederacy and Republicans loyal to the Union—in ways that would affect even the investigation of a young VISTA worker's murder a century later.

≡≡

In the presidential election of 1868, Republicans took Madison County by just seventy-one votes, but they hung on to it for much of the next hundred years. Until the 1930s, GOP adherents in Marshall marched behind a Union army drum during election season. The first two Democratic votes cast in cantankerous, Unionist Shelton Laurel were not recorded until 1910.

A seismic shift struck Madison County, like much of the rest of the country, after World War II, when a cohort of young men came back from military service to take a more active role in the way things were run. Their leader was Zeno Ponder, a soil chemist with a college degree who had spent the war years as a deferred civilian, separating uranium for the Manhattan Project at the Oak Ridge National Laboratory in

Tennessee. Born in 1920 as the youngest of thirteen children, Zeno seethed at conditions he found when he returned and at the way he felt local Republican bankers maintained political control through debts and mortgages on houses and even livestock. "The people of Madison County, without knowing this, were living in semi-slavery, or worse, in a free country," he said.

Even as a boy during the Great Depression, Zeno Ponder had known instinctively that he was no conservative. "We had very little to conserve," he told an interviewer with the University of North Carolina's Southern Oral History Project. "We were liberal, and the Democratic Party was liberal in its views, nationally, state and county. So we were for that form of government which would give us a better opportunity to involve ourselves and enjoy some of the goods, some of the good things in life." He knew what it was like "to live right on the edge of hunger. And if you've ever been there, you just don't want to go back."

Despite the strong Republican registration in Madison County, Zeno sensed he should stick with the Democrats. The party controlled both the state legislature and the Governor's Mansion, and the state capital served up significant financial aid to the localities. "To me it made good sense that if you wanted something from Raleigh, you needed to be in tune with Raleigh."

Zeno farmed in the evening and started teaching classes during the day to returned veterans through the GI Bill. He leavened his lessons in vocational agriculture with New Deal ideology. "I had a little education [and] a whole lot of desire to make a difference in Madison County. . . . That gave me a base to establish some leadership." In 1948, when Zeno won the position of election registrar for the town of Marshall, one of the first things he did was memorize the poll book. He soon sent his students out to the coves and hollers to register anyone who could make his mark.

By 1950, Zeno and his older brother, Elymas Yates Ponder, known as E. Y., were ready to move under an insurgent Democratic banner, beginning with their support for liberal United States senator Frank Porter Graham in his party's primary runoff. Challenger Willis Smith, a conservative state legislator, waged a textbook campaign of race- and red-baiting, aided by a young activist named Jesse Helms. "We carried it heavy for Frank Graham in Madison County," said Zeno. But despite garnering 90 percent of the county's vote, the statewide effort failed.

Locally, the Madison County Democrats' standard-bearer was E. Y. Ponder, who served as his precinct's Democratic chairman and who had first won election to the county school board in 1941. His target in the 1950 general election was the historically powerful job of "high sheriff." In a sparsely populated county like Madison, which had no resident district attorney, it was up to the sheriff to recommend what criminal charges, if any, should be brought when wrongdoers were caught. Together with a local doctor who served as medical examiner, the sheriff held responsibility for saying whether a death was natural or accidental, suicide or homicide. His choices could make the difference between freedom and prison, even between life and death. More often, the sheriff's decision was between when to mediate and when to prosecute.

"I didn't expect to be elected when I first started," E. Y. admitted. The hard-fought campaign was about as close as possible, and guns were everywhere. Zeno, wearing a .38 pistol on his hip at the poll on Election Day, carried his Marshall precinct for his brother by two votes.

In the end, E. Y. Ponder won county-wide by thirty-one votes. The incumbent Republican sheriff, Hubert Davis, had no intention of giving up power and charged the Ponders with fraud. He and his heavily armed deputies barricaded themselves in the jail, setting up a .50 caliber machine gun on a tripod outside the front door. E. Y. opened a rival office up the street in the courthouse. Nightly, boisterous supporters of E. Y. and Zeno drove back and forth before the Republican guns, tossing firecrackers and corncobs wrapped in red masking tape, made to look like dynamite sticks with lit fuses attached. Taunts and catcalls flew both ways. For a while, it looked as if the Civil War were about to erupt in Madison County again, almost a century after Appomattox. But no one pulled a trigger.

The Ponders took their case to Raleigh and ultimately to the state supreme court. There, a little-known justice named Sam Ervin—who would go on to the United States Senate and Watergate fame—wrote the order in support of the Ponders. The brothers wasted no time implementing the ruling. "We stripped about a four bushel sack of pistols off the Republican deputies and sent them back to plowing," Zeno said.

E. Y. offered a contrast to his gregarious, flamboyant younger brother. Zeno was a dapper man with a mustache and string tie who invited comparisons to a circus ringmaster. The sheriff, diminutive and soft-spoken, wore glasses with thick black frames and rarely donned a uniform or carried a gun. He drove an unmarked car. He found he was less likely to get shot that way while making an arrest. "If you treat people right, you don't need to do too much. I'd rather have one friend as ten guns," he said.

Once E. Y. was safely installed in the sheriff's office, Zeno moved quickly to consolidate his control of the county Democratic Party, ousting what he saw as the complacent, conservative old guard in Mars Hill. He strengthened his hold on appointed county boards and offices. "I was named to the county board of elections, and subsequent to that the other two members elected me chairman," he recalled decades later. In the 1954 general election, he said, "we put out a full ticket again and elected every single Democrat who was running for office." Zeno also focused on the five-member school board, often serving as its chairman. Teachers paid kickbacks, usually collected by the superintendent of schools, and school administrators were told to pad their student enrollments so state funds would allow more teachers to be hired. Building more schools also meant building more roads, because the state required safe roads for buses to transport students. Extracting roads from Raleigh became Zeno's claim to fame to such a degree that it entered the realm of legend.

Sometimes, in their enthusiasm to acquire and consolidate power, the Ponder brothers overreached. In the wake of their 1954 electoral sweep, Zeno, E. Y., and eight of their family and allies were indicted by the Eisenhower Justice Department for vote fraud. A federal jury in overwhelmingly Democratic Asheville, in neighboring Buncombe County, acquitted all ten after fifteen minutes of deliberation.

In the face of endemic and intractable poverty, the Ponder machine focused on the concrete: jobs, housing support, surplus food, roads, and law enforcement. Like their big-city counterparts, the brothers were pragmatic, rather than ideological. They based their approach on pork and patronage. "If the people didn't have it, and it was available, then we had to get it for them," said Zeno. "Roads or sewers or sidewalks. Whatever the issue was."

E. Y. earned support through his quiet philanthropy and good deeds. It was said that, together with Marshall storekeeper George Penland, E. Y. had teachers at the school serving Shelton Laurel draw outlines of the feet of students too poor for shoes. The two men then supplied the shoes anonymously. Once, when a sharecropper from Tennessee was accused of murder in Madison County and his impoverished family members came to Marshall for the trial, E. Y. paid to put them up in a rooming house so they wouldn't have to sleep on benches on the courthouse lawn.

Over the next dozen and more years, the Ponder family and its allies accumulated posts, both elected and appointed. The princelings were everywhere. Madison County began to look like a miniature Saudi Arabia with voting machines—which were largely decorative. According to Joe Huff, a Mars Hill attorney and longtime Ponder adversary, locals "would go in the voting booth and officials would let them mark the ballots of other people, and it was just so obvious it was dishonest."

"They had everything set up to where you had to go through them to get a road or a job," recalled Dedrick Brown, the Republican deputy who challenged E. Y. Ponder in a number of sheriff's races.

Clyde Parks, a military retiree and a Republican, had the same experience. "They controlled lives. I couldn't even get a job in Madison County." In order to survive, he had to commute to work in Tennessee. "I don't like socialism," said Parks, "but I don't like dictatorships either. And I honestly to God believe that's what we've had in Madison County since the Ponder family took over."

The same held true for dissident Democrats like Joe Huff. "It was the worst damn dictatorship you'd ever seen," he said. "If you weren't one of the faithful, you didn't get a job."

A relatively bright spot in the Ponders' record was their support for civil rights in the 1960s. Their stand was no profile in courage, since few African-Americans lived in Madison County. When the United States Supreme Court ruled in 1954 that schools should be integrated, Zeno ordered the county to do so immediately. Until then, Madison County had sent its black students to Asheville to attend segregated public and private schools. Busing them "was just morally wrong. It was financially wrong," Zeno said. His identification with African-Americans was deep, visceral, and instinctive, rooted in his class consciousness. "I'm in the deepest of sympathy for the blacks, and I hesitate to say right now that I would have been even half as tolerant as they were for the hundred years they were in semi-slavery. . . . If I'd been black I'd of raised hell a long time before they did. . . . I just couldn't have been content to take that kind of treatment."

E. Y. Ponder's views on race were not as uniformly progressive as his younger brother's. The sheriff often boasted of his pure Anglo-Saxon blood. "The only thing the Civil War did was freed the nigger—the colored person, which should have been freed—and then enslaved the

Southern whites." E. Y.'s vocabulary notwithstanding, he claimed an African-American, Everett Barnette, as his great fox-hunting buddy. And
in the 1980s, E. Y. made it a point to carry across the street the robe and
briefcase of a visiting African-American superior-court judge who had
been insulted in nearby Avery County.

Zeno never apologized for his pork-and-patronage policy. "I can
always find a Democrat that's just as good, or a little bit better, than a
damn Republican," he said. In 1960, he backed his high-school buddy
Liston Ramsey for a seat in the state legislature. Under Zeno's patronage, the former Marshall alderman rose to become one of the longest-
serving speakers of the North Carolina House of Representatives.

One key post often eluded the Ponders—district attorney for the
larger, multicounty judicial district, which usually voted Republican.
Given the number of times the Ponders and their allies ended up in
court, often but not always on vote-fraud charges, this was a critical
post. Yet despite numerous indictments and trials, neither Zeno nor
E. Y. ever spent a night in jail.

Even without control of the district attorney job, the brothers had
a reputation for influencing Madison County jurors by packing the
spectator section of the courtroom in Marshall with menacing-looking
supporters. Another favored location was the chamber's second, dupli-
cate jury box, facing the first. It was used in cases that required two
separate panels to hear the same evidence. "Big rogues filled up that jury
box," said Joe Huff, the lawyer. "Court would recess, and these henchmen would run out and I'm sure meet jurors in the hall out behind the
courtroom and going down to the bathroom."

As a result, Ponder allies usually prevailed in both civil and criminal
cases. "Sheriff Ponder could pretty well be depended on to take care if
any of his henchmen got in trouble," said Huff. "Everybody said you
couldn't get a fair trial in Madison County."

The antipathy between Huff and the Ponders lasted throughout their lifetimes. The feud would ultimately play a key role in the Nancy Morgan murder case and would in turn help determine the fate of the Ponder machine.

In 1970, after Nancy's murder, Roy Roberts acknowledged that the sheriff's office was considerably more stressful than he had expected, and he chose not to run for reelection. E. Y. Ponder sought his old position and was elected by a substantial margin. The sheriff-in-exile had returned.

As part of his campaign, he vowed to settle the outstanding questions about Nancy's death.

Part Two
The Trial

10

By 1982, E. Y. Ponder had been reelected sheriff twice but had yet to deliver on his promise to speedily solve Nancy Morgan's murder. The Pondercrat patriarchs, Zeno and E. Y., were aging, and since no strong members of the family's next generation had emerged to take over for them, support for their machine was eroding. Now, facing a challenge from an older, wiser, and more experienced Dedrick Brown, the Republican deputy he had handily defeated in 1970, E. Y. needed campaign ammunition. Again, the Nancy Morgan case gave him leverage. "That was always a burr under his saddle, the fact that he could not solve that murder," said Sheila Kay Adams, the singer and folklorist who knew Nancy. Promising voters for at least the second time that he would solve the VISTA case, he defeated Brown, though by a smaller margin than previously.

Once in office, Ponder again defaulted on his campaign pledge. By 1984, he recognized that Dedrick Brown would no doubt be gunning for him again in 1986. Many observers in the county predicted that the rematch would be close. George Peery, the longtime Mars Hill College political scientist and VISTA liaison, explained, "As the Ponder organization began to lose its power, one of the things that continually floated around had to do with the Morgan murder." Rumors circulated that the Ponder Democrats knew who had killed Nancy but had not pursued the case after winning office in 1970. Now, opponents were saying that "a new sheriff or a new faction within the Democratic Party would pursue this more successfully than had been done in the past."

Suddenly, in the spring of 1984, E. Y. got what seemed a tremendous break. A man named Johnny Waldroup, who was serving time in the Madison County Jail, said he had information to share about the murder. This was the same neighbor who had awakened Ed Walker the morning after Nancy was last seen alive. Now, Waldroup stepped forward with a very different tale from the one he had told in 1970—a tale that implicated Walker.

E. Y. Ponder kept the peace in Madison County largely through a web of informers. According to Harold Bailey, a longtime court administrator and deputy in both Madison and Buncombe counties, E. Y. "had the greatest rat network during his tenure I've ever encountered anywhere. People in Madison County, if they knew anything, they'd report it to him."

Sheila Adams had told her father that the night before Nancy's body was found in her car on Hot Springs Mountain, she and her cousins had searched the area and not found the vehicle there. Adams's father did not take her to Sheriff Roberts to report her story. "It was Sheriff Ponder I told," she remembered.

Ponder dispensed justice selectively. Outsiders with no local political ties were targets for immediate suspicion. This was more than a matter of prejudice; one of E. Y.'s nephews had been murdered by a hitchhiker. Dedrick Brown, unsurprisingly, was a critic of the way E. Y. ran his office before and after the VISTA murder. "We had a lot of things happen in the county during that time that was pretty clear-cut homicide, and it was ruled suicide." Brown claimed that many people in the county believed "a lot of things happened that no one ever got tried for." For example, E. Y. was said to take a flexible view of rape, depending on the status and standing of the woman who brought the charge and of the man she accused.

Political allies tended to benefit from Ponder's discretionary law enforcement. Nowhere was this truer than in Hot Springs, a town that was the subject of much talk because of the sheriff's friendship with Leroy Johnson, the longstanding chief of police. Johnson, according to Dedrick Brown, "was the one who would get the vote out, haul people, set up things for people to get to the polls." In return, E. Y. extricated Johnson's errant son, Richard, and his friends from scrapes with the law. Richard Johnson, like Johnny Waldroup, served as one of Ponder's regular informants.

Johnny Waldroup, by his own later admission, told E. Y. different stories over the years about his involvement—or lack thereof—in the Nancy Morgan case. According to investigators in 1970, Waldroup's account at the time of the murder corresponded to Ed Walker's—namely, he dropped by on the Monday morning of Nancy's disappearance to wake up Walker. In the spring of 1984, facing further jail time and perhaps prompted by the sheriff, Waldroup dramatically changed his story.

⇒⇐

Johnny Waldroup, in the eyes of pretty much everyone who knew him, embodied the term *ne'er-do-well*. In the late 1960s, after a stint in reform school, he came to the attention of Dedrick Brown, then chief deputy sheriff. "We had Johnny in jail a lot for breaking and entering and larceny," he said. And Johnny had a propensity for fanciful tales. "Johnny would tell anything to get attention." Neighbors said he was so stupid that he once set his own pants on fire.

Waldroup made enemies of many of his neighbors in the Bluff and Spring Creek communities through petty theft, vandalism, burglary, the killing of domestic animals, and generally threatening behavior. One former neighbor, Tracy Caldwell-McElroy, said years later, "When I was little, he scared me to death. I remember when he would get out of jail from time to time and walk up and down the road. That was the only time we ever locked our doors. My dad was always afraid he would rob us blind."

In November 1972, David and Camille Shafer arrived in Madison County, part of the first wave of the local back-to-the-land movement. They had discovered the area while walking the Appalachian Trail. "There was talk about the VISTA person that was killed, and it was really in the mind of a lot of people," said David. "Of course, we were warned. They told us to be very careful. People had been very traumatized by it."

They soon met one of their neighbors. "We were naïve," said Camille, a French immigrant. "We were young, we had just arrived here. So Johnny Waldroup would come around our place often. At first, we had some kind of pity about him because we thought the guy didn't have a chance."

They soon recognized their mistake. On one occasion, Waldroup, carrying a six-pack of beer, came over and asked to buy one of the couple's geese. The bird was sitting on her eggs, so Camille said no. Two days later, the goose was gone.

Even more alarming, certain friends "wouldn't come in our house" when Johnny was around, Camille said, for reasons they were reluctant to share. The couple felt they had to make a choice, "and that was definitely that Johnny was out and our community was in."

In the late summer of 1974, Nancy Darrell and her husband came to Madison County, like the Shafers looking for a place to settle in the mountains. When they drove into the Spring Creek area, they picked up Waldroup, who was hitchhiking. Right away, he wanted to talk about Nancy Morgan's killing. Darrell paid little attention to him at the time, but she came to know Waldroup better when she and her husband settled in Spring Creek. Mostly, they knew him as a chicken thief. "He was kind of a notorious character, and there seemed to be some speculation about Johnny in relation to the Morgan killing," she said.

Tom Moloney, an air force retiree, moved to Madison County in 1979. In the Bluff community, where he settled, he heard the story of Nancy's death. The account piqued his interest because, in a previous job in Florida, he had headed the city of Titusville's social-services department, where he supervised VISTAs, including one who had known Nancy. In the early 1980s, talk about the case arose from time to time in Bluff. "The pot seemed to get stirred up every time one of the local desperadoes would get into trouble and would want to turn or provide some evidence on the Nancy Morgan murder," Moloney said. "It all seemed to be coming from the same rumor mill, the same type of people, and Johnny Waldroup was always right in the middle of it," hinting darkly that he knew more than he let on.

Moloney and his wife, Barbara, had repeated problems with Waldroup and filed charges several times against the man for threatening them. Waldroup was "harassing us, continually telling us he was going to burn us out," Moloney said. The most serious episode took place in 1983 at a country store, where the Moloneys ran into Johnny as they went to buy groceries. According to Moloney, Waldroup stepped in front of him, snickering, and Moloney said, "Get out of my face." Waldroup then reached into a neighbor's parked car, pulled out a .22 rifle, and put it to Moloney's head. "I turned around at that point and started to walk back," said Moloney, "and I heard a click. There was no bullet in the chamber." The neighbor came out of the store and took the gun away from Waldroup.

Moloney filed charges with the sheriff's office and soon received a personal visit from E. Y. "Ponder said he knew Johnny had just lost it for a little bit there. Waldroup was just a good ol' boy. He didn't have a very good upbringing, and we needed to give the local fellows a break. Why wouldn't I just drop the charges?" Moloney replied that enough charges had been dropped, and he was not going to do so this time.

Waldroup, who was already on supervised probation for a church break-in that had earned him a suspended five-year sentence, learned somehow that he was in big trouble. Another conviction would send him to state prison. To compound his troubles, he then stole a red pick-up truck from "Uncle" Howard Finley, who lived next door to him in Bluff, and took off for Texas. There, Waldroup ran out of money and called Ponder. Johnny proposed that the sheriff send him enough money for gas and travel expenses, and he would drive Finley's truck back to Madison County (even though he had no driver's license). E. Y. refused and told Waldroup to turn himself and the truck in at the nearest Texas jail. Ponder wanted to let the local authorities pay to send Johnny home, and he would arrange to have the truck returned to North Carolina.

Back in jail in Marshall, Waldroup faced Finley's charge of auto theft as well as Moloney's assault charge, to which he pleaded guilty and no contest, respectively. For some unexplained reason, he remained in the Madison County Jail for a year, rather than being sent to state prison.

At that point, in the spring of 1984, still facing another four or five years of incarceration, Waldroup unexpectedly felt moved to offer up a new account of Nancy Morgan's death. In his revised story—just as E. Y. Ponder had suspected all along—she died at the hands of former VISTA worker Ed Walker.

With Waldroup's information in hand, the wheels of prosecution began to turn. James T. "Tom" Rusher, the district attorney for Madison and a few neighboring counties, wrote to Abigail Morgan, Nancy's mother, on April 27, 1984, that he, Sheriff Ponder, and an agent of the SBI "have reviewed the old investigation and have in some instances re-interviewed persons. I do not seek to kindle any false hope. There are now still no specific leads which we feel justify prosecution."

Years later, the prosecutor explained that he was not being disingenuous in his letter to Abigail Morgan. He was constrained by what he cryptically called "the vicissitudes . . . in Sheriff Ponder's investigative conclusions." In any event, both Rusher and Ponder became convinced, on the basis of Johnny Waldroup's jailhouse testimony, that a case existed against Ed Walker, the last person known to have seen Nancy Morgan alive.

The sheriff decided it was time for a trip to Florida.

11

The late-night knock at the Florida beachfront condo came, as planned, unexpectedly. Ed Walker opened the door and saw a small, older man in a rumpled suit. Behind him stood two other men, one wearing a police uniform. When the strangers said they wanted to talk about the murder of Nancy Morgan, Walker was taken aback—exactly the reaction Sheriff E. Y. Ponder hoped for.

Then thirty-four and living on the Gulf Coast with his wife and adolescent daughter, Ed Walker was working as an auto-parts supervisor at a Dodge dealership, where he was considered one of the company's best employees. He had no inkling of what was happening in North Carolina. At ten o'clock on the night of August 14, 1984, he was at home with his daughter and niece as his wife worked the night shift as a police dispatcher.

"It was the sheriff, E. Y. Ponder," Walker said. With him were an agent from the North Carolina State Bureau of Investigation and a local deputy. After the latter two men identified themselves, Walker invited the three inside. "My first reaction was . . . that they had found who killed Nancy and were coming down to ask me to go testify in a trial. That was my first impression."

Recalling the night years later, Walker was able to pinpoint the date because his wife's birthday was the next day, August 15. Inside the house, he offered the men seats in the dining room and asked the children to go into the daughter's bedroom so the four could talk. One of the men explained that they wanted Walker to come with them to the local sheriff's office. Walker replied that his wife was at work but would be home by eleven, "and then we can do whatever you want to do." He was still under the impression the lawmen were "just going to ask me my recollections, to come testify about everything that happened."

Once Walker's wife returned, the men took him to the nearby sheriff's office, where a deputy read him his rights and asked him to sign a paper. Walker signed, thinking, *This is just so I'll be truthful and they can use it in case I decide to change my mind and not testify.* The agents asked him questions, and he willingly shared his recollections—until it struck him that the questions were beginning to sound accusatory. "Wait a minute," he asked. "What's going on here?"

One of the men replied, "We have information from a person who has told us who committed this crime."

Walker said, "Great. If you want my cooperation, I'll be more than happy to go testify."

Then came the punch line: "The person has said he is an eyewitness. He said you killed Nancy Morgan."

At that point, Walker asked for a ride home. The SBI agent and the local deputy drove him the four or five miles in the backseat of a police car. On the way, he asked the SBI agent, "What does this really mean? What are you telling me?"

The agent, according to Walker, answered, "Well, you're in a world of shit, and if you can't afford F. Lee Bailey, you'd better get the best lawyer you can."

Walker said, "You guys are nuts. You are just absolutely nuts."

Walker was unimpressed by his first encounter with E. Y. Ponder. Like many before him, he underestimated the lawman. Although Walker admitted he was being "socially judgmental," he said Ponder struck him "as kind of a bumpkin." Indeed, Walker didn't even know the man was Ponder until the formal interview began. The SBI agent "identified himself early, but I just thought Ponder was somebody with him. It was during the interview that he identified himself. He was unremarkable. Just sitting there, not saying much."

Back at home, severely frightened, Walker told his wife what had happened. He wasn't convinced the law-enforcement officers were telling the truth. He thought they might just be on a fishing expedition, trying to see if he still told his original story consistently.

At two-thirty that morning, he called Richard Haimes, his former Madison County VISTA supervisor, at home in Atlanta to ask if the North Carolina authorities had talked to him about the accusation. Haimes had heard nothing.

At six in the morning on his wife's birthday, Walker met his best friend for breakfast at Howard Johnson's, explained what had happened the night before, as well as in Madison County years earlier, and asked for advice. See a lawyer immediately, his friend said. Walker, who had never been in trouble with the law, knew no criminal attorneys, so he called his real-estate lawyer, who had been a judge in Ohio before moving to Florida. The lawyer asked if the men who had come to see him had an arrest warrant. Learning that they didn't, he suggested Walker sit tight.

Soon, however, matters took a turn for the worse for Walker.

In Madison County five days later, on August 20, after hearing testimony from Sheriff Ponder, Johnny Waldroup, and agents from the FBI and the SBI, a grand jury indicted Ed Walker for first-degree murder, rape, and obstruction of justice. In his press release, prosecutor Tom Rusher, a Republican, gave credit for the indictment to three previous sheriffs, including fellow Republicans Roy Roberts and Dedrick Brown, for their work over the years. But almost immediately, Sheriff Ponder claimed primary credit for breaking the case, to Rusher's chagrin. The district attorney felt that, in hogging the credit for the indictment, Ponder risked polarizing the community and turning the upcoming trial into a political fight, in which Democrats would line up behind the prosecution and Republicans behind the defense—Rusher's own GOP affiliation notwithstanding.

Ponder told the grand jury that in December 1983, while Waldroup was in jail, he had first heard Johnny's story implicating Walker, although he later told reporters it was May 1984. "Time sometimes causes people to change their minds about things," the sheriff explained to reporters at the time of the indictment, referring to Waldroup's surprise confession.

Charlie Chambers, the SBI agent involved from the beginning, told a reporter for the Asheville newspaper that the case had been broken when an unidentified eyewitness came forward to "clear his conscience."

Sheriff Ponder told the weekly Madison County *News-Record*, "What we have done today is the result of a lot of effort since the time of the crime. Hardly a week has gone by in the last twelve years that I didn't receive some information on the case. With the erosion of time, a man that was in a position to know what happened has come forward." The sheriff said he had gone to Walker's home in Florida "to see if he wanted to change his story" about Nancy Morgan's killing. "We talked some and he never elaborated on anything."

The next day, August 21, Walker learned from his old VISTA supervisor that a story about his indictment for first-degree murder had appeared in a Charlotte newspaper. First thing that morning, Walker was back in his lawyer's office. Again, the attorney checked the local sheriff's office for a warrant. This time, one had been issued. The former judge offered to arrange for a local public defender, according to Walker.

"How can I qualify?" Walker said, bristling. "I own two houses, a boat, and a car. I've got a bunch of money in the bank."

The attorney said, "You can't afford what you're about to get into. . . . You're looking at twenty-five to thirty thousand dollars' worth of legal expenses."

After his lawyer made an appointment for him with a public defender, Walker told the whole story again. By now, he was feeling panicked not only for himself but also for his family. The public defender called the district attorney's office in North Carolina and "finally got somebody in Madison County, who told us the warrant had been mailed to Florida." According to Walker, the public defender said he would arrange for Ed to return to North Carolina, where he would immediately be released on bail. Prosecutor Tom Rusher had, according to his own recollection, agreed with the Florida attorney that if Walker were to come to North Carolina at his own expense, "we would arrange for some kind of bond, and he would not be required to be incarcerated."

By this time, the story had hit the local Florida newspaper. Walker recalled that the public defender warned him about how the publicity would affect his wife and daughter. He advised Walker to "get them put in a safe place so they won't have to be harassed by all this. It's going to be an ugly thing." Walker quickly arranged for his daughter to stay with his mother and other family members, although for a time his wife "had to stay and work and get things squared away."

According to Walker, the attorney advised him to take a polygraph test and, upon Walker's agreement, sent him to a firm that administered the procedure. Later, the lawyer informed his client that he had passed the test, Walker recalled, and that he showed no stress and was not being deceptive when he said he had no involvement in Nancy Morgan's death. Walker said the public defender advised him to fly to Asheville and present himself to the authorities. Walker remembered, "I flew to Asheville thinking . . . *I'm going to go up there, and we're going to talk about this, and they're just going to say, 'This is crazy.'*" He still did not know who had brought the allegations against him.

Walker found himself thinking about the movie *Deliverance*. He felt the film portrayed an extreme stereotype of people he had met in Madison County. But returning to the southern Appalachians to face a murder charge made him think twice about what he was getting into.

"Strange things happened up there," he said. "You never do get into that society unless you're born into it. Nobody ever assimilates into it."

12

Ed Walker's Florida public defender notified Madison County prosecutors that his client would arrive at the airport in Asheville. Walker packed three suits, took some coupons for discounts at the Holiday Inn, and told his boss at the auto dealership he was going to North Carolina for a long weekend. He also brought five thousand dollars in traveler's checks for bail. Tom Rusher's office arranged to have a Buncombe County public defender meet him at the arrival gate.

Walker expected he would meet the public defender and someone from the prosecutor's office, that they would sit down and talk, and that he would convince them he had nothing to do with Nancy Morgan's death. He imagined staying at a Holiday Inn, visiting a few friends in Madison County, and returning to work in Florida. But as he and the public defender picked up his bags, Walker asked the man what would happen next.

The lawyer replied, "Well, they're going to put you in jail."

Stunned, Walker protested that he had returned voluntarily and that he had an agreement with the prosecutor. He had come to straighten things out.

The public defender said, "They're going to jail you. They ain't going to put you up anywhere. They're going to put you in jail, and they're going to keep you there until they try you." He told Walker that he didn't practice law in Madison County, but he knew it was "a lot different than Buncombe County."

Walker's first thought was, *There go my Holiday Inn coupons.*

On the forty-minute drive from the airport to the courthouse in Marshall, Walker sat in the back of the sheriff's car, without handcuffs, and declined to make small talk with the deputies. They escorted him into the courthouse through a crowd of reporters and photographers shouting questions. Inside, E. Y. Ponder read him his rights for the photographers as Walker, dressed in a pale summer suit and striped tie, stood before a bank of filing cabinets and looked on grimly at the documents.

But however low his expectations might have been about the Madison County Jail, one of the oldest still in use in the state, they weren't realized when he was booked in about noon. The squat red-brick facility along the French Broad River and the railroad tracks had a strip of white wood running up one exterior wall noting the high-water marks from historic floods. But inside, Walker said, it was "like visiting somebody's house," or a college dormitory. "The sheriff said, 'Why don't you have somebody show him his room and get him something to eat?'"

Walker thought, *Show me to my room?*

A deputy took him up the fifteen steel steps to the second floor and directed him to a cell. Someone brought him food and then didn't lock the cell door.

The seven cells ranged from claustrophobic two-man arrangements to several designed for four inmates to one dormitory-style enclosure that could hold eight. But there was also a high-ceilinged, well-lit day room. Inmates were usually free to come and go, wandering from cell to cell. Walker didn't want anyone walking into his cell. So when a deputy came to pick up his dinner tray, he insisted the door be locked and kept that way.

"They didn't search me, didn't make me change my clothes," Walker remembered. Ponder had his luggage sent up without searching it. The sheriff asked if he had a knife. Walker replied that he didn't carry one, and Ponder said, "Okay." Walker found the exchange bizarre. "I could have had a gun and a whole arsenal with me."

That kind of jailhouse informality was nothing new in Madison County. Early in the twentieth century, a Shelton Laurel man who admitted killing six men in the county testified that he had been made to feel at home by the sheriff, who allowed him to "keep a gun . . . , drink whiskey in the jail, and eat at table with the family of the sheriff."

E. Y. Ponder wanted a calm, relaxed jail and sometimes went to extremes to achieve it. According to one frequently told tale, seized marijuana plants stored in the jail in an unlocked downstairs closet disappeared leaf by leaf over several months, apparently consumed by savvy inmates—and perhaps deputies—right under E. Y.'s nose.

One of the inmates already walking around upstairs was the son of E. Y.'s old buddy, Hot Springs police chief Leroy Johnson. Richard Johnson was awaiting trial for poisoning his five-year-old daughter to death in a horrendous effort to win back his estranged wife. Johnson introduced himself to the new inmate and tried to engage him in conversation, but Walker rebuffed the effort at small talk.

Once Walker was settled at the jail, Ponder took him up the street to the courthouse and the county clerk's office, where the assistant district attorney awaited him. On the advice of his Florida public defender, Walker asked to have an attorney appointed for him. The county clerk telephoned superior-court judge Charles Lamm for approval. And at that moment, on what was probably the worst day of his life, Ed Walker caught perhaps his luckiest break ever. Judge Lamm assigned his case to Joe Huff, the lifelong opponent of the Ponder regime, who accepted his new client by telephone.

The rivalry between Huff and the Ponders dated to the time Joe and Zeno were teenage students at Mars Hill College. Zeno, the poor farm boy from the holler, and Huff, the middle-class son of a patrician college professor, rubbed each other the wrong way. Until then, Huff said, "he was down there, and we were up here, and not much did we mix. We've got higher class."

People from Mars Hill, Huff insisted, had fought in the Confederate army, while people "down that way" joined robber bands and "pillaged while my grandfather and others were out fighting the war." Huff's charges notwithstanding, both the Huffs and the Ponders had ancestors who fought on the Confederate side at the Battle of Chickamauga. But Huff maintained that "the people back in the Laurels and that way didn't serve. The [Mars Hill] men were gone, and so they could come over here and do what they wanted to do. And that caused a big schism between this part of the county and that part there."

The breach between Joe and Zeno was deep, personal, and entirely mutual. After the Korean War, Huff moved his law practice from Asheville to Marshall, said Steve Huff, Joe's son, also an attorney. "Zeno showed up in his office and tried to tell him how to handle a case. As you might expect, my father threw him out of the office." Nobody was going to tell Joe Huff how to practice law. Over the years, Huff became convinced that the Ponder brothers intimidated jurors when they had a personal interest in the outcome of a trial, and he claimed to have tried cases in which he had no doubt the jury was fixed.

Later, Joe and Zeno came to blows, engaging in a fistfight in the courthouse. Both claimed to have won. In typical Madison County fashion, the literal truth of the incident remains elusive. "We were in the center of the courthouse, and Zeno and a bunch of his henchmen were standing around," said Huff, who was a boxer in college. "I walked in, and he had something insulting to say to me—it was this way all the time. I hauled off and knocked the hell out of him. He had a black eye for weeks."

The encounter was entirely in keeping with Joe Huff's nature, his son Steve said, despite the fact that Zeno was a bigger man. "My father was the kind of man who would knock you down if you pushed him."

Zeno always maintained he won the fight, waving off the Huffs' account as "a pack of lies" in an interview with historian Hunter James. "Hell, everybody in that courthouse was fighting to keep me off him."

No one was going to tell Joe Huff how to vote either. In a Mars Hill precinct in 1964, the lawyer took part in another melee with Ponder loyalists. Zeno had run in the primary for the Democratic nomination to the state senate, and in Mars Hill, a stronghold of the conservative anti-Ponder faction, tempers were spiking as partisans for both sides counted—and disputed—ballots in an elementary-school classroom. The shouting escalated into a fistfight and then a brawl. Someone knocked open a closet door, and out tumbled several stuffed ballot boxes. Pistols were drawn, but before any gunfire erupted, a group of E. Y.'s deputies filed in, weapons in hand, and hauled off the boxes to the sheriff's office. To no one's surprise, Zeno carried the precinct.

Normally, Zeno had some good words, or at least faint praise, for his adversaries, even Madison County Republicans. But not in this case—and Huff was a fellow Democrat. "Joe Huff is what we call a revolving son of a bitch," Zeno said. "Any way you look at him, he's a son of a bitch."

On the way back to Ed Walker's cell from the courthouse, the sheriff handed the Florida man a copy of his indictment. "I'm reading it, and I see Johnny Waldroup's name, and I thought, *This is just absurd*," Walker remembered.

Huff, then sixty-five, soon arrived at the jail to meet his new client. Walker described the scene: "Joe comes in, in khaki pants, hiking boots, and an old plaid shirt that my dad wouldn't even wear." An avid outdoorsman with ruddy cheeks and piercing blue eyes, Huff was a familiar sight in the more remote areas of the county, dressed in work clothes and riding in a four-wheel-drive vehicle, often with a young local guide impressed into his service. Walker thought he was doomed. "They appoint me an old man who don't have a clue."

Huff hardly reassured his client when he asked if Walker would like a radio or some books. When Walker asked why, he said, "You're going to be here awhile." Huff was not optimistic that the judge would release Walker on bond. He said, "It won't be too bad after a while. They'll probably make you a trusty so you can just walk around and do what you want."

Walker showed Huff the indictment and asked if he knew "this son of a bitch" Johnny Waldroup. Huff replied that he did, and Walker said, "Well, this is absurd. . . . He's the village idiot. How can they indict me on what this crazy bastard says?"

Huff did his best to soothe his client. He told Walker he had been in the courtroom the day the grand jury indicted him, waiting at the back to see a judge. "I saw the sheriff come in with Johnny Waldroup, and I said, 'Well, you got your stool pigeon here today, must be trying to indict somebody.'"

Walker by that time was on the verge of tears. He thought, *I've got to get to a phone. Get my brother on the phone. Get everybody I know. Get everything going. Get me the hell out of here.* But he realized that Labor Day was approaching and guessed that no judge would be in town until after the holiday. He felt increasingly helpless. His call to Jeffrey Hammer, who was still with VISTA, asking for some higher-priced legal talent was rebuffed. Politically, having Joe Huff defend him in Madison County was a double-edged sword because of the attorney's well-known enmity toward the Ponders. "It didn't help Walker any that he had me for his lawyer," Huff admitted, "because they hated me worse than God hates sin."

Ultimately, Judge Lamm set bond at one hundred thousand dollars. When Walker was arraigned on September 4, the day after Labor Day, it was reduced to fifty thousand, but 15 percent of that had to be in cash or secured North Carolina property, a seemingly impossible hurdle for Walker.

Help soon came from an unexpected quarter. Tom Moloney, the retired air force officer from Spring Creek, to whose head Waldroup had held a gun, contacted Sheriff Ponder as soon as he heard that testimony from his old nemesis had led to Walker's arrest.

"There's some pretty damning evidence here against him," E. Y. said.

When the sheriff confirmed that the evidence came from Waldroup, Moloney asked if E. Y. had any objection to his coming over to speak to Walker. He told Ponder, "I used to work in social services, and we may have some mutual friends." The sheriff agreed to Moloney's request, and he visited the jail over Labor Day weekend.

"Ed was just beside himself," Moloney remembered. "He still at that point didn't understand what was going on." Moloney then talked to the sheriff, telling him he wanted to discuss with his wife, Barbara, the possibility of paying Walker's bail. Barbara agreed, and the two put their house up to guarantee the bond. "We didn't know Ed," said Moloney, "but we knew Johnny, and the fact that Ed was a VISTA worker said enough, as far as I was concerned." After talking with Walker, Moloney felt Waldroup's story was "all too pat and too clean, and there was not a bit of truth to it."

Walker was grateful but also wary of this stranger. "I was suspicious of him at first because he wasn't an original mountain person. I thought, *Why would this guy be doing this?* I thought maybe he was a shill put there by Rusher or E. Y."

Moloney visited Walker during the ten days before he was released on bail, bringing him newspapers and taking messages to his friends in Bluff. Upon his release, Walker left immediately and drove back to Florida with his brother.

As it turned out, Johnny Waldroup was a greater flight risk than Ed Walker. The trial was originally scheduled for April 1985, but as the date neared, Waldroup, who had been released from jail for time served on the truck-theft charge, was nowhere to be found. Then he called the sheriff's office from Salt Lake City, where he said he was stranded. A gullible deputy wired the wayward witness bus fare, whereupon Waldroup disappeared again. He next contacted Sheriff Ponder with the story that he had mistakenly boarded a bus heading west instead of east, and was then in Los Angeles. Would E. Y. send him some more money? This time, the sheriff had a contact in Southern California put him on a bus back to North Carolina. Ponder told the newspapers that the request for a new trial date was the result of an "ill witness." The change cost Walker's family, who had already returned to North Carolina, precious resources.

After Walker's indictment and arrest, his life in Florida hurtled downhill. His boss at the car dealership said he would have to let Walker go. His wife, who was still on probationary status with the sheriff's department, was fired. Trying to survive on unemployment, the couple cashed in their retirement accounts and insurance policies. Walker's wife sold her jewelry. "We used up all the money we saved," he said. In short order, he lost his house, his condo, his boat, and his two cars.

The family moved from its upper-middle-class neighborhood to a small apartment in a sketchy part of town. "Around Thanksgiving time, we just gave up," Walker said. "We stopped paying bills and didn't make an effort." In hindsight, he thought he should have declared bankruptcy, but at the time he was "imbued with the Protestant work ethic. You owe the money, you pay it." By the time of the trial, the Walkers were down to fifty-two dollars and an ancient Cadillac. They had given up their apartment. "We were truly homeless people," Walker said. When the trial was postponed, they moved their few remaining pieces of furniture into a garage apartment at Walker's sister's home, which they renovated themselves.

To save on expenses, Joe Huff traveled to Florida to consult with his client, but the visits did little to lift Walker's spirit. He wanted his attorney to try to quash the indictment, but Huff argued that would be a mistake; even if he was successful, it could be revived later. Only a not-guilty verdict would drive a stake through the heart of the prosecution and let Walker get on with his life.

For Walker, that was not the worst of it. There was collateral damage to his adolescent daughter, who had been inside the condo when E. Y. and the SBI agent came calling. She took the arrest and the upcoming trial especially hard. "Having to uproot a nice middle-class family and a little girl who lived on the beach like a little princess, grabbing her up when she's about twelve years old" caused her great anguish, Walker said. The family had moved into a cramped, run-down apartment, where she roomed with her cousin. "No friends. No money. She just couldn't cope with it." And her dad was about to be tried for murder.

13

The stately Madison County Courthouse, a red-brick building in the Neoclassical Revival style, dates to 1908. Impressively traditional, it fronts the French Broad River and features a four-stage polygonal cupola painted silver. Atop the dome rises a statue of Lady Justice. For many years, the goddess was missing her blindfold, and local people liked to speculate why. Storekeeper and former Marshall mayor George Penland suggested that "maybe it's because she'd better keep her eyes open in Madison County." Others said the statue should have been holding her nose—although if she had, she would have missed the whiffs of smoke from periodic attempts to burn the structure down. During one post-arson renovation, Lady Justice was found to have at least three bullet holes.

Spectators entered the second-floor courtroom from the rear of the chamber. Laid out arena-style, the courtroom was like a university lecture hall with gently sloping aisles. The floors squeaked. Along the right wall were three large floor-to-ceiling windows that looked into a wooded hillside. Along the left, an equal number of double-hung windows with half-round tops looked out over a Corinthian portico, where pigeons waddled on sunny afternoons. A chandelier hung from the thirty-foot ceiling, a square grid of dark-stained beams. Dark wooden panels topped with elegant old wainscoting rose from the floor to about chest level. Behind the two facing jury boxes, each containing fourteen green leather chairs, ancient, rattling metal radiators provided heat.

The spectator area was comprised of three sections of blond-wood folding seats trimmed in black wrought iron. On the first day of Ed Walker's week-long trial before Judge Robert D. Lewis, all 160 seats were occupied. More people stood at the back of the courtroom and spilled onto the street. At the time, first-degree murder was a capital offense in North Carolina, but District Attorney Tom Rusher announced he would not seek the death penalty. In fact, he had no choice in the matter. The United States Supreme Court had declared the state's previous death-penalty statute unconstitutional, exempting all crimes committed before the new law was enacted in 1976.

Rusher, a Republican elected in 1982, served as district attorney for five western North Carolina counties—a job held two hundred years earlier by an ambitious young Democrat named Andrew Jackson. Rusher had known about the Nancy Morgan case since early 1971, when he was a young assistant district attorney in the same jurisdiction. In the second chair for the prosecution was James Baker, a Madison County native who would later be named a judge.

Naturally, the Walker family and its camp of Madison County supporters were anxious as the trial neared. Walker was an outsider—and a mouthy, longhaired one at that—facing small-town justice. Solving the case was a major plank in Sheriff Ponder's campaign platform. In a defiant—if reckless—move, Walker decided not to trim his hair in deference to local sensibilities. Instead, he wore his standard coiffure, a Caucasian version of an Afro that made his head look like a two-tone Tootsie Pop.

Since Walker was down to his last fifty dollars, his sister and daughter came by Greyhound bus. The family, including his mother and aunt, stayed at a private home. Walker's father was too ill to travel, but Ed's brother flew up for one day.

From that first Monday, Walker and his attorney established a morning ritual: Ed would meet Joe Huff at his office, and they would walk across the street to court together, joining the other members of his family. Walker's initial skepticism about his lawyer had by now evolved into confidence.

The Morgan family had a reduced presence at the trial. Since Nancy's murder in 1970, her father had died of stomach cancer. And her younger brother, George, was touring with a rock band, hoping for a big break. But her mother, Abigail, her brother John, and her aunt Katy Boulden came to Marshall to attend the trial. They all stayed at an Asheville motel after driving together through the mountains of Tennessee. Abigail, who was known for bottling up her emotions, remained silent throughout much of the ride.

In court, the Morgans sat on the right, directly behind the prosecutors, whose table almost abutted the jury box used for the trial. On the first morning, the two middle-aged, middle-class sisters realized they had overdressed. Unlike the other women in the courtroom, Abigail and Katy wore fashionable suits, hats, and makeup. They shared some of the same cultural concerns about Madison County justice as the Walkers. The two women felt like outsiders and at times found the proceedings almost farcical, the opposing lawyers characters out of some rustic drama. In the relaxed way of things in Madison County, Walker's wife and daughter joined him at the defense table that Monday morning.

Outside the courtroom that first day, Abigail Morgan said, "Naturally, we would like to see justice done," but she didn't reveal if she thought Walker was guilty.

Nancy's brother John seemed to lean toward the prosecution,

telling a reporter that "fourteen years ago, Walker was the prime suspect. The FBI was pretty sure he was their boy, but they didn't have enough evidence on him."

Although some members of the Bluff and Spring Creek communities were excused from jury service because they knew either Ed Walker or Johnny Waldroup, Rusher and Joe Huff wasted little time picking a panel before lunch. It included five men—one named Ponder—seven women, and one male and one female alternate.

Rusher gave an opening statement that painted the crime as one of unrequited love, a familiar theme he hoped would resonate with jurors.

Huff declined to address the jury—and in the process tip off Rusher to his strategy. "We have nothing to prove, Your Honor," he said dismissively.

The prosecution's first witness was former sheriff Roy Roberts, who testified under direct examination that he had questioned Ed Walker at the murder scene.

Huff cross-examined Roberts, asking if he had spoken with Johnny Waldroup. Walker shot a skeptical look at his one-time neighbor, who was sitting in the courtroom but avoided the defendant's gaze. Roberts said he hadn't questioned Waldroup directly. He had interviewed Ed Walker at the scene where Nancy's car was found, but he had not arrested anyone at the time because he had insufficient evidence.

Waldroup, a hard-faced man with sharp features, then in his thirties, was next on the stand that same Monday afternoon. He had been kept under guard the last two days, in light of his previous unannounced jaunts around the country. Wearing a yellow knit shirt that had seen better days, he began his testimony standing next to a crude diagram of the neighboring Waldroup and Walker houses in Bluff. Waldroup said he had met Nancy Morgan at Walker's house the Saturday before Nancy's final Sunday dinner, while mowing Walker's lawn—a sighting of Nancy not reported at the time or corroborated by anyone since. At times, Waldroup spoke so softly the judge had to ask him to raise his voice.

Late Sunday night, after hearing a noise, Waldroup said, he went to Walker's house. "I walked around to the side of the house and looked through the window, and I see'd two people in the house and one on the couch."

Waldroup said he recognized Walker but not the second man. The woman on the couch was Nancy.

"She didn't have no clothes on. She had a cord running from her neck to her feet," Waldroup said, not mentioning if her hands were also tied, as they had been when the body was found.

Waldroup testified that when he entered the house to come to Nancy's aid, he saw her eyes moving, the lids fluttering. But before he could release her, the life seemed to go out of her. Then, suddenly and without provocation, Walker punched him in the nose, drawing blood. The VISTA worker, who was unarmed, told Waldroup that "if I didn't help them dispose of the body, they was going to kill me. I was told if I didn't drive the car, I'd be killed, too."

Convinced the threat was genuine, Waldroup said, he drove Walker's car while the defendant got behind the wheel of Nancy's gray Plymouth, followed by the second man in a third car. The caravan proceeded to Tanyard Gap. There, he testified, "I sat and waited on him." At no time, Waldroup said, did he ever touch Nancy's body following his failed effort to release her.

After he and Walker returned together to Bluff, they sat in Waldroup's car in a fork in the road. Walker didn't explain Nancy's death. "I didn't ask him," said Waldroup. "He was in an outrage. He said he loved her."

Later that Monday morning, after a few hours of fitful sleep,

Waldroup said, he returned to Walker's house, which had been cleaned since the killing. There, he saw Walker burning papers he thought were letters.

By this point in his career, Joe Huff had given up suits for blazers and slacks. But for the Ed Walker trial, he wore his one summer suit and an out-of-fashion square-bottomed black tie. All the time Waldroup was testifying for the prosecution, Huff was thinking, *Let me get at him.*

When it was his turn, Huff launched into a cross-examination sometimes so blistering it caused jurors to grimace. The rituals of courtesy were immediately dispensed with; there were no "mister" honorifics. From the outset, Huff addressed Waldroup as "Johnny." The witness called the attorney "Joe," "Huff," or simply "you." The contest was the legal equivalent of hand-to-hand combat, and as the cross-examination gathered steam, it threatened to become physical.

The first question went back to 1970: "Why did you tell Sheriff Roberts that you were not up there [at Bluff] and you didn't know anything about what happened up there?"

Red-faced, Waldroup shot back, "I wish not to answer that question."

Why, Huff asked, didn't he tell the sheriff's deputies who questioned him at the time anything about Walker's involvement in the killing?

Slumping in his chair, Waldroup replied barely audibly, "I didn't tell them nothing."

Had the witness ever told his story to the then–district attorney, Clyde Roberts?

"No!" Waldroup shouted.

In this first stage of the cross-examination, which lasted more than an hour, Huff shifted to Waldroup's criminal history, both to undermine his credibility and to establish a motive for him to lie—namely, the desire for special treatment from Sheriff Ponder. With Waldroup's criminal records stacked high on the defense table, Huff began a recitation of the witness's offenses, starting with his juvenile record at Stonewall Jackson Training School and moving quickly to weightier matters, including the theft of his uncle's truck and, before that, the church break-in for which he had been sentenced to five years in prison. Huff asked how he had been able to get that sentence suspended—by ratting out an accomplice?

"I guess E. Y. Ponder could answer that," Waldroup said.

At one point, the judge reminded Huff that only convictions or guilty pleas were admissible from Waldroup's criminal record, which included numerous arrests for offenses that never came to trial. So the defense attorney asked Waldroup to list his convictions.

"I don't know," the witness snapped. "You got the brains. You look it up."

In light of Waldroup's previous convictions, Huff asked, and the fact that he was supposed to be on supervised probation at the time of the truck theft, why wasn't he in custody now? "Why are you walking around here today when you've got a five-year sentence you ought to be serving?" Huff demanded. "I say you didn't tell anybody [about the Nancy Morgan murder] until you had been down there in jail for about a year and couldn't get out."

"No," Waldroup replied.

Huff: "Who's taking care of you, Johnny? What did they promise you if you testified? . . . They brought you up here and gave you a year and gave you credit for ten months and sixteen days served in jail and let you out, didn't they? So you bought your way out of jail on a lie? You were between a rock and a hard place, and that's all you could do?"

Waldroup gave no ground on this barrage, replying rapid-fire: "No." "Lie." "Lie." "*You* are lying."

Huff challenged Waldroup about things he had told the defense attorney during earlier courthouse encounters, before Walker was charged. "You also told me you didn't know a thing about Ed Walker, that you were not up there, and that you might be a low-down son of a bitch, but you weren't *that* low-down. You weren't going to come into court and swear that—didn't you [say that]?"

The witness asked Huff if he, Waldroup, had been drunk when he said that.

Huff replied, "Well, you told me that you were on drugs the whole time you were down in jail—that you didn't know what you were saying."

Huff wanted to know if Waldroup had just told another scheduled witness, Marie Osteen, in the courthouse lobby earlier that same day that "they had you hung up on a hook, and that you could not get out, and that they thought you were going to come up here and swear lies on Walker, and that you would not send your soul to hell by swearing a lie to send somebody to the penitentiary."

Initially, Waldroup's mumbled answer was inaudible.

As Huff pointed to the woman sitting in the courtroom, all Waldroup could say was, "I don't know. I don't know, Huff."

The defense attorney wondered aloud why the witness had not been charged as an accessory after the fact in the Nancy Morgan killing, in light of his account of helping Walker.

Huff hammered away at other inconsistencies in Waldroup's testimony.

Waldroup said he had seen Walker cooking dinner for Nancy, rather than the other way around, as Walker had told investigators at the time. In fact, Huff declared, Johnny had told investigators he was spending time with prostitutes in Asheville that evening.

Waldroup also said Nancy's face had turned black-and-blue, a statement not borne out by either police reports from the death scene or autopsy photos.

"Johnny, Johnny," Huff asked wearily, "can we tell the truth for a minute?"

Waldroup stewed. The courtroom had no air conditioning, so the windows were kept open. Every time a freight train came roaring through town, the proceedings had to pause.

Not content with detailing Waldroup's criminal history, Huff circulated Johnny's rap sheet to the jury. The defense attorney asked if the witness had been confined several times in a state mental hospital.

"They found out I wasn't crazy," Waldroup shot back.

Huff appeared unconvinced. "You told me that they harassed you in the jail until you thought you were crazy, didn't you? Isn't that right?"

While on the subject of health, Huff asked Waldroup the whereabouts of his mother, Ada.

"My mother's in the hospital, where you put her, big boy, badgering her," Waldroup snarled.

Not rising to the bait, Huff asked, "You would sell your mother into prostitution for five cents, wouldn't you?" And by the way, hadn't Johnny once taken a pipe to his "poor cousin Elmer Waldroup," breaking his ribs and his arm?

The witness was silent.

Throughout the cross-examination, the pressure on Waldroup grew. And as it did, the witness alternately flew at and retreated from his tormentor verbally. He repeatedly asked the judge to be excused to go to the bathroom. When the judge did not immediately agree, Waldroup stepped down and walked out of the courtroom, forcing Judge Lewis to call a hasty recess.

A few minutes later, one of the spectators looked out the window and noticed that Waldroup had left the courthouse and was strolling down the street.

Deputies retrieved him, but Waldroup was losing patience. At one point when the cross-examination resumed, he told Huff, "I'm not answering no more of your damn questions."

The attorney fired back, "Are you afraid you might tell the truth if I ask you enough?"

No, said Waldroup, wagging his finger in Huff's face, "I'm just afraid my nerves will make me choke you to death."

The jurors were shaken by Waldroup's reaction to the cross-examination. And they weren't the only ones. Waldroup "was just bouncing off the walls, literally flailing himself around the courtroom," said Tom Moloney, who attended parts of the trial after putting up Walker's bail.

Harold Bailey, who had been a court administrator and sheriff's assistant in both Madison and Buncombe counties, was disgusted. "The state's key witness made the poorest witness I have ever seen in all my years in any case, civil or criminal, anywhere in any court I've ever been in. He's a criminal. He's a convicted felon. At one time after the murder, the sheriff wanted to indict him. . . . He's the least credible person I can think of."

The prosecutor—the man whose entire case rested on Waldroup's testimony—felt most unnerved. "I was really embarrassed," Tom Rusher said years later. "We weren't altogether sure that he was giving the truth, and in fact, when he made himself heroic, that to me did not sound believable."

The second time Waldroup walked off the stand to go to the restroom—again without the judge's permission—the district attorney admitted that he felt the proceedings might be headed for a mistrial. Rusher thought Waldroup wouldn't come back, even though he was accompanied this time by several deputies. "I sat there thinking, *This trial's going to end. This is going to be a huge embarrassment.*"

After a two-and-a-half-hour cross-examination, Waldroup was finally excused from the witness stand that afternoon. To avoid waiting reporters, he climbed out a back window of the courthouse and ran down the street.

Much of the prosecution's remaining case seemed anticlimactic. When FBI agent John Henninger, who had been at the site where the body was found, took the witness stand, Rusher tried to conceal—and

Huff later did his best to reveal—that Nancy's clothing and jewelry were now missing. So was the seven-strand nylon cord that caused her death, which Henninger had cut at the scene with a borrowed knife.

Charlie Chambers acknowledged that all the physical evidence from the scene, which the FBI had turned over to state investigators, had disappeared, probably when the SBI's Asheville offices flooded. The agent also undermined Waldroup's testimony by recounting contradictory stories the man had told about the killing.

On the second day of the trial, Dr. Page Hudson, the state medical examiner who performed Nancy's autopsy, testified that death had occurred at least twelve hours before the body was discovered. At the time of the autopsy, Hudson had said Nancy died sometime Monday. He testified that Nancy had been alive when she was tied, but that she would have lost consciousness within seconds. Huff—perhaps wary of the medical examiner's reputation—did not challenge him.

The prosecution scored some points. Dewey Griffey, a former Madison County deputy, testified that Ed Walker had been asked to identify Nancy's body at Memorial Mission Hospital in Asheville and had run out of the room shouting, "I didn't do it! I didn't do it!" That testimony would later be contradicted.

Nancy's former landlady, Glendora Cutshall, one of the last people to see her alive and to know where she was going, took the stand for the prosecution, testifying that the young woman had been "like my daughter."

In his cross-examination, Joe Huff did his best to undermine Nancy's character, implicitly blaming the victim in order to open the door for the possibility that other men might have killed her. "It's true that Nancy Morgan was very friendly to men?" he asked Cutshall, who was not easily led.

"She was friendly to *everyone*," Cutshall replied stiffly.

Huff asked, "She was known to make slightly risqué remarks, wasn't she?"

Rusher objected to the question, and Judge Lewis sustained the objection.

"Wasn't she known to pick up strangers on the road?" Huff asked, which also drew an objection.

Huff was able to get Cutshall to confirm that, on one occasion, she had denied a request from Nancy and Diana Buzzard to allow two men, out-of-town visitors, to spend the night at their cabin.

Nancy's family was outraged by this questioning of her reputation, at the time a frequent defense strategy in rape cases.

The prosecution then called Stan McElroy, a local man who had driven VISTA workers on several occasions. He claimed he had once seen Walker put his hand on Nancy's breast, but "she asked him to take it away. It was not the time or place for that." Later, he said he had seen Walker kiss her.

Velma Shetley, whose husband was a Baptist minister in Spring Creek at the time of Nancy's disappearance, lived not far from Walker's house. She testified that late that Sunday night, she heard a car that might have been Walker's drive down from the direction of his cabin. Headlights flashed, a horn sounded, and another car pulled up behind the first. She heard at least three men talking or shouting. All of this, Shetley testified, she told SBI agent Charlie Chambers in 1970. What she hadn't told Chambers, she said, was that later that week, Johnny Waldroup informed her he had witnessed a murder and swore her to secrecy. When Waldroup finally released her from her vow fourteen years later, she told the whole story to Sheriff Ponder. Shetley's testimony seemed to support Waldroup's account, but it further locked the prosecution into a scenario in which at least a third participant was involved in the killing.

Huff, his blood still up from his cross-examination of Johnny Waldroup, mocked Shetley for her late-night car identification, undermining her credibility.

James Waldroup, Walker's roommate (and no relation to Johnny), was Rusher's last witness on Tuesday. The prosecutor did not press the former Mars Hill College student on any involvement in Nancy's death. But he did ask about a recent visit James Waldroup had in Georgia, where he now lived. E. Y. Ponder and Bill Guillet, the SBI officer who accompanied the sheriff on the late-night visit to Ed Walker's Florida condo, had come calling unannounced. There followed, James Waldroup testified, an almost word-for-word duplication of the threatening confrontation Walker had experienced in Florida. He said the two lawmen had told him that an "eyewitness" had placed him—James Waldroup—at the scene of the killing. The sheriff told James Waldroup he might be indicted for the crime if he did not cooperate.

On cross-examination, Huff alleged that when Ponder and the other investigators learned James Waldroup had a strong alibi, they tipped Johnny to change his identification. The implication was clear: Sheriff Ponder was willing to use Johnny's account to bully anyone into a confession. During James Waldroup's testimony about the meeting in Georgia, E. Y. Ponder looked away and combed his hair.

On Wednesday morning, the prosecution called Ponder to the stand. Joe Huff couldn't have been happier, even though in past courtroom encounters the sheriff had proven hard to pin down, recalled Steve Huff, who was informally assisting his father. "It was a challenge for my father to deal with E. Y. Ponder to get at the truth." Still, the elder Huff relished the opportunity to have one of the hated Ponder brothers right where he wanted him—under oath and having to address charges of corrupting the judicial system for political purposes.

But the sheriff did not crack, though several times Judge Lewis had to ask him to speak up. Ponder denied offering Johnny Waldroup immunity from prosecution in exchange for his testimony, and in general batted back Huff's questioning.

The defense lawyer began his cross-examination by asking if the sheriff's prosecution of the Nancy Morgan case had been a campaign priority dating back to the 1970 race. Wasn't the sheriff's campaign pledge in November 1982 to solve the case his motivation in accusing Walker?

Ponder was unflappable. "I only agreed to give it my undivided attention," the sheriff replied blandly.

Behind the scenes, the prosecution had more trouble. Sheriff Ponder told Rusher he had come into the possession of what he believed to be Nancy Morgan's belt, broken in two, and an Avon fragrance bottle he said belonged to the woman. This evidence, he said, had been recovered by a neighbor from Ed Walker's backyard following the killing. But Rusher said he could not put the Avon saleswoman who had delivered the perfume to Nancy on the witness stand, since she was too ill to testify. Just as well. Ponder would have had to explain his gathering of this evidence in 1970, when he was not the sheriff—and where it had been since then, what is called the "chain of custody."

Years later, Rusher suggested his case was subtly sandbagged by county Republicans. While not suggesting they committed perjury, he felt that three of his Republican witnesses testified in court somewhat differently from when he had interviewed them before the trial. As he conducted each direct examination, Rusher was increasingly flabbergasted at the almost imperceptible ways the three undermined his case, especially regarding the time of Nancy's death.

When the prosecution rested, Huff moved for dismissal of all charges. Judge Lewis agreed to drop the rape charge, since the prosecution had presented no evidence connecting Ed Walker to any assault. But the judge ordered the trial to proceed on the murder and obstruction of justice charges.

Outside the courtroom, Rusher admitted to reporters that his case was based on circumstantial evidence. Yet he insisted Walker had committed a "cruel, calculated, premeditated murder."

The prosecutor might have been trying to convince himself, knowing what was to come.

14

Throughout the trial, Joe Huff alternately prowled and stalked the courtroom with a slightly bent, stiff-backed walk. Rail thin and silver haired, he reminded many of the actor Jimmy Stewart, who was nominated for an Oscar for his role as a defense lawyer in the 1959 film *Anatomy of a Murder*. At sixty-six, Huff was a little past his prime, yet the attorney was invigorated by the case, combative as ever, and still sharp enough to recognize the opportunity for a last hurrah. He wasn't concerned about the time and cost of the trial.

"He genuinely felt his client was innocent and was eager to help him," his son Steve recalled. "He was passionate about the flimsiness of the state's case. He was aware of the significance of the unsolved case and the eagerness of the sheriff to solve it. My father did what he needed to do to defend his client."

On Wednesday of the trial, Ed Walker was the first witness for the defense. He remained composed as he testified in the sweltering courtroom. He said he had not killed Nancy Morgan and had not been in love with her or had sex with her. Unable to tie anything more complicated than his shoelaces, Walker testified that he would have been incapable of hogtying Nancy.

Part of Walker's time on the witness stand was devoted to rebutting prosecution testimony. He attributed Stan McElroy's account of his having made a groping pass at Nancy in the car to an old jealousy. Walker denied Dewey Griffey's testimony for the state that he, Walker, had gone to the morgue and then run from the room shouting, "I didn't do it!" It was Richard Haimes, Walker said, who had identified the body in Asheville.

Walker seemed to be holding up well. But during a recess that broke up Rusher's subsequent cross-examination, Huff cautioned his client that he might be sounding a little glib, answering the prosecutor, "No, you're not correct." Walker should be succinct and not try to match wits with the prosecutor.

On Thursday, a parade of witnesses proceeded to demolish what remained of Johnny Waldroup's credibility. His own family members, neighbors, cellmates, and acquaintances in one way or another corroborated the defense's contention that Johnny had made up the story to get out of jail. "Nobody would believe him on a stack of Bibles," said Joyce Reece of Bluff.

Even Johnny's mother, Ada, released from the hospital where she was being treated for stress—and driven to court that day by Ed Walker himself—testified that her son was a habitual liar. Johnny, she said, had informed her that his account of the murder was untrue, that he had "told a story to get out of jail" on the stolen-truck charge. She said she urged him to tell Sheriff Ponder that he lied. The night of the killing, she said, Johnny would have had to go through her room in order to leave the house, and she did not hear him do so.

Three more witnesses repeated the story they had told authorities at the time of the killing—that they had seen Nancy driving her government car with two other "hippies" the day before her body was found.

Jeffrey Hammer was among numerous character witnesses for Walker, from both Florida and Madison County—so many that Judge Lewis ruled no more could testify.

The condition of Nancy's body became a key point of contention as the forensic portion of the prosecution's case continued to fray. In order for Rusher's scenario to jibe with Johnny Waldroup's account, Nancy Morgan had to have been killed no later than early Monday morning. If she had left Ed Walker's house alive, he couldn't have committed the murder.

Huff recalled Dewey Griffey, the former deputy, who testified that the county coroner at the time, who had since died, told him at the crime scene that Nancy had been dead for three to four hours when her body was found Wednesday morning. He was merely reporting the coroner's spoken opinion at the time, however; the local physician had said nothing about time of death in his one-page handwritten report.

Yet photographs taken at the time and shown to the jury clearly demonstrated that the body was in pristine condition, without swelling, discoloration, or flies or maggots. He had smelled no odor, the deputy said. Huff hammered away that the body was in a car with the windows rolled up in the middle of June in partial sunlight. Had Nancy's body been there since early Monday morning, it would not have looked the way it did.

Not everything went smoothly for the defense. Although Jeffrey Hammer testified on Walker's behalf, Richard Haimes, the VISTA resident Madison County supervisor, did not.

Rusher had contacted Haimes several times before the trial, asking him to be a witness for the prosecution, but the former supervisor re-buffed him. "I have nothing to say to you," Haimes told the prosecutor. "If you call me as a witness, I'm going to testify on Ed Walker's behalf."

Which was what was supposed to happen. Haimes was scheduled to take the stand after Hammer. But "Richard took offense, thinking that Jeffrey had made him look bad," Walker recalled. Haimes had let Nancy live alone in Shelton Laurel after her roommate quit the program and went home to Pennsylvania. Haimes felt Hammer's testimony "had made [him] look like he didn't know what he was doing," Walker said, "or didn't do the right thing."

According to Joe Huff, it quickly became apparent that "Haimes was stuck on defending his role." The defense attorney told him not to worry—to go home to Atlanta, which he immediately did.

Another prospective witness, Harold Reed, had come to Huff during the trial with a story a local man had told him. The man, who was never identified, told Reed he had seen several cars, including the government-owned Plymouth, late Tuesday night near where the body was found, and that he had recognized some of them as belonging to young men from Hot Springs. But Reed was not permitted to take the witness stand, perhaps because the testimony would have been hearsay. Huff stayed unperturbed, according to Walker. "Joe said, 'We don't need it. We don't want it. Let it go.'"

Friday morning was devoted to closing arguments. James Baker, who spoke first for the prosecution, had the onerous task of defending Johnny Waldroup. Speaking from notes, Baker criticized Huff's cross-examination, claiming that Waldroup, not Walker, seemed to be on trial. "Johnny Waldroup has been humiliated and ridiculed," Baker said. "He has been discredited, he's been insulted." Although Waldroup might have been "untruthful in many things," Baker said, "I would argue that that doesn't mean that every single thing he says has to be considered as untruthful."

The young prosecutor went a step farther: "If you find Johnny Waldroup's testimony to be untruthful, [does] that mean that Mr. Walker is not guilty of this crime? Absolutely not. Even if Johnny Waldroup is being untrue, there is still a lot remaining in this case, a lot of evidence that points to Ed Walker beyond any reasonable doubt."

Joe Huff, up next, began a long, folksy, sometimes rambling summary of his case. In a classic example of mountain storytelling, the defense attorney launched into a vivid mini-lecture about the signing of the Magna Carta and how it led to the modern jury system. Later, Huff proffered a mildly racist anecdote to illustrate his lonely task of defending Ed Walker in the face of the resources marshaled by the prosecution. "I feel like the darkie that was called for trial out in Texas, and the bailiff called, 'The state against Rastus Jones,' to which the defendant replied, 'Lordy, what odds!'" Walker, Huff said, has "got to rely on you, the jury, and Almighty God for his deliverance."

Huff begged the jury's pardon "if I cross-examined Mr. Johnny Waldroup in a way that you thought was not proper." Still, the primary thing Huff wanted the jurors to do was contrast Ed Walker with Johnny Waldroup.

"Here, you have a fine man, Ed Walker." Just look at his family, Huff suggested, and consider his work record since he left Madison County. Consider the witnesses from Florida who testified about his excellent character and his nonviolence. Walker's life "has been shattered," he said, "shattered by the lies of a man who did it for personal gain."

Huff pounded away at the forensic evidence and testimony from the trial. Walker had testified that he detested carrots and would not serve them at his house, yet they were found in Nancy's stomach. "Where did the carrots come from? I don't know where the carrots came from—she didn't eat them there. And she didn't die on Sunday either." He urged the jury to think about the pictures of the body. "There's no way that I'll ever believe that she had been dead since sometime on Sunday night or Monday morning, because the human body just does not work that way. And you, every one of you, know it."

He also wanted to know why prosecutors had not taken the abundant sperm found in Nancy's vagina and rectum and tested it against Walker's. Although clinical DNA typing in 1970 had not reached its current level of sophistication, scientific tests could have generally included or excluded the defendant.

Huff seized on a critical gap of logic in Johnny Waldroup's account of the killing, one he had not raised during his cross-examination. Waldroup testified that he had acted as an accomplice only because Walker threatened to kill him if he did not help dispose of Nancy's body. That might have held true while the two were together, Huff reasoned, but what about when, as Waldroup testified, they drove in different cars to Tanyard Gap to leave the body?

"He was driving a separate car. Why didn't he go some other way? It doesn't make sense." The route from Bluff to Tanyard Gap, about eight miles away, passed numerous turnoffs. All Waldroup had to do "was turn off in Hot Springs, gone up Spring Creek, gone anywhere he wanted to, and yet he says he drives over there."

And what about Waldroup's visit to Walker's house the next morning?

"He testified he was right back up there the next morning, at Ed's house, hanging around. Now, ladies and gentlemen, do you believe that? Do you believe that somebody would threaten me and cause me to help take somebody's body, that I would be up there the next morning palling around with them? That's absolutely absurd."

A navy veteran of World War II and Korea, Huff closed by comparing his client to someone at sea about to be overcome "by the raging current of the storm." For the benefit of the religious members of the Madison County jury, he recited a verse from the "Navy Hymn":

> Eternal Father, strong to save,
> Whose arm doth quiet the restless wave,
> Who bids the mighty ocean deep
> Its own appointed limits keep;

O hear us as we cry to thee
For those in peril on the sea.

The summation, said Ed Walker, "had me in tears. I mean, it was like he was reciting poetry. It was definitely Clarence Darrow stuff."

Last up was Rusher, the district attorney, who began by complimenting the skills of his adversary, something by this time obvious to everyone in the courtroom. "As a lawyer," he said, "there is none better than Mr. Huff."

Still, before Rusher could attempt to salvage what was left of his case, he had to address the political dimension that seemed to overshadow the trial. Huff, he said, "would have you as the jury of Madison County put Sheriff E. Y. Ponder on trial. He would have you believe that in this case the defendant was arrested merely because Sheriff Ponder wanted to further his political career."

Huff not only wanted to focus on the sheriff, the prosecutor said. "He would like you to find Johnny Waldroup guilty. He would like for you to find me guilty. He would like for you even to find Nancy Morgan guilty, and somehow in all of that process you would forget about your actual duty, and that is to consider the guilt of Ed Walker."

Rusher admitted to the jurors that he was to some degree frustrated by his star witness and his motives: "I don't know whether Johnny Waldroup's telling the truth or not." But he urged the panel to "take Johnny Waldroup out of it and consider that for fifteen years Walker has been the suspect."

Arguing that Walker had murdered Nancy because she rejected his advances, Rusher seemed to resort to the type of lyrics characteristic of mountain murder ballads: "When it became clear that he could not have her, it became clear that no one else was going to have her." The prosecutor also defended Nancy's character, which Huff had undermined. The defense attorney had portrayed her, Rusher said, as "some kind of a wanton person" who had liquor bottles in her house and was too friendly to men. Rusher gestured to the Morgan family members in the courtroom and asked, "Wasn't Nancy Morgan innocent? We're talking about a real live person, the life of one who was loved, and these people have come here from Louisiana to see justice done."

The timing of Nancy's death was crucial, Rusher repeated. He said he was confident in relying on Dr. Page Hudson's testimony, given his stature and reputation. The medical examiner said that the woman had eaten carrots between thirty minutes and two hours before her death, despite Walker's assertion that he hadn't served them. Rusher insisted that Nancy had eaten carrots with the defendant. But even if she had eaten them at nine o'clock Sunday night, she was still alive six hours later, at three o'clock Monday morning, according to Johnny Waldroup's testimony.

Stress, the prosecutor said, could have accounted for the time discrepancy. If the jurors did not believe Nancy's death occurred on Sunday night or Monday morning, "then by all means, ladies and gentlemen, come in and say, 'We find him not guilty.'"

15

When at the outset of the trial Rusher announced the death penalty was off the table, he lost a valuable card. Wily—or unethical—district attorneys in North Carolina often announced before a trial that they would seek capital punishment. This enabled them to "death qualify" a jury and effectively exclude all unalterable opponents. In practice, this meant many blacks, liberal whites, and those with religious objections to the death penalty were excused for "cause." This often left a jury predisposed to convict a defendant, even when the prosecutor decided not to ask for the death penalty at the conclusion of the trial. In addition, without the death penalty, there was also likely to be less media interest—and scrutiny—outside the immediate area.

Judge Lewis excused the jury for lunch at midday Friday, after the prosecutor finished. He then called Rusher and Huff into his chambers to discuss the jury instructions.

The prosecutor chose not to argue for the judge to offer jurors the choice of several "lesser included offenses"—voluntary and involuntary manslaughter and second-degree murder. In this, Rusher said he relied on Dr. Page Hudson's opinion that the death was intentional. But that precluded the scenario of rough sex gone wrong, or that Nancy had been tied up to restrain her and then her captors simply wandered off, not intending for her to die. Thus, jurors were essentially boxed out of any verdict other than first-degree murder, a premeditated act.

For his part, Huff was happy that the jury would not be able to compromise with a "split-the-difference" verdict.

During the trial, Pat Franklin, a young political protégé of E. Y. Ponder and a good judge of opinion in Madison County, had warned Rusher that she didn't think he would be able to win a first-degree murder verdict, based on the testimony she had seen. "He seemed shocked by my observation," she recalled. "I think he couldn't comprehend anything but first-degree murder, that consensual rough or reckless sex was something he could not fathom."

In chambers, Judge Lewis had some bad news for the prosecutor. Huff came out of the meeting and shared it with Walker: "The judge said to Rusher, 'Tom, when I was a young lawyer, one time I disavowed a witness, my primary witness.' Rusher asked him, 'What happened, judge?' Lewis replied, 'My ass was creamed.'" Huff chuckled as he confided to his client, "What the judge was saying was [that] you can't win a case if you disavow your chief witness."

That afternoon, Lewis charged the jury members and sent them to deliberate. They filed into the jury room, just a quick right turn out the door and ten steps from where they had been sitting. It was a long, narrow, high-ceilinged room with two windows that looked out back on to the hillside. A small bathroom was at one end of the room, with a sink outside. Cracks in the plaster crept up the walls like spider webs. Jurors sat around a brown wooden table that barely seated ten, forcing the rest onto chairs along the wall.

The first order of business was to select a foreman. They chose Anthony James of Little Pine.

One juror was troubled about the victim's stomach contents and the time it would have taken to digest her last meal. But for the most part, the members of the jury focused on the two major weaknesses of the prosecution's case: Johnny Waldroup's credibility and the condition of Nancy Morgan's body.

"There was a lot of the stuff that didn't make sense, that I didn't believe," said juror Barbara Penland, the former mayor's wife. "The whole trial was based on Johnny's credibility, and as far as I know, none of us could believe him too well."

If Walker were guilty, Penland said, then the body had to have been "closed up in a car for two or three days on the mountain" in hot weather in the spring. But in the crime-scene photographs, it appeared to be "in perfect condition. The only thing she had was a little scratch on the back of her heel, maybe on the elbow, and that was about it."

Juror Harry Payne, a tobacco farmer, agreed. Walker's character witnesses also influenced Payne. Loyalty, even to an outsider, still counted in Madison County. "He seemed innocent to me, and all the people on Spring Creek [near where Walker lived] seemed to think he was innocent. They had known him for a long time and really thought it wasn't him, and they showed their support by being there with him."

Spectators congregated outside the courthouse during recesses and adjournments to weigh in on the proceedings. Rusher fared poorly there, too. For centuries, court sessions had provided free drama for the people of the southern mountains. Rusher himself, in his book *Until He Is Dead: Capital Punishment in Western North Carolina History*, wrote, "Lawyers often hear their performances critiqued by citizens sitting on park benches outside the courthouse. Madison County citizens were among the most devout in attending and following criminal proceedings."

While the jury deliberated Ed Walker's fate, the courthouse cognoscenti competing for the sparse shade outside suggested that Rusher and his prosecution team might have read too many Perry Mason novels. Someone thought they lacked the courtroom finesse of first-year law students. Back in the courtroom, John Morgan, Nancy's older brother, told James Baker that even he had not been convinced by the state's case.

The jury was out a little more than an hour before returning with a verdict. Judge Lewis admonished everyone about emotional reactions. Joe Huff stood with his client.

When Anthony James announced the not-guilty verdict, the entire courtroom seemed to sigh. Walker rolled his eyes to the ceiling. His wife and daughter burst into tears and embraced as Walker's friends from Florida and Madison County mobbed him, along with people he didn't know, who said they had been praying for him. Outside the courthouse, Walker held his wife's hand and said, "I'm going to celebrate. You can believe that."

John Morgan worked his way through the crowd to shake Walker's hand. Nancy's younger brother, George, remembered years later that John thought "the guy was probably guilty." But John admitted that if he himself had been a member of the jury, he would have had to vote not guilty on the strength of the evidence.

The family was ushered into the prosecutor's office, where Katy Boulden, Nancy's aunt, watched from the window as Walker left the courthouse. "Well," she told James Baker, "he'll have to answer to a higher authority than this court." Years later, she said, "I thought he was guilty. Maybe I just wanted him to be guilty to close it up."

In the years that followed, the family members essentially sealed off the murder and the trial in an effort to allow their pain to heal. "My mother could not, and still cannot, speak of it," George Morgan said in 2009.

"Had I been on the jury, I would have just done what the jury did,"

Sheriff Ponder said, "because you're sworn to give the benefit of the doubt to the defendants, which is right. I'd much rather let a guilty man go unpunished as for some innocent person to be punished." But the sheriff remained adamantly supportive of his primary witness. "I wasn't manufacturing witnesses. I was using those that were there. Poor old Johnny Waldroup was our witness, and he never lied. . . . I was convinced beyond a doubt that Johnny was not lying."

The day after the verdict, Walker took his wife and daughter to the Bluff community to thank his old friends. Without their support, he said, the experience would have been "totally unbearable."

A week later, he told reporters he wasn't bitter toward police and prosecutors, despite the fact that he had been forced to sell his house, car, and boat to defend himself. "My life has changed quite a bit," he said, noting that he had moved to another part of Florida between his indictment and the trial. "I'm sort of starting over. One reason for moving was so we would not have to dwell on it constantly. We're not trying to forget it, but we're not trying to make it the focus anymore."

In fact, Walker *was* bitter, and would remain so for years. In Florida, the acquittal did not get nearly the news coverage the indictment had. Back home, he was still receiving the *News-Record*, Madison County's weekly newspaper. When he read an article four months later about an unrelated murder that portrayed Sheriff Ponder in a favorable light, he wrote a letter lacerating the lawman and the district attorney, Rusher. "I will always feel that I was a victim of the criminal justice system run amuck in Madison County," Walker wrote.

The residual bitterness went both ways. Two weeks later, the newspaper published a reply to Walker's letter from Faye Reid, a Ponder ally and former police chief of Marshall. Reid's reply amounted to a broadside against all the VISTAs. "I'm sure Mr. Rusher and a lot of other people don't care what you think of Sheriff Ponder. We didn't want you people here in the first place. We can't see any good you did, except be paid with taxpayer's money."

Most people in Madison County agreed that the acquittal was a factor in E. Y.'s defeat in the election for sheriff in November 1986, the year after the trial, when he ran against a determined and invigorated Dedrick Brown. It didn't help that in 1985 E. Y.'s brother Zeno was again indicted, this time on federal charges that involved using insider knowledge from the state highway commission to buy up property where a road was to be built. Well before the voting, it seemed to E. Y.'s supporters that he had given up. On Election Day, when he would normally have been on the hustings, the sheriff was seen moping in the courthouse.

Ed Walker had been accepted and embraced by the people of Bluff and Spring Creek, so it was no surprise that they came to his defense. E. Y., normally an astute politician, should have factored that into his recommendation that Rusher prosecute Walker. "Everyone attributed [Ponder's defeat] to that," said Walker. "In the community where I was from, in that part of the county, he lost by a large majority."

That same year, the Democrats lost control of the Madison County Commission, and with it the jobs they commanded. "I didn't understand how the Ponder dynasty could be crumbling around the edges," said Tom Moloney. "I think the acquittal was the single event that really started the slide. Sheriff Ponder at that time was in contention for National Lawman of the Year, going up against a fellow from Texas. It looked to me that he needed that one case solved, and he would have gotten it"—and with the honor, reelection.

Despite the numerous charges pending against him, Johnny Waldroup did not return to jail. Instead, he took off for Newport, Tennessee. Moloney recalled, "It was after Sheriff Ponder lost the election and the day that Dedrick took office. Johnny was seen leaving the Bluff community with a pack on his back and his cowboy hat on, his cowboy boots on. He said he was never coming back to Madison County until Sheriff Ponder got back in office."

That never happened.

Everyone in Madison County seemed relieved the trial was over, and most accepted that Ed Walker was not guilty. But many continued to wonder, *Well, then, who did kill Nancy Morgan?* That mystery remained.

Nancy Morgan
Courtesy of George Morgan

The government Plymouth in which Nancy Morgan's body was found
News-Record of Madison County

Zeno Ponder in his native mountains
Photograph by Mark I. Pinsky

Madison County Courthouse in Marshall
Photograph by Sarah M. Brown

E. Y. Ponder on the sidewalk in Marshall

E. Y. Ponder

E. Y. Ponder (*center*) and his men posing with a backwoods moonshine still
Courtesy of Pat Franklin

Nancy Morgan
Courtesy of George Morgan

Nancy (*center*) with George Morgan, Abigail Morgan, Rosemond Morgan (*Nancy's aunt*), and John Morgan, 1970
Courtesy of George Morgan

Richard Johnson
Courtesy North Carolina Department of Corrections

Part Three
Reinvestigation

16

I knocked on Ed Walker's office door, not certain anyone would be on the other side. It was a Sunday afternoon in 1995, and the modernistic suburban Florida complex was nearly deserted.

About two years after Nancy Morgan's murder—and the time I clipped the *Durham Sun* article while sitting in the student newspaper office at Duke—the case had come back into my life in an unexpected way. The Southern Oral History Program at the University of North Carolina at Chapel Hill was looking for a researcher, and I persuaded the director to hire me. Soon, I was sitting at a long table lit by a row of green-shaded desk lamps at UNC's Wilson Library. In front of me were three-by-five note cards and a tall pile of thick file folders of newspaper clippings held in the North Carolina Collection. My job was to use the yellowed articles about the state's prominent political figures to prepare cards with questions for the project's interviewers.

One day, I opened a file marked "Zeno Ponder." The man with the funny first name, I read, was the legendary boss of Madison County, then an isolated, impoverished, and corrupt pocket of the southern Appalachians. I immediately thought of Nancy Morgan and her murder there. The articles described Zeno as a political wheeler-dealer who, with his older brother, the sheriff, exercised nearly complete control over a county of just seventeen thousand people. A classic southern Gothic scenario leapt to mind and sent my imagination into overdrive.

Did the Ponder brothers, their power somehow threatened by the VISTA workers, contribute to Nancy's killing? Still too quick to judge motives, and all too eager to construct a dramatic narrative without evidence, I decided that if the Ponders were not themselves responsible for Nancy's murder and for driving the VISTAs out of Madison County, then they must surely know who was. And yet the Ponders remained silent. I made some notes, copied the clips, and took them home to add to my Nancy Morgan folder.

However, I missed one 1972 article in *Official Detective Stories* magazine that dealt directly with the murder: "Dixie Riddle of the Hog-Tied Nude." In it, Sheriff E. Y. Ponder boasted, "We'll solve this one, and it won't take long."

≡≡

Covering sensational murder cases around the Southeast as a freelance writer in the 1970s led to some unusual experiences for a committed lefty like me. Cop reporters too long on the beat tend to burn out or become law-enforcement groupies and end up wanting to be detectives or private investigators. No matter how many murders I covered, I thought that would never happen to me, perhaps because of my extensive experience on the other side of law enforcement during scores of riotous marches, protests, and demonstrations in the 1960s.

But along the way, some forensic education almost turned me around. While covering murder trials, I kept running into Herbert Leon MacDonell, an eccentric blood-spatter expert and the author of *Flight Characteristics and Stain Patterns of Human Blood*. As sometimes happens with trials, we hit it off outside the courtroom. Herb invited me to take his week-long course in death-scene analysis—the forerunner of the various *CSI* television shows—in Corning, New York, as his guest. In 1975, I accepted.

The short course for homicide detectives and coroners included sections on photography, ballistics, and fingerprinting, but its centerpiece was blood-spatter analysis. We used expired human blood from the Red Cross for experiments in which we flung blood against the wall and hit blood-soaked sponges with sharp or blunt objects in order to analyze the patterns left behind. We fired a .22 rifle bullet into a blood-saturated sponge to record the forward and backward high-velocity impact spatter.

But the most important lesson I learned from MacDonell was that, much as in political reporting it's always a good rule to follow the money, so with murder the wise course is to follow the forensics. Science may be imperfect, and it can be manipulated and even falsified, but it doesn't lie. This lesson would serve me well when I returned to the Nancy Morgan murder.

As I gained knowledge and experience in reporting criminal cases, I felt the inexorable tug of the case. In 1978, I made my first trip to Madison County, to visit an old Duke friend, Elmer Hall, who had just bought an inn in the spa town of Hot Springs. The inn, called Sunnybank, was more than an old bed-and-breakfast. It was a chunk of American cultural history. Built in 1875 at the dawn of the spa's heyday, the white Victorian house with gingerbread trim was listed on the National Register of Historic Places.

Elmer had been the assistant Methodist chaplain at Duke in the late 1960s. His outspoken support for activist and radical students in battles over civil rights, union organizing, apartheid, and the Vietnam War probably cost him the job of university chaplain when it came open. Forced off the university staff, he later moved to Madison County and bought the century-old hostel overlooking the Appalachian Trail not far from where Nancy's body had been found.

In Madison County, Elmer bumped heads with the Ponder brothers, who tended to be suspicious of outsiders. Amid the parlor clutter, Elmer told me local tales and said he wanted me to write a book about the Ponders, with whom he had clashed over his plans for the inn and over his liberal politics. Once, he said, the sheriff had prevailed on him not to file criminal charges after some items were stolen, in exchange for their safe return. I told him I was more interested in Nancy Morgan and wanted to know if he had heard anything about the murder since his arrival in Hot Springs.

In fact, Elmer had learned of the killing during a dinner at which someone talked about recent local history, including the VISTA experience—which was shared as a cautionary tale for newcomers. "There were several people who actually knew her who were at the potluck supper," he recalled. "I remember very clearly because someone said, 'Oh, it was very near to you. It's in Mill Ridge,'" next to Tanyard Gap. Elmer shared what little he knew and promised to find out what he could.

Two decades later, Sunnybank Inn would be my base in trying to solve the case.

≥≡

Ironically, I missed all coverage of Ed Walker's murder trial in Marshall. In the early 1980s, I was working as an editorial advisor to the Xinhua (New China) News Agency in Beijing. A year after my return to Durham, I was hired as a staff writer, based in Orange County, for the *Los Angeles Times*. For more than a decade, I honed my craft mostly on the religion beat, investigating nearly a dozen televangelists and broadcast ministries based in the area. Then, a combination of staff cutbacks, my earlier courtroom and investigative skills, and some ill-advised run-ins with editors propelled me back to the criminal beat at the *Times*. Violent death was once again how I made my living and forged my professional reputation.

This time, I didn't like it one bit. The killings were of the most gruesome and meaningless sort, and the *Times*'s intense competition with the *Orange County Register*, a successful daily, made the coverage only more unrelenting. Initially, editors assured me the murder beat would be a short-term assignment, three months at most. But three months became six months and then a year.

I was fed up with murders. Except for one —Nancy Morgan's. Her killing was somehow different from the cases I covered every day at the high-rise Orange County Courthouse in Santa Ana. It seemed incongruous, but the now twenty-three-year-old case gripped me again. That unpunished killing represented unfinished business. Its mystery held the kind of meaning and personal connection that pulled me back to a time when I felt my working life had greater, political purpose. With the experience and skills I had acquired since her death, I felt I had a chance to bring those responsible for her death to justice.

I contacted newspaper librarians in North Carolina, who sent me clippings about Nancy's murder and Ed Walker's arrest and trial. I filed a Freedom of Information Act request with the FBI, asking for anything the bureau had on the case. And I obtained a copy of Nancy's autopsy report, which included disturbing photographs of her body.

With the help of Sheila Kern, a savvy and sympathetic research librarian in my *Los Angeles Times* office, I was able to locate Walker in central Florida. He didn't reply to my letters, but that could wait. I quit my post at the *Times* and took a job covering religion for the *Orlando Sentinel*, not far from where Walker lived.

Journalists looking into old cases often begin with an assumption of a wrongful conviction and build their cases with that in mind. Otherwise, they have no story. But ever since the 1970s, when I seemed to be investigating a murder case or covering a trial almost monthly, I had imposed an intellectual discipline for myself, one different from that of other investigative reporters. Oddly for a political lefty like me, whenever injustice or exoneration was at issue, I approached the case with a strong bias for the prosecution. I assumed that the accused person I planned to write about was guilty. If the defendant had already been convicted, I presumed he or she had received the benefit of appropriate due process. In that way, I first had to persuade my skeptical self that the accused was innocent—or that some serious defect had marred the investigation or the prosecution—before I could ethically and convincingly argue the point to readers.

In the case of Nancy Morgan, this meant that, before turning elsewhere, I would look closely at Ed Walker and decide if he was in fact the killer.

━━═

A voice invited me into a cramped office with pale blue walls. The middle-aged man with a hawkish nose, his brown hair hung with limp curls, greeted me warily. He took a seat in a rolling chair behind his desk, which featured a photo of his grandchild. His smooth, tanned hands, a high-school ring on the right one, contrasted with his rough complexion. With great reluctance, he was about to return to the most traumatic period of his life, and to have it all tape-recorded. I wanted to know if Ed Walker had anything to do with the death of Nancy Morgan.

After his acquittal, Walker had returned to Florida, but almost immediately moved from the Gulf Coast. He enrolled in a paralegal program at the University of Central Florida, thinking he might become a lawyer and fight injustices such as had been visited on him. But he decided it wasn't for him. Walker and his wife divorced. Eventually, he remarried and carved out a new career in academics and emerging Internet technology.

Walker felt in no way vindicated by the jury's verdict because he had won nothing. "I just didn't lose as much. . . . There's no winning involved, it's just less losing." Few congratulations were in order, he believed. It was simply a matter of "thank God it's over. . . . It should have stopped long before then."

He said he still had nightmares that he was facing murder charges. "I have this dream. There's this microsecond when you come from unconsciousness to consciousness, when your brain boots up every morning. Sometimes in that little period, I forget who I am. I wake up thinking I have to go to this trial. I'm still trying to prove I didn't do this."

Well before our meeting that Sunday, while I was still at the *Los Angeles Times*, I had written to Walker, asking to arrange an interview. For a year, he declined, saying he didn't want people he had known for years to learn about this bizarre chapter in his life. He had moved on, or tried to. But I wouldn't let him.

Journalistic intimidation isn't pretty, and is nothing to be proud of, regardless of how much one rationalizes it, pretending it's for the greater good. More often, I have found, it's for one's own good. Janet Malcolm, in an infamous essay in *The New Yorker* about the murder trial of Green Beret doctor Jeffrey MacDonald, the same case I covered in the late 1970s, wrote that all journalism is betrayal. That is indeed one of the unpleasant aspects of the craft, although one I assiduously tried to avoid throughout my reporting career.

For me, the unsavory professional sin was intimidation, which I resorted to sparingly and reluctantly. But I was at a point when, in order to find out who killed Nancy Morgan, I needed to talk to Walker, one of the last people to see her alive. Whether he wanted to speak to me or not.

So after more than a year of fruitless phone calls and e-mails, I had left Walker a voice mail informing him that I was going to tell the story of Nancy's life and death, and that his trial was a part of the story I could not leave out. If the former VISTA worker chose not to participate, I would rely on the public record and the memories of others, and I'd note the Florida town where he resided and what he did for a living. However, should Walker agree to a series of interviews, I promised that I would share with him all the documentary evidence I turned up in my research. Under this duress, he agreed.

Our meetings usually took place on Sunday afternoons, when no one was around Walker's office. "Every time we get into this interview stuff, it disrupts my life," he wrote after one meeting. "I'm only doing this because it is better than not doing it. I wish it wasn't happening."

At our first interview, before I could even turn on my tape recorder, Walker handed me a copy of a Florida polygraph examination from the 1980s that showed no stress in his answers about any involvement in Nancy's killing. This finding seemed to contrast with the result of the earlier FBI-administered test, yet that was not surprising. I knew that differences in the personnel administering the test and its location could color the results. Polygraphs detect stress, not lies, which is one reason the results are not admitted in court.

"I didn't do it," Walker said by way of introduction when I switched on the tape recorder. "Nancy left my house, and that's the last time I saw her."

Ed Walker was raised in a small town in Florida by socially liberal parents. He went all the way through public school in one building. In 1969, when he was twenty and attending a local community college, a VISTA recruiter visited the campus. Rather than a higher mission, VISTA for Walker was "the alternative to just backpacking and hitchhiking around the United States." It was his first time away from home. Although he hoped VISTA would send him to an Indian reservation somewhere in the West, he willingly accepted the Madison County assignment.

The VISTAs learned nothing about local politics during their weeks of training at Mars Hills College, after their ten days in Atlanta—nothing about the county's power structure or the long reign and influence of the Ponder machine. Most of the preparation was about mountain culture. Once settled in the Bluff and Spring Creek area, Walker easily made friends with his neighbors and found ways to be useful, especially with young people.

As he relaxed, the memories began to flow. He recalled the point after Nancy's murder when his fears grew. "I think it wasn't until the next day that I really got scared personally. I thought, *Well, now, wait a minute, she left my house at two or three in the morning. I am obviously the person they are going to be looking at.*"

Once Walker learned that no one had been arrested for the crime or had come forward to confess, he understood he would likely be the prime suspect. "I'm the last person who admits seeing her alive," he said, and the authorities could do "whatever they want." He tried to convince himself he was being alarmist, but he felt frightened. He confided in the other volunteers, "You know, this could be a big deal for me."

"Oh, no, that's not going to happen," one reassured him.

In the immediate aftermath of the killing, Walker's Bluff neighbors doubted the crime would be solved. When the topic came up for discussion, they voiced the belief that no one would ever know the truth, especially if the killer was a local person. "Everybody had the same theory I did," Walker said. "The only way it would ever be solved is a deathbed confession by someone, when they wanted to meet Jesus."

Still, people speculated. "Nobody knew if this was a random act against Nancy or against VISTA or against outsiders." It did not take long for Madison County sectional prejudices to surface, Walker recalled. "The Bluff people thought it was something to do with that bad bunch in Shelton Laurel. That's a quote: 'Bad bunch in Shelton Laurel.'" Shelton Laurel had the reputation in Walker's part of the county of being a rough place: "Bad dudes, bad people, lots of fights." People told him that VISTA "should never have had a young girl out there in that mean old Shelton Laurel by herself."

One of the things that puzzled Walker from the beginning was that Nancy's shorts—the shorts her landlady, Glendora Cutshall, remembered her ironing before she drove over to Bluff—were found with her body. Walker recalled that Nancy was wearing long pants when she arrived at his house.

"I know that she had on slacks. Long slacks. I know that for a fact because there's no way at all Nancy would go in the community, particularly over to my community, into my house, in a pair of shorts," her appearance in cutoffs at the Marshall skating rink notwithstanding. The only place a volunteer would have worn shorts, Walker insisted, was at home or perhaps around Mars Hill College. "But a woman would not go around in shorts. That was just an unwritten rule."

After the murder, resident VISTA supervisor Richard Haimes, Walker, and some of the other volunteers went to Atlanta for reassignment and were sent back to the mountains, this time to East Tennessee, where they rebuilt a project that had recently fallen apart. Haimes became obsessive in lecturing the female volunteers about personal security. Walker taught seventh- and eighth-grade math at a school in the town of Crossville. "I just wanted to do something," he said. "There was no organized community group, no chance of organizing one. I just volunteered to work in the school, and I taught remedial math." Early in their Tennessee stay, the Madison County VISTAs returned voluntarily to North Carolina for polygraph tests.

After finishing his VISTA service, Walker worked briefly for a foundation in Washington, then signed up as supervisor for a VISTA project in Florida, where he met his first wife.

He made three visits to Madison County during the 1970s, the last with his then two-year-old daughter, and he continued to write to his friends in the Bluff community until his arrest in 1984. These relationships ultimately saved his life, Walker believed. "The target could have been anyone. They chose me because I was the outsider and I had, as far as they knew, no ties with the community at all." But when he came back for trial, "literally hundreds of people" publicly supported him. "That's why the whole thing fell apart."

So strong was the support of Walker's friends in Bluff that Stan McElroy, who claimed during the trial that he had seen Walker making advances toward Nancy, said years later that he was shunned by the community for testifying against the VISTA. Twenty years after the trial, he said, some people in Madison County still would not speak to him.

From the first, in exchanging e-mails with Walker, talking with him on the phone, and meeting with him in Florida and again in Madison County, my sense was that he was not responsible for Nancy's death. He seemed guileless, open, and uncalculating, and his account of his arrest and trial rang true as the nightmarish experience of a terrified victim. Still, I knew that a feeling, an impression, could not sustain a verdict—even a journalistic one. I had been around this track dozens of times with people accused of murder, and I knew better than to reach a conclusion until I had seen and heard all the available evidence and testimony.

Yet at one point, when he asked me point-blank what I thought, I hedged. In such situations, the journalist's playbook says to show empathy and imply sympathy without committing oneself. The goal is to avoid shutting off future contact by giving the wrong answer. I said, as honestly as I could, that I didn't think he had any role in the murder, but on the basis of my experience covering criminal cases, I couldn't exclude that possibility. Walker seemed a bit disappointed, although he said he understood.

The jury that tried him in 1985 found that insufficient evidence was presented to find him culpable in Nancy's death. Still, as many Americans forget—but Walker remembered—a verdict of not guilty is not a determination of innocence.

Yet if Ed Walker didn't kill Nancy Morgan, who did?

17

In 1996, I began devoting two weeks a year to sleuthing into the Nancy Morgan case in North Carolina. The other fifty weeks, I lived with my family in flat, suburban central Florida, reporting mostly on religion for the *Orlando Sentinel*. My life was Scouts, synagogue, sports, and PTA meetings. Autumns, I got to pull my Timberland hiking boots out of the back of my closet and the flannel shirts out of mothballs.

My trips were far enough apart that I never lost an outsider's sense of wonder about the natural beauty of the place. The view always began with rushing water. In particular, the French Broad River—and the road and rail line that grew along its banks—was for many years the main artery. Throughout Madison County flow smaller roadside tributaries and creeks, stony and mostly unpolluted streams. The footpaths, worn by Cherokees walking the Warrior Trail, ultimately gave way to packed-earth and gravel tracks, then two-lane roads tracing many of these capillaries of tumbling water.

Over time, technology inexorably has been reducing the county's rural isolation. Large satellite dishes began sprouting in front yards in the 1990s, replaced over the years by smaller white ones attached to walls and rooftops. Other scenes seemed timeless—stone chimneys, the only remains of burned and ruined cabins; sure-footed mountain cattle grazing on the slopes as the sun faded; tobacco drying from barn rafters, visible through open lofts. Around one bend, I encountered a crew of county jail inmates, overseen by two guards with shotguns, doing maintenance on the road.

Residences ranged from century-old two-story houses to mobile homes to lavish custom homes and gated communities. These last were bemoaned by many natives as well as the "old newcomers," who had arrived as part of the 1970s back-to-the-land movement and built exquisite handmade dwellings fit for *Architectural Digest*.

When I returned in 1994 for the first time since 1978, it was natural that it would be to Elmer Hall's Sunnybank Inn. In Madison County, I felt—rationally or otherwise—that I needed a safe, private place to return to year after year for my research, a base from which to venture out and pry into a murder for which no one had been convicted. Conceivably, Nancy's killer or killers—and likely their families—were still around and would not welcome an outsider digging up the story. Sunnybank qualified as just such a bunker. Worried about my safety, I told no one but Elmer exactly when I would arrive.

On that first return visit, while I was still job hunting, I found that the former chaplain supported the book project enthusiastically. Even better, he had tantalizing news of something he had heard while working as a poll watcher some years earlier. "When everybody's voting, you just tell stories and gossip, and somehow this story came up, the murder of the VISTA worker as one of the unsolved murders in our county." According to Elmer, a local man had recounted a vague version of the crime for his coworkers, "and that's when I first heard the story that there were Hot Springs people involved." He had nothing more specific.

Since 1978, Elmer had transformed the upstairs bedrooms to a condition much like a century earlier. An integral part of the restoration effort was to keep alive Sunnybank's musical tradition. Early in the twentieth century, the inn's original proprietor, Jane Gentry, had collected and preserved English ballads with British folklorist Cecil Sharp. Both are honored with a state historical marker outside the inn. In one of the first-floor parlors, Elmer encouraged his guests to choose from a collection of donated, discarded, and collected instruments and play away. Some nights when the inn was full of trail hikers, or when a social gathering took place, the room would come alive with music and singing and dancing, shaking the whole house with rhythmic stomping that sent up a surreal, white, dusty haze.

On my first, week-long reporting visit, I sat in the middle of my antique bed, surrounded by yellow pages torn from my legal pad, scanning lists of names and phone numbers, trying to figure out whom to contact first. The ancient metal springs squeaked every time I leaned over to retrieve one of the papers for a closer look.

Doubts washed over me from time to time, and I would be struck by the absurdity of what I was trying to do. I felt alternately like I was in a movie or a mystery—or a delusional farce. Other times, I couldn't decide if I was Philip Marlowe or Walter Mitty.

In addition to keeping my visits unannounced, I took other precautions. Even if Nancy's killers, their families, or their friends were still around, I reasoned, bad things were unlikely to happen in the sunlight. I tried to stay off the roads after dusk, and I always let Elmer know where I was going and when he should expect me back. Whether these precautions were melodrama or simple prudence, I remained uncertain. Elmer was neutral on that point.

Associating myself with Elmer provided me a secure credential and allowed me to draw on his hard-earned credibility in the county. His knowledge of its people, generously offered, guided me as I tried to organize my brief, sometimes frenetic visits. Calling from my room at Sunnybank, I was never certain how people would respond, or even if they would listen long enough to my pitch before hanging up or turning me down. I had no color of authority—no badge, no gun, no subpoena power, not even a book contract. Plus, I was an outsider asking about an event that had done Madison County's reputation harm.

Some of the people I most urgently wanted to interview—including Myrtle Ray, Nancy's VISTA coworker in Shelton Laurel—declined to speak with me, pleading age or illness. Others were reluctant to talk. I also encountered the problem of memories fogged by time or colored by self-interest. In some cases, I had to race to reach people before their recollections slipped behind the curtain of dementia. So when they did agree, my reception by the elderly was especially heartening. For the most part, the seniors I contacted shared what they knew.

Madison County's old-timers were generally gracious about seeing me. It seemed that the more advanced in age they were, the more hospitable they proved. Perhaps they were simply grateful for a visitor who wanted to listen. Almost without fail, they invited me into their homes, whether they were rich or poor, living in rickety old cabins, mobile homes, or modern ranch houses. Oddly, the interiors often looked and felt much the same regardless of the owners' economic status— cozy, dusty, overheated rooms crowded with overstuffed chairs and sofas accumulated over a lifetime. Frayed carpet or linoleum on the floors. Bulging cabinets and stacks of papers everywhere. Most often, we sat around chipped Formica kitchen tables or in front of smooth river-rock fireplaces.

I began with those most directly connected to the Nancy Morgan case: Glendora Cutshall, Nancy's landlady and surrogate mother; E. Y. and Zeno Ponder; Joe Huff; Clyde Roberts, the district attorney at the time of the killing; and Dr. Page Hudson.

Glendora Cutshall sat with me many times, in her now-shuttered grocery store and in the refurbished cabin nearby where Nancy lived. Clear-headed into her late eighties, she answered all my questions, recreating the time Nancy and Diana Buzzard lived with her. She even guided me to the overgrown site of the Shelton Laurel Massacre, just up the road.

Despite older folks' general hospitality, I sometimes met with reticence or even refusal to answer specific questions. Clyde Roberts and his wife invited me into their home, set in the woods, and served me cider from their own press. But every question I asked about the Ponder brothers caused Mrs. Roberts to stifle her husband's response, cutting him off before he could speak, sometimes just by putting her hand on his arm.

I met E. Y. Ponder, the former sheriff, in 1996 at his mobile home on Star Mountain, where he had moved after a fire of suspicious origin burned him out of his house. Recently, he had done something he never had to do while he was a lawman—shoot someone, in this case a fleeing burglar, he told me.

When we talked of the VISTAs, Ponder stated his belief that much of the evil that took place in the county came from the outside. "That was the beginning of the drugs being introduced in Madison County," he recalled. "That crowd is the one that brought it in."

Standing in his front yard, E. Y. stuck to his original version of the Nancy Morgan killing. He described a big party that he said had taken place at Ed Walker's house in the Bluff community the night before the murder, with both locals and outsiders present—what E. Y. described as "a damn multitude."

When Johnny Waldroup returned from Asheville that night, he "see'd all these lights on. He went up to see what was going on. He got up there, and they was all having a big dance and all drunk, and Johnny told me that he sit down there in the yard, outside the window, and smoked a pack of, I believe it was Pall Malls. Anyway, he smoked a pack of cigarettes there. Said most of the butts was laying there on the window sill. The investigation showed all that."

Unfortunately, no one could confirm any of what Ponder said. The case file had long since vanished, and former sheriff Roy Roberts was dead.

What the partygoers were doing, Ponder said, "was playing a game of sex." Johnny told him that he had seen Nancy "hollering for help." But when he went to her aid, Walker hit him in the face and "busted his nose." Ponder asked what he did next, and Johnny said, "Well, I went and tried to give her artificial respiration," his nose bleeding all the while. "There was blood on her blouse," said Ponder, "but it wasn't her type of blood. It was Johnny's type," O rather than Nancy's A. (At Ed Walker's trial, Johnny Waldroup testified that he never touched Nancy's body.) The others at the party, including the secretary of a Sunday school, fled, according to Ponder. "All the rest of the crowd was afraid they'd be involved." E. Y. admitted that he never tried to have any of the locals who were there named, much less indicted or called to testify at Walker's trial. "You can't start a blood war in your own crowd," he said. Besides, they were "too damn drunk" to be of any use in court.

The old sheriff still stood by his star witness, even while acknowledging his weaknesses. "I was convinced beyond a doubt that Johnny was not lying. He told the truth about the thing. . . . But hell, I had nobody to back it up." He admitted that Waldroup had a history of mental illness but added, "If you were going to try the devil for any bad crime, you'd be forced to go to hell to get your damn witness." Ponder was also realistic about the devastating effect of Joe Huff's cross-examination. Ultimately, he believed the killing was more likely the result of misadventure than of design.

Sheriff Dedrick Brown, a towering man with a mustache and a

deep voice, was no friend of E. Y. Ponder's. But when I spoke with him, he was still an adherent of the wild-sex-party-gone-bad scenario. One problem with this narrative, apart from the fact that no one ever came forward to prove such a gathering took place, was that too few VISTA women were available to staff an orgy. Of the three female volunteers, one was a newlywed and another was a committed virgin who had already departed by the time of Nancy's murder.

At first, I plotted my interviews along a blacktop axis: Highway 25-70 from Hot Springs to Marshall, the county seat, and Highway 213 from Marshall to the college town of Mars Hill. These main thoroughfares were themselves studies in contrast—in one place, a sprawling auto junkyard on both sides of the road, the lime-green cinder-block building housing Cody's Video; along another stretch, modern whitewater rafting companies.

But over time, I found myself on twisting, unpaved roads where the tableaus deepened my sense of Madison County. Seasons transformed the roads as well as the views from them, mute chronicles of the agricultural cycle. Early in the spring, at the wide places along the roads, the tilled bottom lands were lined with pastel green tobacco plants, set off by the rich brown earth like knots on a quilt. A sudden rainstorm on a hot afternoon could send up veils of mist from the asphalt. Or a sudden swirl of Queen Anne's lace blossoms could sweep across the road like a seasonally out-of-joint snowstorm. My trips in the late fall had a darker feel. After the vacationers and "leaf peepers" left and the last of the Appalachian Trail through-hikers were gone, a timeless melancholy settled over the mountains. As winter approached and the days got shorter, sleet and ice and snow made the roads dangerous, given their steep grades, switchbacks, and hairpin turns. The crops were in, the firewood was chopped and stacked, and people's main concerns were keeping warm and fed until spring. The primary indoor antidotes to boredom—music making and serious drinking—began. In convenience stores in the "back of beyond," idle young men and tired old ones spent the days huddled around wood stoves playing rook—an old game from Puritan days using a "Christian deck" without blasphemous face cards. Complaining about the federal government was another favorite pastime. Should a stranger like me walk in, conversation stopped. I felt all eyes turned toward me, the stares as chilly as the weather outside.

≡≡

Zeno's Ponder's hilltop home—a sprawling, modern house up a long driveway from a mailbox marked simply "Zeno"—was as opulent as his older brother's was modest. It had a circular driveway out front and white pillars flanking the entrance. Just inside the front door, the living room was dominated by a pool table, a piano, photos and framed letters from Democratic presidents, and a bust of JFK. From the swivel chair in his office, the view included both Mount Pisgah and Mount Mitchell.

When we met for the first time, Zeno seemed a bit haggard, probably from chemotherapy treatments for lymphoma. He was long out of power and facing new legal problems. Chief among them was an indictment charging that he had used his position on the state highway commission to buy up land in Madison County for a county road. He brushed aside the charges, as he had numerous others over the years, by comparing them to children breaking wind in bed—"pootin' under the covers," he called it. He said he planned to donate the land to the state to shorten the bus ride for students in the hamlet of Trust, who attended the consolidated Madison County High School. Zeno had also been the object of a raucous protest at the county courthouse over a proposal to sell some of the same land to the state for a prison.

Neither his loss of political power nor the cancer had done much to diminish the old politician's bravado and zest for life. As we sat on the couch, it was hard to resist his charm and persistent smile. His mustache led newspapers to compare him to a riverboat gambler, but he also bore a resemblance to the actor Lee J. Cobb. Between visits, he initiated a lively correspondence. Like Elmer Hall but for different reasons, Zeno thought my book should be about the Ponders—at least one of them—rather than about Nancy Morgan. "Dear Mark," he wrote, "I am optimistic enough to think that a book written by you with the title, 'Zeno Ponder: The Man and the Legend'—think about a title—would sell at least 20,000 copies within six months after being published. I am known in every county in North Carolina as well as Tennessee, Georgia, South Carolina and Virginia. My wife, Marie, and I will travel and hit the road to autograph the books."

Zeno professed no special knowledge about who killed Nancy Morgan. Yet the canny politician, who knew his people as well as anyone, had an informed opinion starkly different from that of his brother. Zeno believed the young woman had run afoul of some local boys, men "with very little respect for themselves and the law," who had a wrong idea about her sexual availability. "Probably she was a little bit ahead of her time, and she partied and drank some." But he thought people who considered her loose were mistaken: "I think she was probably a good girl."

Page Hudson, the former medical examiner who testified at Ed Walker's trial, had retired to an elegant two-story mountainside home above the French Broad River at Marshall, up the road from E. Y.'s mobile home. Hudson greeted me dressed in a button-down shirt, khakis, and athletic shoes. A tall man then sixty-seven with receding, unruly white hair, he spoke in a deep, measured voice that retained traces of a Tidewater accent. The Nancy Morgan case, he said, was one "I haven't forgotten and don't expect ever to forget." One of the reasons he remembered it so well was that it was officially "an unsolved mystery."

Another reason the memory remained indelible, Hudson said, was the unprofessional way the investigation had been handled. "One, I would have taken photographs of the ropes on the body and around the neck. Two, I would have been able to give these directly to the law-enforcement officers involved and would be in a position to testify that these were the ropes that produced the death."

Hudson defended his testimony during the Walker trial regarding the time of Nancy's death. "Determining time of death is a relatively subjective thing," he said. "There's no good way, even under the best of circumstances, of coming to any exactitude about time of death. A body can start to swell in two or three hours, or a body can be in a location for weeks and not swell. There are too many variables to really give you a good answer to that question."

Reviewing the copy of his autopsy report that I had brought with me, Hudson shared some reminiscences of the trial, getting up from his easy chair to call his old Chapel Hill office in an effort—ultimately futile—to track down the fluid slides that might be tested for DNA. If the technology now available had been used at the time, he said, it would have been a relatively simple matter to determine who had sex with Nancy just prior to her death.

Before long, Sheriff Ponder's name came up. Hudson had a generally high opinion of the lawman, who had helped him find the property where we were then sitting. Hudson told a story about working years before in his lab. One Saturday, the sheriff and a deputy arrived unannounced, carrying a bag. Inside were three skulls that had been recovered from the banks of the French Broad River after a break-in at a Hot Springs mausoleum. Ponder wanted Hudson to help identify the skulls, including one that had belonged to the son of President Andrew Johnson, from photographs, which the medical examiner did.

When I called Joe Huff, he was—unsurprisingly—enthusiastic and even exultant to talk about the biggest trial in his legal career. "That case caused more notoriety than any case I tried and I would gladly see a story written about it," he said in a subsequent letter before we met. Huff even wrote to Ed Walker on my behalf, when I told him of Walker's initial refusal to agree to an interview. "It was the outstanding victory of my legal career and I would be proud to have my name appear," he wrote Walker. On the front lawn of the lawyer's Mars Hill home flew a good-sized Confederate flag. Huff told me it was there to honor his ancestors who fought in the Civil War, but African-American students from the school across the street sometimes tore it down.

Like his longtime adversary Zeno Ponder, Huff claimed no insights about Nancy's killing beyond what he had learned during Walker's defense. But as a lifelong observer of the underside of Madison County, he offered the theory that "local rednecks," accepting the fantasies of the VISTAs' lifestyle, were responsible. "The men resented the fact that they had parties. It was talk that sex was pretty cheap, so the men resented that." He thought the issue of class might also have played a role. "The VISTAs didn't talk the same way that local people did. They were hoity-toity rich people, educated." But ultimately, he believed "it was sex that got the girl killed. I'm sure the redneck boys thought that they did more than drink at these parties, that there was sex going on in these things."

In a subsequent letter, Huff wrote that he thought the sheriff knew all along who the real culprits were. And he was not surprised by the jury's verdict: "The people that had no ax to grind as far as the Ponder ring was concerned did not think that he was guilty."

But if Joe Huff and Zeno Ponder were right that local men were responsible for Nancy's death, I wondered, why had no sympathetic soul come forward with information that might have led investigators to her killers?

18

One of my earliest and most valuable interviews was with Sheila Kay Adams. She is a rugged mountain beauty, her long raven tresses mostly gone to silver, her once-glowing face still compelling but now creased by a life touched by tragedy. After graduating from college, she taught eighth grade for seventeen years in Madison County. She is a proud and articulate advocate for mountain culture and over time has become a folklorist, telling, writing, and singing her people's story without compromise or apology.

As a teenager, Adams knew Nancy Morgan. One of her stories, "When the Snake Handlers Come to Sodom," was based, she said, on a true incident from Nancy's summer in Madison County. Six snake handlers from Tennessee crossed the mountains to hold a service in the hamlet of Sodom, just up Lonesome Mountain Road. Adams and her cousin Inez Chandler joined a large gathering at Shady Grove Low Gap Primitive Free Will Baptist Church. While Adams didn't recall if

Nancy was also there, this was still a part of the culture the VISTAs encountered in Madison County.

As Adams told it, the church's spirited bedrock faith provided comfort and community to people used to living a hard life in what some called "the Land of Do Without." Yet even the church's location was precarious, planted atop a steep knob with barely enough level space at its base for a narrow footpath to circle the white, steepled structure with a rough plank exterior. Out back, two weathered brown outhouses hovered above the precarious drop-off. Since the congregation was too poor to afford pews, the church had only eight short rows of backless benches, divided by a narrow center aisle.

The crowd quickly filled the seats and then lined the walls and plunked down on the floor in front of the benches. Latecomers lingered on the front porch and peered in through the open, unscreened windows.

Adams explained that the crowd had come out of curiosity, wanting to observe an unadulterated religious experience straight from the Bible. As the service began, three men and three women filed through a narrow door near the front of the sanctuary, sharing the weight of several hinged wooden boxes. Taking their seats at the front of the room, they began loudly breathing in and out and humming in the rhythmic practice known in the mountains as "huffing." Their knees began to bounce. One of the men, a preacher dressed in lime-green polyester slacks and a pale yellow shirt buttoned at the throat, delivered a long prayer denouncing sin and abomination, twitching and jerking his body, chanting as his eyes rolled back in his head. The others joined him, standing and ranting in the ecstatic gibberish known as "speaking in tongues." They ran around the room, frightening even some of the county's devout citizens.

Suddenly, the Tennessee preacher flipped open one of wooden boxes and pulled out two rattlers—their tails "in full sing," as Adams told it—and waved them high above him. One of the women grabbed two copperheads and started running around the sanctuary.

"Them's real snakes!" somebody shouted, and the congregation exploded, turning over the benches in a mad rush for any way out. When the doors couldn't handle the traffic, people headed for the windows. Those too bulky to make it through themselves tossed their children down the hillside. "Catch little Floyd!" Adams remembered hearing before grabbing on to the back of her cousin Inez's voluminous polyester dress as her formidable relative plowed a path from the front bench to the double doors at the rear like a crazed fullback.

At first, just as I feared, Adams advised me against dredging up the past. "It's like my father said, 'Hell, she's been dead over twenty-five years.' Why do you want to scratch around in that old stuff? You ain't gonna bring her back." Adams warned that I might run into resistance and was concerned that reviving Nancy's story would only perpetuate unflattering stereotypes of Appalachia. "Mountain people are just often misportrayed," she said. "They're portrayed as being suspicious and closed and narrow-minded and having teeny little visions when it comes to the world, and that's not the way it is at all." She said it broke her heart that "these wonderful, warm, loving, caring people, with the best senses of humor in the whole world," were so often misrepresented.

Yet the more she thought about it, the more she felt resolving the murder case might not be a bad thing. "It's so distant now, I don't think that it would be the community trauma that it would have been twenty-five years ago, because so much has gone by. My granny used to say that time was a great healer, but it was not a very good beautician. Enough time has gone by to where definitely the wound is gone." People in the community, she said, felt badly about what had happened to Nancy. "They hated it. That's what they would say. 'Boy, I hate what happened to that girl.'"

However people felt about my poking into the murder case, they seemed willing to talk about their memories of Nancy, sympathetically but not always uncritically. Adams described the locals as Nancy's protectors. "Nancy Morgan was accepted into this community. She was taken care of by members of the community. She was looked after. Even though they had what possibly was wrong ideas about her moral conduct, they still took care of her." Adams recalled that cousins of hers had invited Nancy to meals and family gatherings and had tried to introduce her to other locals. They felt sorry for her: "She's off up here by herself, and she ain't got no people here," Adams said.

Still, the sentiment persisted that in some way Nancy had brought her death on herself. "Mountain girls grow up knowing that there's a certain amount of distance that you have to maintain with the male population, because that's just the way it is. In the mountains, if you behave in a certain way, they can very well assume what they assume, based on their own upbringing," said Adams. People thought that "if she'd have been down there with her people, if she had stayed where she was born and raised, where somebody could see about her and look after her, then this would have never happened."

Not being part of mountain culture, Nancy "made some mistakes," said Adams. "She had sort of the reputation of being right loose. That's what was kind of talked about here in the county—that she cussed in front of men and she drank. This kind of behavior was not done overtly in mountain culture." Women did not drink with men "unless they were loose women." Adams had never heard any rumors of Nancy's actually "going out and having these wild sexual experiences with local boys. But there was always that kind of underlying implication that she was loose morally."

Ellen Banks rejected the notion that Nancy was raped and killed because of her reputation. "The loosest, drinkingest, cussingest women in Madison County—and there are plenty of them—are still not tied up and murdered because of it." Although violence against women was far too common, she said, "there's also respect for women" in Appalachian culture—even for "bad" women.

Banks, a Madison County activist who knew Nancy Morgan, said, "We'll never really rest in Madison County about Nancy's death. People really liked her, and it was an awful thing. It has, I'm sure, ruined Ed Walker's life and has made a terrible stain on Madison County and Madison County people. We've had enough problems since the Shelton Laurel Massacre."

Banks, like Adams, was born and bred in Madison County, left for a time, and then returned to settle. The experience of living elsewhere gave each woman a perspective that enabled her to offer incisive views of the place she loved so much.

I spent most of one trip tracking down surviving jurors from Ed Walker's trial. I found Harry Payne in his two-acre tobacco patch on bottom land across the road from his home, amid pale green plants sprouting in the brown loam. A laconic man at first unwilling to allow himself to be recorded, Payne stopped his tiller to speak, then sat on the dropped back of a nearby pickup truck. "I'd just love to know who done it," he said, pushing back his cap and mopping his brow on a hot spring afternoon. "I don't think this is a county for people to kill and get away with it. I'd rather for someone to be tried for it and convicted. Madison County is a real fine county, and there's a bunch of the nicest people in the world there. I think it's a real dead shame that it happened in our county."

In the subtle way that information sometimes suffuses southern mountain communities over time—tentatively, even timorously, by inference and indirection—a vague alternative scenario of Nancy's death gradually emerged from my interviews. Echoing what Elmer Hall had first heard and what Joe Huff and Zeno Ponder both believed, it centered on "local boys." Specifically, people kept guiding me toward one group of young thugs in Hot Springs.

At first, Clyde Parks, a native who retired to Madison County after a military career, was circumspect. "Just say it was the local people, local boys who liked to party in a rough manner," he said as he sat in the sun-drenched front yard of his mountaintop home near the Tennessee border. "Now, I won't name names because I don't know." But when I read him a tentative list of suspects I had gathered, men from both Hot Springs and Shelton Laurel, Parks dismissed those from Shelton Laurel and said I had missed one of the likely Hot Springs participants.

Parks then named Richard Lewis Johnson, the Hot Springs police chief's son and one of E. Y. Ponder's regular informers. This was the same man who with his father chanced on the crowd where Nancy's body was found, and who met Ed Walker in the Madison County Jail in 1984. Johnson had a rough reputation.

"One of my sons went to high school with him, and I've heard more than one tale, because I've had run-ins with Johnson before, and I know that he would be capable, personally, of this killing," Parks said. Once, when he tried to collect a debt from Johnson on behalf of a tire company, the younger man denied that he owed the money and threatened Parks. Johnson "didn't scare me personally, because I've protected myself during two wars and in and out of a third one, so that didn't bother me," Parks said. One nickname for Johnson was "Firebug." He was suspected of burning down the Hot Springs Hotel—the latest incarnation of many resorts built to take advantage of the riverside landmark that gave the town its name—in 1976.

My interest surged because some Madison County old-timers, although they had no proof to offer, also seemed to be guiding me toward Johnson, a perpetual thorn in the county's side. George Penland, former mayor of Marshall and owner of Penland and Son Grocery and General Store, where Nancy shopped, said he wouldn't be surprised to hear that Richard Johnson had been involved in her killing.

"Everyone always knew Richard Johnson had something to do with it," recalled Lynn Steen, whose husband was Hot Springs's longtime dentist. She said she once loaded a pistol because she thought Johnson was lurking outside her Hot Springs home.

Charlie Chambers, the retired SBI agent who had investigated the murder in 1970 and testified against Ed Walker, still wasn't willing to accept anyone else as the culprit. But my mention of Richard Johnson struck a nerve. "That boy gave me a lot of grief," Chambers said.

Clearly, here was someone I needed to know more about.

19

While I faithfully pounded the religion beat at the *Orlando Sentinel* through the 1990s, I used Internet databases to locate Nancy Morgan's old friends and colleagues, now scattered around the country and the world. Some did not respond to my inquiries or declined to participate, pleading that the murder was still too painful to discuss. But many helped fill in the blanks about Nancy and her life before and during her VISTA experience, sharing their memories of her and her letters they had saved. Before I could figure out who killed Nancy, I had to figure out who she was.

At first, reading Nancy's letters and learning about this young woman from her friends was, frankly, disappointing. I hoped a heroine for my story would emerge—a rebel, a crusader, someone fired by the anger and idealism that had burned in me and my friends at Duke in the late 1960s. Instead, Nancy wrote to her friends from 1965 to 1967 mostly about academic news, cooking, the clothes she was making, and the men she was dating. I had imagined her as a fighter and a feminist, and instead she seemed to be searching for a man to complete a life that was on its way to becoming conventional. I was depressed that, at least in her letters, she wasn't the generational avatar I wanted her to be. But like many of us, her growing concerns about civil rights, the Vietnam War, and economic and social justice crystallized in the late 1960s on campus.

≥≡

The sprawling, modernistic campus of Southern Illinois University at Edwardsville looked like it had sprouted in the middle of a cornfield—which in a sense it had, the product of a backroom patronage deal in the state legislature. The grounds had the look of an overgrown community college, built as much for job creation as for research and education. Its student body of more than thirteen thousand started classes in 1965, the year before Nancy enrolled.

During the second half of the 1960s, the campus was bubbling with rock concerts and small demonstrations. In one celebrated off-campus incident, an antiwar professor smashed a picture of Richard Nixon hanging in the post office. Yet there was no serious campus upheaval after the 1968 assassination of Martin Luther King Jr.

Nancy began commuting to classes in the summer quarter of 1966 and immediately encountered a student body far more diverse than she'd been used to at Radford in Virginia. After completing her required classes, she gradually shifted to courses on the French Revolution and Latin American history, as well as one in pre-nursing. She switched her major from history to social work—and made dean's list—and told a friend she was interested in finding a job in that field. Intellectually, she was evolving. She earned one of only four As in her Western Civilization course.

Nancy's brother George saw clearly her developing political consciousness. He and Nancy were close "theologically and philosophically," as well as personally, he said. "The difference between us was that she wanted to save the world, and I felt that that was unrealistic and it was better to improve the world while taking care of your home team, a less ambitious but reachable goal."

Inevitably, Vietnam arose as a topic of Morgan family conversation. Nancy was against the war, George said, but he didn't recall that she upset their parents with her views. Growing up in the military, the two siblings had heard over and over from their father that the United States had "signed a treaty that obligated us to defend South Vietnam as we had with Japan and most of Europe." Then there was the argument that "the communists will take over the world if we don't stop them right here and now." Colonel Morgan had bought into all of it, George said, so perhaps Nancy censored herself in conversations with her family.

Martin Luther King Jr.'s death deepened Nancy's thinking about race. She was a great admirer of MLK, George said, recalling favorable comments his sister made while the family watched television coverage of the civil-rights movement. Their parents were nominally Democrats but were not strongly affiliated with the party. "On race, I suppose for the time period my father was rather liberal, but he came from the South, and there was definitely a little racist undertone."

In the 1968 presidential campaign, Nancy supported the antiwar Robert Kennedy and then, after his assassination, George McGovern's short-lived run. "I think she actively campaigned for Kennedy," said George.

But however politically active she might have been, Nancy "always had a social conscience and wanted to help people," according to Rita Weiss, the wife of an SIUE professor.

Another faculty member, Patrick Riddleberger, was not surprised that she later joined VISTA. She was a compassionate person, Riddleberger recalled, "an idealist and a young lady who was trying to do good in the world."

An affair with an older professor led to an abortion. Nancy was a longtime supporter of abortion rights, George said. She went to Chicago with a friend, underwent the procedure there, and didn't inform her parents until afterward. "I recall my parents ranting a bit about it because it was dangerous, and the fact that there was a prohibition at the time and it was illegal meant you had none of the legal protections," George said. Nancy wasn't herself when she returned from Chicago. "I think one of the reasons she had to come clean with it was there was some physical trauma," he remembered. "It was primarily the health issues. My father was very strong about obeying the law, but that was a secondary concern to the health issues."

To all appearances, Nancy recovered from the trauma emotionally as well as physically. But after finishing at SIUE, she seemed to drift, skipping commencement ceremonies. She decided she wanted to go to graduate school in nursing—"but probably not for a year and a half," she wrote in a 1968 Christmas card. She also considered studying psychiatric social work as preparation for working in a hospital or women's prison. After moving back to Washington, she briefly took a series of clerical jobs with nonprofits, searching for something meaningful to do before going back to school. By September 1969, she decided she was prepared to make a one-year commitment to VISTA.

"In part, it was a search for significance," said Nancy's older brother, John. "The American government was presenting VISTA as a way to make a contribution. That was something she was struggling with." The decision was not unlike his own around the same time to attend the Air Force Academy at the height of the Vietnam War. While on leave from the air force, John took United States Army Airborne training at Fort Benning, Georgia. "I tend to think we both had a sense of invincibility, a sense of adventure. I'm sure she went with high hopes and expectations. I think the sixties time frame had something to do with it, but I think it was part of the human condition. It manifests itself in people differently, and in different cultures differently. At the same time, if she had found Mr. Right, she might not have gone to VISTA."

≡≡

My visit to Southern Illinois University at Edwardsville in 1999, for what would have been Nancy's thirtieth college reunion, brought unexpected results. While there, I dropped by the offices of the campus daily, the *Alestle*, and for the first time told for publication the story of my effort to solve the case. I hoped the *Alestle* article might shake loose some memories in the university community. The story ended up on the Internet, under the headline, "Grad Case Unsolved."

At the time, anyone trolling the Web and using the keywords *Nancy Morgan* and *murder* would call up the article. The *Alestle* story dealt with my search for whoever was responsible for Nancy's death and my growing suspicion that someone local was responsible. Several of Nancy's good friends and acquaintances contacted me, including her school friends Kristin Johnson and Marty Tyler, who each mailed me photos and e-mailed their recollections.

Kristin met with me in San Francisco and brought along a cache of Nancy's letters to her from the late 1960s. In one, dated February 12, 1970, Nancy wrote that she had taken the Graduate Record Exam in preparation for applying to nursing school, and was waiting for results, uncertain where the money would come from. Work was "picking up a bit but since we're the first VISTAs in Madison County we're starting from scratch." Nancy was concerned that she and Kristin would be the last in their group to marry. "I still like being single and free," she wrote. "Either I'm not ready to settle down or just haven't met anyone who could tie me down. There are still a hundred things to do first— like nursing and Europe and working in poverty. So many things that couldn't be done as a married person."

One former Madison County woman who stumbled across the *Alestle* story on the Web contacted me to say that, while in therapy, she had recalled an incident from the week Nancy's body was discovered. The woman was eight years old at the time and riding in the backseat of a car with her father and his cousin, both occasional armed robbers and both now dead. The only thing she could remember about the conversation was that the two men discussed whether or not Nancy's underpants had been found, in a way that suggested they knew something about her abduction. Her note lent another angle to the local-boys theory about the murder.

I decided early on not to approach the surviving members of the Morgan family—Colonel Earl Morgan had died. Not until I reached the end of my research would I ask them to relive this traumatic episode in their lives. I wanted at least to be able to present them with my findings before I asked for their help.

But Nancy's younger brother, George, came across the *Alestle* article and wrote me. I immediately replied, explaining why I had not yet contacted the family members, and he agreed to be their primary spokesman. "I think we are similarly motivated," he wrote. "We'll never know what Nancy would have done with her life, but I feel confident that her loss was a loss to all." Via e-mail, the Internet, and surreptitious looks at his elderly mother's address book, George helped track down some of his sister's other friends. He passed my contact information along to his older brother, John, who at that time declined to participate in the project (but years later agreed to an interview). I decided not to trouble Abigail Morgan, then in her eighties. Years later, before I could revisit my decision, George wrote to tell me that his mother had retreated into Alzheimer's. It was sad news, but on a certain level I confess that I was relieved.

I encountered some frustrating blind alleys. Nancy's VISTA supervisor, Richard Haimes, declined to be interviewed, without explanation, as did Nancy's roommate, Diana Buzzard, who wrote me an angry letter that instructed me not to contact her again. Ron Bedrick, another Madison County VISTA, did not respond to repeated contacts, and I could not locate Peter McDermott, another volunteer in their contingent.

Several of Nancy's other acquaintances from outside North Carolina fed my growing suspicion of Richard Johnson and his Hot Springs gang as possible killers. Nancy's VISTA colleagues Frank and Peggy Breckenridge were now living in an improbably leafy, rural, creek-side oasis tucked among the Cincinnati suburbs. All these years later, they remained haunted by their friend's death, although they were no longer in Madison County or VISTA when it happened. Already weary of the VISTAs' ideological bickering, they had been further frustrated when they were unable to convince their county project supervisor, Richard Haimes, to pull Nancy out of her Shelton Laurel cabin after her roommate quit the program.

There had also been less substantive omens. Three weeks before Nancy's disappearance, they "woke up in the middle of May and realized it was time to get out of there," said Peggy. "To this day, we call it 'the Arm of God.' Frank had this dream, and he sat bolt upright the next morning and said, 'We're leaving. We're getting out of here.'" The couple's chief reason for going was that they felt the other VISTAs' political truculence had made it unsafe for the two of them in Hot Springs. "It was real clear that certain VISTAs were making enemies of the power structure," said Peggy, whose social conscience had been nurtured at Quaker summer camps.

As I shared with the Breckenridges what I had learned about Richard Johnson and his associates, they grew more animated, suddenly looking at each other, excited. Barely containing themselves, they recalled an incident that had taken place in Hot Springs in 1970, not long before they left Madison County, and several months before the murder.

Frank's movie theater restoration project had become a victim of

its own success, provoking jealousy in the community. A group of local men in their late teens and early twenties, older than the kids with
whom Frank was working at the theater, complained to anyone who
would listen that it was unfair that they had enjoyed nothing like this
when they were younger. The resentful crowd included Richard Johnson and his good friend Henry Sharpe, among others who were known
for cruising around Hot Springs on weekend nights. "They had gotten out of high school and were rattling around and generally causing
trouble, because we kept hearing about it," said Frank.

Late one Saturday night, as the theater was closing, a car containing
a group of these men, including Sharpe and Johnson, pulled to the curb
beneath the marquee. The gang, obviously drunk, piled out of the car
and waded into the unsuspecting teens, throwing fists and pounding
on nearby parked vehicles. When Breckenridge tried to stop the attack,
one of the drunks grabbed him by the shirt and threw him against the
wall.

Peggy was home sick that night, but another person who remembered the incident was one of Frank's friends, John Barnes, a Harvard
graduate from northern Virginia who had been invited to the theater
that night. In the late sixties, Barnes had found his way to Madison
County and was teaching school at Spring Creek in order to maintain
his draft deferment. When I reached him by phone, he recalled the
group as mean, "dumb, hard-drinking, wild guys who caused trouble"
and were known for their propensity for violence.

"They came up drunk, and they stayed out front," Barnes said. "They
were beating on cars, and they were driving around in the car really fast
up and down the street, just threatening and nasty." A town deputy was
on hand but refused to intervene against the police chief's son and his
friends, despite Barnes's demand that he do something. "I remember
not asking [but] saying to the cop, 'You ought to do something.' And he
told me I ought to shut up and put his hand on his gun."

Henry Sharpe in particular made a lasting impression on Barnes. "I don't think he did anything" by way of work, Barnes said. "He just hung around, and you'd see him on the weekends, drunk and strutting around. Blue jeans and boots and greased hair. Not a farmer. He was the bad guy in town, getting drunk, causing trouble, getting in fights with people." Barnes remembered Sharpe's companionship with Richard Johnson and another young man. "They hung out together, and then they'd be in fights with each other. They were the town thugs."

Getting no help from the deputy, some of the younger kids—none of whom was seriously hurt—ran around the corner and called their parents. The attackers jumped in their car and drove off. In minutes, four carloads of angry parents arrived with chains and dogs in their vehicles and took off after the thugs. The troublemakers crossed the raised railroad tracks—their car going airborne—and then came to the bridge over the French Broad River. They abandoned their car on the bank, swam across the river, and ran home, where, by local custom, they could not be pursued.

Sharpe, who was on probation at the time, said that anyone who swore out a warrant against him was a dead man. Nonetheless, Frank Breckenridge filed charges against the attackers, brought them to court, and promised to testify against them, which led to subpoenas for Barnes and some of the teens to back him up. Although at least one of the defendants was on probation and the others had been in numerous scrapes with the law, the matter was settled in the judge's chambers, and all the young men were freed. The charges were dropped on the day Nancy Morgan's body was found. Breckenridge, Barnes, Leroy and Richard Johnson, and Henry Sharpe were all in the Madison County Courthouse when news arrived of the discovery.

Unfortunately, Frank Breckenridge's action proved costly in terms of the resentment it sparked in Hot Springs. "Things seemed to be going so well and then, after the incident, there was one family with a lot of kids that separated themselves out because Frank took out this warrant against their cousin," said Peggy. "The people that owned the filling station had spent a lot of time at the community center, and all of a sudden they wouldn't let their kids interact with us."

Several years later, after leaving Madison County, John Barnes returned to visit a friend and former fellow teacher and was accosted by E. Y. Ponder, now back in office. "I was walking down the street in Hot Springs, and this guy pulled me over and says, 'Can I talk to you?' It was E. Y. Ponder, and he wanted to talk to me about the murder."

Ponder asked Barnes why he was in Hot Springs, thereby intimidating him "to the point where I felt like he was insinuating that I was involved in the murder. He scared hell out of me."

Then, in 1984, at the time of the Walker indictment, Barnes got a surprise visit at his Cambridge, Massachusetts, apartment by two agents of the North Carolina State Bureau of Investigation. It was virtually identical to the calls paid on Walker in Florida and James Waldroup in Georgia. The agents, together with a Cambridge police officer, took Barnes to an interview at the station house and told him an "eyewitness" had placed him at the murder scene. When Barnes realized that the point of the interrogation was to implicate him in Nancy's death, he broke off the conversation, saying he wouldn't continue without a lawyer.

Later, he was not surprised to learn of Ed Walker's acquittal. "The fact that they came sniffing towards me made me believe that they didn't know what they were doing. They were making it up."

Although Barnes visited Asheville and drove through the state in the years after Walker's trial, he never again returned to Madison County "because I was scared," he said. "Madison County is a weird place, gothic in a different way. Every time I went into that state, I would think about it."

Gradually, recollections of Richard Johnson by people from outside Madison County and revelations of long-held suspicions by county residents grew from a trickle to a torrent, carrying me inexorably in the direction of Johnson, the son of the Hot Springs chief of police.

20

Growing up in Hot Springs, Richard Johnson was surrounded by a pessimism that approached despair. For a few decades, the town had known wealth and even acclaim, but that was long gone by the time Johnson was born in 1948.

In the late 1880s, Hot Springs was one of the premier summer resorts on the East Coast. Its main attraction was the soothing waters that seeped from the banks of the French Broad River. New York promoters changed the town's name from Warm Springs. On the burned ruins of a previous structure, they built the grand, four-story Mountain Park Hotel, spread out on a hundred-acre site. The Swiss-Gothic hotel was the height of Gilded Age elegance, boasting two hundred bedrooms lit by electricity and heated by steam. It had a mansard roof; a tower at each corner topped with a pointed witch's-hat turret; some 1,000 feet of veranda, including 125 feet enclosed by glass; and a hydraulic elevator. Other amenities included an elegantly appointed lobby with leather furniture and potted palms.

A newly completed rail line brought six trains a day, including the famed Carolina Special. Thousands of wealthy tourists came to the spa every summer in hopes of escaping the heat. Clad in daytime whites—flannel and linen—they took advantage of recreational facilities that included a nine-hole golf course, a swimming pool, bowling alleys, and billiard tables. An orchestra played nightly beneath the soaring ceiling of one of North America's largest ballrooms.

In keeping with the custom of the time, African-Americans were imported from the lowlands to work as domestics and liveried staff; waiters served meals in tuxedos and white gloves. But there were also, for the first time in memory, lots of paying jobs for white residents of Madison County, who worked as everything from desk clerks to hunting guides. For a while, Hot Springs prospered. The short-story writer O. Henry honeymooned at the Mountain Park Hotel in 1907.

A long period of economic decline followed. The New York backers gave up and sold out to locals. In 1917, during World War I, the United States government leased the hotel to house German civilian internees, including merchant marines and the crew of the cruise ship *Vaterland*, the pride of the Hamburg-Amerika Line. By the 1960s, bypassed by the new Interstate 40 link, Hot Springs was destitute, nearly a ghost town. It had fallen so low that representatives of the Maharishi Mahesh Yogi scouted it as a site for their cult's headquarters, approaching a local woman who owned much of the town. Only the intervention of her outraged Presbyterian minister, who warned her that she would go to hell if the deal went through, prevented the sale.

The downfall of Hot Springs as a resort, and the despair it inflicted, had many victims, including Richard Johnson. By all accounts, including his own, he was a thug, an arsonist, a rapist, a petty thief, a vandal, and a pathological liar. He was a bad seed who flowered into evil as he grew. As I dug into his history, he seemed increasingly like a grotesque character limned from the pages of Cormac McCarthy, Charles Frazier, Thomas Wolfe, or William Faulkner. And I soon learned that Johnson wasn't thought by only his neighbors to be capable of murder. He was actually serving time for it.

Sitting in the tiny lobby of her motel in Hot Springs, one of his former neighbors, Virginia Anderson, told me that as a youngster, Richard was known for walking around town with his friend Henry Sharpe, carrying a kerosene can, and burning anything inconsequential he could find. Over the years, the boy became a bully at school, where he was known derisively as "Jughead." "He was a trial to his parents," Anderson recalled. Richard stole from his family—money, furniture, tools, food—she said, as well as from the Andersons and other neighbors. He broke into the Andersons' gas station so often they stopped locking it. When residents asked his father, Leroy Johnson, the town police chief, why he didn't do something about the boy, he would reply, "He's my own flesh and blood."

In his early twenties, Richard was suspected of increasingly violent acts. The cases against him that made it into the justice system through the 1970s, after Nancy Morgan's death, involved arrests or guilty pleas for vandalism, assault, trespass, drunken driving, and hit-and-run. Johnson was widely suspected of sexually assaulting single women who lived alone but who, because of their lack of social status, their reputation, or their drinking, were not in a position to bring credible charges. In most cases, Leroy Johnson was able to keep his son out of prison, thanks to his ties to Sheriff Ponder.

As a member of the Hot Springs Volunteer Fire Department, Richard sometimes rode the red truck to blazes he had started. To keep ahead of the authorities, he would monitor the county's police radio from the scanner in his father's patrol car. He also ran political errands. He drove voters to the polls on Election Day for Bobby Ponder, who was E. Y. and Zeno's nephew, the owner of the local hardware store, and the de facto ward boss of Hot Springs.

Richard rarely had a regular job, eking out a living on the dark side of small-town life, serving those he called "high-class people." He made runs to government alcohol package stores for them and also chauffeured cheating spouses to trysts out in the country, so their cars wouldn't be spotted. E. Y. sometimes called on him to pick up respectable folk who had been pulled over by Tennessee troopers for driving home drunk from University of Tennessee football games, occasionally with people other than their spouses.

In the late 1960s, Johnson and his friends abducted a local woman and a boy. Johnson and one of his friends took the young man down to a creek, cut his hair, and dunked him in the water. They later raped the woman and her sister. Leroy Johnson couldn't keep the Republican sheriff, Roy Roberts, from arresting his son. But E. Y. Ponder made a call to a judge in a neighboring county and had the case transferred to a different jurisdiction, after which the charges evaporated. Richard Johnson later described the assault and bragged that the men were charged with it but never tried.

Around that time, Johnson married a woman named Brenda Church, who was sixteen. Their first child, born a year later, lived just nineteen days before dying of natural causes. The couple later had a son, Christopher, and a daughter, Joyce. But the match was a turbulent and troubled one. On at least one occasion, Brenda fled to a domestic abuse center, showing evidence of having been beaten. She finally left Richard after thirteen years of marriage, separating on March 9, 1984. The following month, he was awarded temporary custody of his children, for reasons that are unclear. Richard lived next door to his father, now retired from law enforcement after thirty-one years, and his mother, who helped out with child care.

In early June 1984, Leroy Johnson rushed his eleven-year-old grandson, Christopher, to Asheville's Memorial Mission Hospital. Though complaining of chills, the boy was sweating profusely. His pupils were pinpoints, his chest muscles were in spasm, and his speech was slurred. Emergency-room personnel diagnosed him as suffering from exposure to an insecticide, an organophosphate, which his family had been using around the house that day.

Several weeks later, on June 17, an ambulance brought Christopher's five-year-old, red-haired sister, Joyce, to the same hospital at ten o'clock on a Sunday morning. Dr. Thomas Howald, the emergency-room physician, found that Joyce was not breathing and had no pulse. Her pupils were dilated, she was blue, and she had vomited and was still foaming at the mouth. Howald detected the strong odor of an organophosphate-based insecticide, which he took to be either malathion or diazinon, the only types of poison he believed would cause symptoms like those the girl displayed.

The staff at the hospital, especially Teresa Thornberry, a registered nurse in the pediatric intensive care unit, was familiar with the Johnson family, according to newspaper articles and a trial transcript. She had first encountered Richard and Brenda separately on several occasions in May of that year, when little Joyce was admitted with symptoms including disorientation and hallucinations so severe she had to be restrained. The symptoms might have been the result of insecticide exposure, but Richard seemed more concerned about his ex-wife than his stricken daughter. The first thing he did was show the nurse his custody papers, informing her that he had control over who could and could not see his daughter. His wife could visit, he said, but not Brenda's boyfriend.

Richard worked himself into a rage, telling Thornberry about his disintegrating marriage. "He seemed real distraught over that, the fact that his wife had a boyfriend," she later recalled on the witness stand. Johnson told her that if Brenda "would get rid of the boyfriend that he would take her back, that she wanted the children, but that she was not going to have the children until she got rid of the boyfriend, because she wasn't a fit mother."

On another occasion that May, when Joyce was hospitalized in Asheville for an illness unrelated to poisoning, a confrontation erupted in the hallway. Richard tried to have Brenda barred from visiting her daughter's room, but the medical staff and social-service workers managed to have the two alternate visits. When they passed in the hallway, according to Brenda, Richard asked her if she remembered a Hot Springs man named Jim Ward, who eleven years earlier had killed his two children and then committed suicide. "Yeah, what about it?" Brenda said. "And he told me if I didn't go back to Hot Springs, that was what he was going to do to him and the kids. And I told him I didn't care if he done that to himself, but to leave the young-uns alone." Richard grabbed her by the arm and threw her against the wall.

Richard's lifelong friend Timmy Ramsey later testified that a month before Joyce's poisoning, Richard told him "he would rather see his kids in hell as his wife have them."

Richard, in his self-defense, claimed that what he said was, "I would rather see her in hell than have the kids."

On June 15, Joyce Johnson was brought to Memorial Mission Hospital for at least the third time that spring. She was admitted for nausea and then released. Two days later, on June 17, when she was brought back by ambulance and admitted to the emergency room, the news that she had likely been poisoned reached Steve Huff, Joe Huff's son, at his law office in Marshall. The younger Huff, who had informally assisted at Ed Walker's murder trial, often served as the county's guardian ad litem—a court-appointed watchdog over the well-being of children.

"I usually was appointed to represent children alleged to be abused or neglected," Huff told me, "so when it became evident that Johnson's daughter had been poisoned, I was asked to be the guardian for the little girl and her brother." As a Huff, Steve well knew the close relationship between Richard Johnson's father and Sheriff E. Y. Ponder, who was still in office in 1984. He also knew that Richard was one of the sheriff's informers.

"Having been aware of the players here and how it worked, I saw the need to do several things, one of which was to get the State Bureau of Investigation involved, as opposed to the Madison County Sheriff's Department." Still, for whatever reason, the SBI never requested a search warrant for either of Johnson's houses and never attempted to recover any bottles that might have contained poison or medicine.

On Wednesday afternoon, June 20, physicians withdrew life support from the comatose Joyce Johnson. She died thirty minutes later. Dr. Brian Sudderth, one of those who treated her, asked Richard Johnson if he had any idea how his daughter might have been exposed to the pesticide. "He said that Joyce's mother left behind a suitcase that had some makeup in it, and that the makeup had bugs in it, and that he sprayed it, and [asked] could putting on that makeup cause Joyce's pesticide poisoning."

Steve Huff called the hospital and learned that the child's body was soon to be released to the family's custody for burial. "I talked to Judge Alexander Lyerly by phone, and basically the judge gave me permission and authorization to do whatever was necessary on both the girl's autopsy and her brother's custody, because time was of the essence. The wolves were literally at the door. The timing on this was critical because I was playing catch-up, up to a certain point."

After talking to the judge, Huff called the hospital. Arrangements for the body's release to the Johnsons had already been made. "The Department of Social Services had actually authorized the release of her body without an autopsy," Huff explained. "It was unbelievable. If I hadn't made the call when I did, the body would have been released before anyone could do anything." Much of the credit went to the hospital, he said, because the doctors there were concerned about letting the body get away unexamined. They had no authority to prevent Joyce's remains from being returned to the family, and they wanted someone to stop the release.

What Huff remembered happening next concerned not Joyce but her older brother, Christopher. "The grandparents were doing everything in their power, and the Johnson family in general doing everything they could, to get physical custody of the little boy. They had a lawyer in Marshall who was helping them with that. They were literally trying to get a court order, so that was my next plan of attack, to try to stop that." Huff filed a motion for the Madison County Department of Social Services to take custody of Christopher and place him in foster care. He ran across the street from his office to the courthouse in Marshall to file the papers. "I got in just as the doors were closing for the day. That was how touch-and-go it was. It's like a horror story. The SBI literally had to take the boy and put him someplace where he couldn't be found."

The next day, Judge Philip Ginn granted Huff's motion for protection. "If I had not been on the scene at the time Richard Johnson's daughter was murdered," Huff said, "and if I had not grown up around here and been educated in who the players were and how things worked, then I would not have known what to do to see that the little girl's murder was properly investigated and the evidence was gathered for the prosecution. He probably would have gotten away with it."

Doctors ordered an autopsy the same day. It was conducted at the Asheville hospital. Nonetheless, Sheriff Ponder told the local newspaper that the case was not under investigation. This did not keep Richard Johnson from calling E. Y. regularly about the results of the autopsy in the days that followed, Johnson later testified.

On July 4, 1984, after receiving the preliminary autopsy report, which found the death a homicide, Ponder arrested Johnson for the murder of his daughter and put him in the Madison County Jail. Judge

Ginn ordered Johnson held without bond. On August 20, he was indicted for first-degree murder and was again denied bail.

It was around this time, while Johnson was still being held in the jail, that he met Ed Walker, who had just been arrested for Nancy Morgan's murder. The Johnson case involved some of the same people who would be caught up in Walker's trial the next year: District Attorney Tom Rusher, Assistant District Attorney James Baker, Sheriff Ponder, Steve Huff, Chief Medical Examiner Page Hudson, and Bill Guillet and Charlie Chambers, two SBI agents in western North Carolina. In a county the size of Madison, it was not unusual to assemble the same cast of characters in the same courtroom for different cases.

≡≡

In late August, several days after his indictment, Richard Johnson filed a startling affidavit with superior-court judge Charles C. Lamm Jr. He asked to fire his court-appointed attorney, Eldridge Leake, saying he would defend himself. Asserting his innocence of the murder, Johnson requested a polygraph test. He wrote that, when it came time for the trial, he intended to accept the first twelve prospective jurors called, that he would call no witnesses and not testify himself, and that he would not appeal if he was convicted.

Tom Rusher's assistant, James Baker, told reporters, "I've never seen a defendant make such a bizarre motion." Baker thought the affidavit might be an act of desperation. "He wants to get out of jail, but we're not going to let him proceed with sheer folly like this. The state is serious about its case, and we are going to try it properly."

Seeing Johnson's action in much the same way, the judge ordered him to Raleigh for a psychiatric evaluation at the state mental hospital—where Johnny Waldroup would be sent in 1985 before testifying against Ed Walker. Personnel there found him competent to stand trial.

Richard Johnson, represented by Leake, was arraigned on October 4 and pleaded not guilty. The prosecutor, Rusher, knowing well the ties between Richard's father and Sheriff E. Y. Ponder, the vagaries of Madison County juries, and the Ponders' influence on them, moved successfully to choose the panel from neighboring Buncombe County and to have jurors bused to and from Marshall each day.

The trial began on Monday, December 3, 1984. Rusher opened by telling jurors that Johnson had "used a little five-year-old girl as a pawn, a tool, as a means of getting back at his wife."

Christopher Johnson, now nearly twelve, took the stand as an early witness for the prosecution. He testified that on the morning his sister died, she had seemed unwell. Their father went to the refrigerator, took out a bottle of "medicine," and gave the girl a teaspoonful of white liquid. Then he told the boy to look after his sister while he went into town. Within minutes, Joyce became violently ill, retching and foaming at the mouth. She soon became incoherent and ultimately lay down on the bed and stopped moving. To the boy, the substance "smelled like some kind of bug poison."

The prosecutor called Page Hudson, the state's chief medical examiner, to help explain the fact that little insecticide was found in the victim's body during the autopsy, after the physicians' extensive treatment to purge the poison and save the girl's life. What hadn't been washed out, Hudson said, had broken down chemically.

On Wednesday, December 5, Richard Johnson was the first witness for the defense. In a preemptive move, his attorney had the defendant go through his criminal record in Madison County and surrounding jurisdictions. The list was confined to guilty pleas—his charges had never before gone to juries—and excluded a much longer list of cases in which Johnson was arrested but charges were dropped. One of the latter was the episode in Hot Springs at the movie theater refurbished by Frank Breckenridge and his community youngsters. Leake was also able to conceal from jurors the fact that one of the guilty pleas, for destroying private property, had been reduced from arson. Despite admitting to the long list of crimes, Johnson said he had "never done anything or threatened to do anything to my family."

Under Rusher's cross-examination, Johnson testified that Brenda had left him six or seven times in the course of their marriage—three times for someone in Tennessee and once for someone in Weaverville, in Buncombe County. But he denied Rusher's accusation that he had called the town clerk of Weaverville and identified himself as a Madison County deputy sheriff in order to locate Brenda. He admitted that during fights he had given her "love taps" that sent her to a shelter for battered women. As for why he had checked in with Sheriff Ponder about the autopsy results, Johnson said, "Up till today, I still talk to him for different reasons." Seemingly frustrated by his inability to shake Johnson's story, Rusher ratcheted up his questions about Joyce's death. "You thought she would just hump over and die when you gave her that poison, didn't you?" But Johnson was not rattled.

Altogether during the three-day trial, the two sides called more than thirty witnesses before the defense rested that Wednesday. The jury began deliberating just after two o'clock the next afternoon. By four forty-five, with the weather turning foul, Judge Lamm called the jurors in and told them he was going to send them back to Asheville earlier than usual because the roads were beginning to ice. One of the jurors, however, asked a court officer to inform the judge that they thought they could reach a verdict if they could deliberate another fifteen minutes. Lamm agreed to let them continue. While they were out, the judge, sensing that feelings might be running high over the verdict, ordered the nearly full courtroom cleared. Sheriff Ponder then had his deputies search each person before permitting everyone back in. Just after five, the jury returned. The foreman handed Lamm the guilty verdict.

The judge said that the jury would consider the penalty phase of the trial, including a possible death sentence, the following morning. But when the court reconvened, Lamm cited a recent state-court decision strictly defining what constituted an "especially heinous and cruel" killing. Lamm ruled that he would not direct the jury to consider sentencing Richard Johnson to death. Rusher objected, but the judge then sentenced Johnson to life in prison. Johnson subsequently appealed, in part because the jury had not been instructed that it could find him guilty of lesser offenses, on the theory that his daughter had died as a result of negligence or accident. He also contended that he should have been provided with a medical expert to assist in his defense.

The North Carolina Supreme Court upheld his conviction in 1986.

When I went looking for him about another murder in the late 1990s, Richard Johnson was in the Yancey Correctional Center, a medium-security facility one county over from Madison, well into his sentence for killing his daughter.

21

In May 1998, I made plans to try to interview Richard Johnson. It would be best, I decided, not to let him know why I was coming, so I made no mention of Nancy Morgan and gave him only twenty-four hours' notice of my interest in visiting. As much as possible, I wanted to avoid the rich southern Appalachian tradition of spinning tall tales for gullible outsiders.

The prison, outside the town of Burnsville, on the banks of the Cane River, was primarily a road camp. The fifty other inmates usually worked outside during the day, doing highway maintenance under armed supervision. At night, the men slept in their shorts in bunk beds in two open, crowded dormitories, which was still preferable to some of the closed facilities they had come from. True, the windows were barred, but they allowed a view and the sounds of passing cars and the river's coursing water. For those not working on the roads, the recreation yard was open all day. The prison also had several TV rooms and a canteen for candy and toiletries. The chaplain occasionally showed movie tapes in his office.

The food wasn't bad either. Inmates had their own garden, which provided fresh vegetables, and local church people came in to prepare their meals, served in generous portions. On the other hand, the facility had its dehumanizing aspects: There were no partitions between the communal toilets, and female guards watched the men as they showered. Richard Johnson had regular visits from his mother and his son, Christopher. Considering the different places where he had been incarcerated, he felt he had it made at the Yancey County unit.

The fenced facility had a watchtower at its entrance. After parking in the gravel lot, I put my car keys into a bucket lowered by the guard, but I was not searched as I entered through a modular structure. Inside, I was taken to a common room to wait for Johnson.

As he shuffled in, he looked like a defeated man. By then in his fifties, with more than a dozen years behind bars, he had a beefy build, hazel eyes, a close-cropped fringe of white hair, and a scar on his right cheek. He wore a green prison-issue cap, a white T-shirt, khaki pants, and a slightly quizzical look. He wasn't sure why I was there, just as I intended.

After little in the way of preliminaries, I told him I was interested in knowing about the kidnapping and murder of Nancy Morgan. Johnson didn't hesitate. He began to narrate an account of the event in an eerie fashion, mostly in the third person, as if he had been an observer rather than a participant. Four other men had been involved, he said, three of them from Hot Springs and one from Shelton Laurel.

That Sunday afternoon, as Nancy drove from Shelton Laurel to Ed Walker's for dinner, Johnson and his friends had parked their two cars at the French Broad River just outside Hot Springs. "We were sitting on the edge of the bridge, drinking beer," he said. They recognized

Nancy and were still there when she drove back early Monday morning.

The men followed in the two cars, boxing Nancy in at a wide place on Highway 25-70 outside town and flicking their headlights off and on, in a sign of distress, until she stopped. "She wanted to know what the problem was," Johnson said. One of the men held up a .25 caliber pistol and ordered her to the passenger side. "She was tied up in the vehicle," Johnson recounted.

The abductors then drove the three cars across the state line to Greene County, Tennessee. Johnson remembered, "She tried to pay them to let her go, to contact her parents for money. She offered to leave and not return. She was a young, inexperienced lady who was scared as hell, would be the way I would describe it. Maybe she thought she could talk her way out of it. . . . She had enough sense to know she would have gotten hurt faster if she had tried to run. The odds weren't in her favor."

One reason Johnson and the others waylaid Nancy, he said, was that they had abducted women before, raped them, and gotten away with it. But the VISTA abduction was a crime of a different magnitude, something even an out-of-office sheriff recognized. To E. Y. Ponder, attacking a vulnerable local woman was one thing; abducting a federal volunteer was another. Johnson said that on Tuesday, Ponder contacted him with the message that if he and his friends had Nancy, they had better turn her loose.

On Tuesday night, Nancy, still alive, was brought back to Madison County, to an area near Hot Springs called Mill Ridge, near Tanyard Gap. Johnson would not be pinned down about where the assaults on Nancy took place, and he insisted that he himself was not responsible for her death. But what happened to the woman was horrific, he admitted. "She was all to pieces. She was abused in every way possible. She got violent. They were getting rough with her. She was crying, hollering, everything else." How Nancy died late Tuesday night, perhaps when she lost consciousness or struggled to free herself from the nylon rope when the men left her for a while, Johnson wouldn't say. At about one-thirty Wednesday morning, the men drove her car, with the body in it, to the wooded area of Tanyard Gap where it was later found.

Despite all my experience on the criminal beat, I had no strong sense of whether or not Johnson was telling the truth. His blank look and impassive face throughout the conversation told me nothing. Certainly, he could be playing me. But what did he have to gain by the admission? Clearly, it would be in my interest to wrap up the Nancy Morgan story in just such a neat red ribbon, but I knew from experience that a character like Johnson could recant his confession—which prison officials did not allow me to record, in any event—in a heartbeat.

Still, the scenario fit with what I knew about the case. And Johnson made other admissions that corresponded to stories people had told me about him. Just as most residents of the town assumed, he said he had set fire to the Hot Springs Hotel, called in the alarm, and then returned to watch it burn. He said he set the fire because the owner kept turning down offers to buy it.

Unprompted, Johnson said that while he and Ed Walker were in the Madison County Jail in 1984, Sheriff Ponder asked him to eavesdrop on the Florida man and his visitors, including his attorney, Joe Huff. Johnson expressed remorse for all the trouble he had caused Walker and said that if there was any way to apologize to him, he would be willing to do so.

Ed Walker didn't kill Nancy Morgan, he said.

22

John Morgan, Nancy's older brother, was not surprised by Johnson's account of his sister's actions when I told him about it. "She was in many ways naïve. She would not have had the same fear that some people might have had. That's because she attributed her own good motives to other people."

I thought Ed Walker would be ecstatic when he heard about the confession. Instead, he was cautious. "It's very plausible," he allowed, when we got together in Florida to review Johnson's story. The scenario was one of many his defense team had considered at the time of his trial, but this was the first time he had heard it stated as fact. "The time frame fits. The description is vivid. It makes total sense. Nothing in there would not fit perfectly with what I know about all of this."

Yet some elements of Johnson's story left him unimpressed as definitive evidence. "The time that he claims she was stopped, boxed in, fits absolutely perfectly. But anybody could say that because of knowing the newspaper accounts at the time." Similarly, everything Johnson said about the men hanging around at the bridge would have been known to anyone then living in Hot Springs. "That's nothing special to know. It doesn't indicate truth or not-truth either way."

One part of the account began to persuade him, though. He recalled that the night before Nancy's body was found, the VISTA workers had made an exhaustive search for the missing woman between Shelton Laurel and Hot Springs. "It is inconceivable to me," Walker said, "that that car could have been in the location where it was found at the time we did that search and we could have overlooked it. That's always been my contention. That one little thing he says about returning the car there after midnight or sometime in the wee hours of the day the body was found fits absolutely perfectly." Walker believed Johnson could not have fabricated that detail. "I'm not sure he would have known the times that we did the search. That's a really important element in everything he says."

At the end of our prison interview, Johnson had said he wanted to tell his story directly to Ed Walker, in person and in greater detail than he was willing to offer me. He wanted to apologize for causing the Florida man so much suffering by remaining silent about his role in Nancy's death, and for acting as E. Y. Ponder's jailhouse snitch. I told the inmate I would communicate the offer, but in light of Walker's anguish over my investigation of the case, and his reluctance to speak with me, I thought there was little chance he would accept.

Again, Walker, who once claimed investigative skills, surprised me. "I would be very interested in hearing his total story," he wrote in an e-mail. "It is going to be tough to figure out his truthfulness. Everything I know about the whole matter has been printed in the newspapers. . . . I have no 'hidden' information that could be used to determine his truthfulness." Anyone, he thought, could spin a tale from public knowledge, filling in the unknowns as they wished. Walker wrote, "I would like to be included in a prison interview with Richard. I can get time off and could fly to the prison. I would only like to talk to Richard in your presence."

A long series of rambling letters from Johnson to me followed, full of spelling and grammatical errors, with frequent assertions that he was not guilty of murdering his daughter, Joyce. The letters varied in tone from wheedling to demanding, a tendency familiar to me from the time I taught writing in a federal prison. Johnson tended to avoid addressing directly my follow-up questions about the exact circumstances of Nancy's sexual assault and death—things that could be verified. Some of what he wrote was bizarre. For example, he said he could pick out Nancy's underwear from twenty-five different examples if they were brought to the prison.

Still avoiding any specific reference to what *he* did after Nancy was kidnapped, he dropped some more tidbits. He said Nancy had talked about Walker while the men were holding her. "She kept asking us not to hurt Ed or another [VISTA] lady that was there with them" in Madison County. Johnson mentioned a two-tone Chevy—a 1955 or 1956 model—that might have been in the Bluff area that Sunday night.

In one letter, he included a note to Walker: "I know you didn't hurt her in any way. And she did drive her own car through Hot Springs about 30 minutes after you say she left your house. You may have the right to hate me and I understand that." The other young men with him, Johnson claimed—despite what he had told me earlier—"hadn't known or ever saw Nancy before that night." He added that Johnny Waldroup, the key witness against Walker in 1985, couldn't have driven Nancy's car, as he testified.

The part of the Mill Ridge area where the men brought Nancy when they returned to Madison County, Johnson said, was actually a section of Sheriff Roy Roberts's old farm, on the land that he sold to the United States Forest Service. Two old houses and a barn stood on the property behind a metal gate that could be locked. Somehow, Johnson had a key. If true, that might explain why none of the searchers saw

Nancy's car there. Also, Johnson said, a forest-service car was sometimes parked in the area, so Nancy's government Plymouth might have been overlooked.

Johnson implicated the sheriff, too, this time in more detail. "E. Y. Ponder knew without question what happened to Nancy Morgan within hours, not days or weeks," he wrote. "Not for sure, but they's a good chance they may have knowed before she was found. They was a call made to his house from Hot Springs . . . [and] he did talk with a SBI man for sure the next day."

Richard Johnson said he didn't want to be drawn into any "war" with Ponder—E. Y. was still alive, though now long out of office. Yet he dangled hints of what he knew about other unsavory doings in the county under the Ponders. These included Johnny Waldroup's playing informer; the disappearance of confiscated marijuana from the county jail in the 1970s; tampering with ballot boxes; and a break-in at the district attorney's office in Marshall when the Ponders were under federal investigation for vote fraud.

Johnson wrote that he would agree to only one more meeting. "I would be able to go into more details but not now. . . . [I] will some day, if needed, just like what was in her ears and . . . her female parts." He hinted that any soil found on Nancy's underwear would prove to be different from dirt in the area of Tanyard Gap, where the body was found.

In his letters, Johnson addressed other matters related to Nancy's killing, expanding on what he had told me at the prison. He wrote that he and the other men had raped a number of women in the area, including local married women while their husbands were away. But most of their victims, he said, were outsiders, such as hikers on the Appalachian Trail, which runs through Hot Springs and Tanyard Gap. He noted that one such woman was "turned loose," but had she accused the men, "we would have made her out a liar."

Johnson claimed that "at one time we had a set of keys" to a local retreat "and could go in the rooms late at night and would be with the ladies before they knew anyone was in their room and that's why a lot stopped staying there without someone with them. So again, Nancy wasn't the only one. The only thing different was too many people had to have answers because of who she worked for and who owned the car she was driving and her being on Forest Service land."

Ed Walker was encouraged by Johnson's additional material. He was starting to be persuaded but was still a long way from convinced. "There are several bits of information in there which I believe add credibility to what he's saying," Walker said in an interview after going over the letters. "The accounts that I have of the sequence of events and who might have been involved, which were uncovered during the 1985 investigation—our own investigation—fit perfectly. And I'm not sure that's in the public record anywhere. I'm not sure how Richard Johnson could have gotten that information without personal knowledge. But it's hard to tell from a cold, written record, not being able to see his body language or [hear] his voice tone. It's almost too credible. I can't find anything in there that's wrong."

Walker repeated his belief that if the killer was a local person, the only way the story would come out would be if he were near death or for some other reason needed "to clear his conscience to meet Jesus. Knowing the culture as I know it, and knowing how religion is woven into the fabric of that culture, I honestly believe that's how it would come. If there are local people that have real knowledge, it will be revealed as a deathbed confession to clear their conscience and pave their way to heaven."

Walker thought that Johnson, unless he was telling the truth, was unlikely to remember so many details that fit the known facts of the killing "without slipping up someplace." Still, he couldn't help despairing that the case would ever be resolved. "I mean, this is never going to close, for God's sake."

23

Even though he had confirmed the prison meeting the night before, I wasn't sure Ed Walker, who had flown from Florida to Asheville, would actually show up at the Yancey Correctional Center on October 5, 1998, to meet Richard Johnson. But less than two minutes after I got out of my car at nine-thirty that morning, Walker pulled up and waved. We dropped our car keys into the bucket, the guard in the tower pulled it up, and the door to the fence, topped with razor wire, slid open.

Inside a modular building, the Reverend Claude Vess introduced himself as the prison chaplain. He explained that Johnson had asked him to sit in, which I said was fine with me. We were shown into the same sparsely furnished room where I had met Johnson the first time. As late-morning sun shone through a row of windows, Johnson walked in, wearing a knit shirt with the number 480 stenciled on it. He sat on one side of the long table, across from me. Ed Walker sat on the same side as Johnson, at the other end, his metal folding chair turned so he faced the inmate across the top of the one chair that separated them. Chaplain Vess sat across from Walker.

"It was a weird feeling," Walker recalled afterward. His reaction was remarkably similar to when he was jailed in Madison County in 1984. "First of all, it was not what I expected—the more stereotypical institutional prison. This was like going to someone's house and just sitting around and talking. Nobody was searched.... [We] just kind of walked in. 'Hello guys,' you know, slap on the back, and people just kind of wander around." He had expected something more sterile, a "more Hollywood-type prison.... I actually had visions of sitting on one side of a glass window talking through a telephone."

Having heard Johnson's story before, I planned to let Walker carry the conversation. Again, no recording was allowed. Walker began on a discordant note, appearing close to tears and slapping his left hand against the table. "No good can come of this book," he said, getting what already promised to be a strange interview off to what I thought was a rocky start. Unknown to me, Walker had come with his own strategy for the interview. Later, he told me, "I didn't want to react to anything. I didn't want to ask questions. I wanted him to talk, and when he started talking about people, you started asking questions about those people. I just kind of wanted to lay back and let him do a monologue because I was afraid if I asked any question or said anything, it might be leading, and I didn't want to lead him in any manner."

Picking up on Walker's reluctance, I began the interrogation as delicately as I could. Again, Johnson seemed eager to talk about his role in Nancy's abduction. In this second telling, he included more details and narrated the story mostly in the first person.

Johnson began by acknowledging that, when he had spoken with me the first time and later in his letters, "I left my part out." Turning to me and then to Walker, he said, "This man had nothing to do with it."

As in the earlier interview, he gave a disjointed, sometimes contradictory account, but he named each of the other men he said was involved, including his best friend, Henry Sharpe, who was still free. He believed the others had since died, disappeared, or were in prison.

After Nancy passed the group at the bridge en route to Walker's house, he said, the men followed her up the mountain in a two-tone Chevy—apparently the one he had hinted about in a letter—and another car, leaving Johnson's own red Mercury behind. "They got behind her below the Bluff community to see where she was going." One of the other men followed her in his Chevy. If Nancy had mistakenly driven into a dead end—and if it had not been daylight—the abduction would have happened then, Johnson said.

Hours later, after Nancy passed them on her way home, the men jumped in their vehicles. At the first wide part of the road, they boxed in her Plymouth. "I came up behind her. [The other driver] was in front of her," Johnson said.

In this account, Johnson said he himself pointed the gun at Nancy, and the other men drove her car. And he made no mention of an excursion into Tennessee, as he had in his earlier version. He did admit that he had keys to the forest-service gate at the old Roy Roberts farm on Mill Ridge. Nancy, he said, "wasn't the only lady they took up there."

The mention of the car that followed Nancy into Bluff struck a chord with Walker, who recalled a neighbor's remarking that he had seen a strange vehicle in the community around that time. Soon, Walker was hooked. "When he started naming names," he said, "I tried to keep a poker face and just be nonchalant about it so he'd keep talking. I didn't want to make him think he'd impressed me or shocked me in any way. I just wanted him to talk. I wanted to keep it on a personal level because I figured if you made it personal, he'd say more."

Walker also wanted to separate himself from me in Johnson's eyes. "When we started out, I wanted to make it really clear that I wasn't there as your buddy," he later told me. "I was there as somebody who had an interest in this because of what was going to happen to me because of all of this, and that's why I intentionally sat on the opposite side of the table from you." He didn't want to give Johnson the appearance that he and I had been collaborating for any length of time. Instead, he wanted to convey that he didn't "really like this son of a bitch"—meaning me—but that he and Johnson "together gotta go through it." Walker said he thought that if he came in as my friend or collaborator, "then it would be us against them again," and Johnson, who might have a hidden agenda, would be uncooperative.

Nancy was not bound during the initial sexual attack, Johnson said. "The first round, the one I was involved in, she was free." Then he and another of the men left the area, he claimed. Johnson said he had picked up the discarded cord used to hogtie Nancy in the trash of Hot Springs Elementary School.

When it was light the Monday morning after the abduction, the men examined Nancy's handbag and wallet and found her government identification. "That's when everybody panicked," Johnson said. Their intention then was to hold the VISTA worker long enough to decide what to do with her, to figure out a way to get rid of her without going to federal prison. Nancy, meanwhile, tried to talk her way out of the situation. "She said she would pay us and she wouldn't say anything." Another of the group, a man from Shelton Laurel, tried to get her to write a note to Diana Buzzard, unaware that Nancy's fellow VISTA had already moved away. It would have been in Nancy's interest to let them think there was someone back in Shelton Laurel who would miss her.

At this point, Walker became more engaged in Johnson's story. "Richard's account of Nancy's behavior is perfectly in character with Nancy's intellect," he wrote to me afterward. "I believe she would have behaved exactly as Richard described. His account suggests that Nancy was frightened, but she 'kept her cool' and tried to talk her way out of her dilemma. She was too smart to fight—she would have tried to persuade these boys to let her go, bribe them, promise them anything."

He noted that Johnson never mentioned anything about Nancy's becoming hysterical or screaming, something the inmate had indeed described during my first interview with him. "I don't recall any factual evidence indicating that she was slapped, hit, or physically abused in any manner except for the gross sexual abuse and the abrasions on her elbows from being dragged," Walker wrote. If she had become hysterical, if she had spat on or bitten her attackers or resisted violently in any other way, Walker thought, "these boys would have slapped her around and bruised her up pretty badly. There is no evidence of any such physical abuse."

Johnson said he and another man left and returned to Mill Ridge three different times, first at ten o'clock Monday morning and then several times on Tuesday.

"The Mill Ridge location, Richard's detailed description of the location, and Richard's account of Nancy's treatment there were all very significant," Walker believed. "His graphic, detailed accounts explain another factual detail that has, to my best recollection, never been revealed in printed accounts of the events in 1970 or 1984, and it was never mentioned, as I recall, at the trial."

The detail was that if Nancy had in fact been tied up and held captive in an old barn, that would account for the abrasions on her elbows. "Every old barn I have ever been in [in] Madison County," Walker said, "had a floor of hard-packed claylike soil of the region with rocks and stones embedded in it."

An SBI report on the nylon cord used to tie Nancy had found stains on it described as having been made by "dirty oil or grease" and "reddish brown modeling clay," along with strands of "yellowish brown animal hair." This seemed to jibe with Johnson's account of Nancy's being carried or dragged by her legs with her elbows on the ground, and with her having been raped on a barn floor.

On his second visit the Tuesday after the kidnapping, Johnson said, he took Nancy some chili or soup in a Styrofoam cup from the café in Hot Springs. Almost without thinking, I asked if there might have been carrots in the food, recalling Walker's insistence that he had not served Nancy the carrots that medical examiners found in her stomach. As I asked the question, Walker shot me a glare, as if I were leading the witness. Johnson said only that the food might have contained carrots.

Continuing his story, Johnson said he came and went several more times from where Nancy was being held, as did the other abductors. That Tuesday night, Johnson said, while he was at home in Hot Springs to eat and establish an alibi, "E. Y. called me. He said, 'If you know anything about that girl, you better get her to where she can be found.'" In that call, or what might have been a second call, Ponder directly asked Johnson if he knew anything about Nancy, and Johnson said it was a possibility. "E. Y. said, 'They better find that girl pretty soon, because all hell's getting ready to break loose.'" The problem was that "we were afraid to bring her off the mountain," Johnson said.

Nancy's death, which occurred sometime after his second visit on Tuesday, was unintentional, Johnson maintained. "No one forced her into choking like that." He would not speculate about how it occurred, insisting he was not present when Nancy died. "I won't add nothing I don't know for a fact."

The men eventually drove the Plymouth, with Nancy's body inside, a short distance and abandoned it early Wednesday morning in another part of Tanyard Gap.

Throughout the search and the subsequent investigation in 1970, an SBI agent kept E. Y. Ponder informed, Johnson said. During Walker's 1985 trial, Johnson tried to tell his story to the sheriff. "E. Y.'s heard my story several times," he said. But the sheriff always told him to stay away from the investigation.

Digressing, Johnson revealed more about his relationship with the Ponders. At one point, he explained in detail how he had burned down the Hot Springs Hotel. After setting the fire, he got into the city night officer's police car and reported it by radio, he said. He later learned that while committing the arson, he had left footprints, and that the sheriff had made a mold at the scene. Shortly afterward, Johnson got a phone call. "E. Y. told me to get rid of the damn shoes."

Johnson said he played both sides of the political system in order to curry favor with the law. On another occasion, a Hot Springs city official who was E. Y.'s niece was suspected of embezzlement. Johnson said he broke into city hall to steal records, which were then turned over to Republican prosecutors.

"There ain't a thing in my life that I'm proud of, that I've accomplished," Johnson said. "At one time, I could have been anything I wanted to be. I could have followed in my father's footsteps. . . . I was E. Y.'s right-hand man in that end of the county. . . . I've helped E. Y. fingerprint places I've broken into."

I asked if he felt sorry for what he had done and for what happened to Nancy Morgan.

"Yeah," he admitted, his vacant eyes downcast, his hands slightly trembling.

Ashamed?

"Yeah. If my story gets me time, then I deserve it."

≡≡

After the interview, Ed Walker left the correctional center, but I hung around and paid a visit to the facility's acting superintendent, Robert Cooper. We met in his office, a small paneled and carpeted room around the corner from the interview room in the same portable structure. His future in the prison was so uncertain that Cooper had no business cards on his desk, only a soft pack of Winstons. A soft-spoken man who exuded reasonableness, he was willing to talk about Johnson, whose life sentence carried a twenty-year minimum but did not exclude the possibility of parole.

Since Johnson had come to the road camp in 1986, Cooper said, his only visitors had been his mother and son. Around the facility, Johnson did general maintenance, changing light bulbs and working on the ground crew. Noting Johnson's many disciplinary offenses, Cooper said he was "one of the hardest people that I have been able to deal with." Cooper described him as antisocial but not aggressive, prone to verbal confrontations but not violent ones. He said Johnson was not considered an escape risk.

Later, at lunch, I discussed the interview with Walker, who still had some doubts. He admitted that Johnson's story made sense. "All the puzzle pieces are revealed, they all fit, and a complete, clear picture emerges." However, Walker still wondered about Johnson's motive in offering his confession. "I don't know that I really believe that he's doing a repentance thing. Yet I think there's a hidden agenda somewhere."

Whatever Walker's doubts, I urged him to phone Joe Huff, which he did from a pay phone on the street in Mars Hill. His attorney from 1985, by this time over eighty, invited both of us to visit. The scene at his house was intense and, for me, saddening. Huff's focus and memory came and went, and Walker seemed overcome with emotion.

At one point, Walker knelt in front of the lawyer. "I owe you my life," he said, weeping, trying to convey the depth of his gratitude.

Joe Huff, his mind suddenly clear, gripped the arms of his easy chair and tried to reassure his most famous client. Walker shouldn't be troubled by what people might say about him, the old lawyer insisted, his voice rising.

A few minutes later, the tension drained and the pair drifted into reminiscences. "I didn't like you when we met," Walker told the lawyer. "You were cocky."

Huff relived his moment of glory, reflecting on the Ponder dimension of the trial. "You were lucky to come out of it," he told Walker. "They hated my guts, and I hated theirs. It's the most important case I ever tried."

Walker lamented that, regardless of what Johnson had confessed to that day, half the people in Madison County would always think he was guilty of killing Nancy Morgan.

"You don't listen to them," Huff admonished him vehemently, his mind again sharp.

After the cathartic meeting, Walker seemed anguished. "What a dilemma," he wrote me later. "I now know what happened, but I have no one to share it with. Joe Huff, the only person in the whole world I could really talk about this in intimate detail with, seems to have little more than a few connected, lucid moments in the course of a conversation."

Early on, Walker had held low expectations about Johnson's confession. "I figured he was going to start out with this story and it was just going to fall apart." Somehow, it would turn out that Johnson simply thought it in his best interest "to make up another damned tale. And it didn't turn out that way. It didn't turn out that way."

In the weeks following the second interview, Walker wanted to talk more about it with me. He seemed to be convincing himself of the truth of Johnson's account. "I believe the guy," he told me. "I think he was plausible. . . . He named names. They rolled right off his tongue. They're people dead and alive." These were people Walker said he could identify as part of the bad crowd in Hot Springs in 1970.

"I realize that I, of all people, want to believe this," he wrote, "but I'm telling you it's not just me wanting to believe it, it's hard to dispute what he says."

24

One afternoon in Orlando in March 1999, my son, Asher, came home from middle school, walked into the kitchen, and started at the sight of two unfamiliar middle-aged men sitting at our table. Dressed in white shirts and ties, jackets draped over the backs of their blond ladder-back chairs, they were leafing through stacks of papers, going back and forth to their brown accordion file. Open pizza boxes littered the counter, which normally would have been enough to draw the boy's attention. But the wide-eyed adolescent zeroed in on something else: Both men were wearing guns.

The two agents from the North Carolina State Bureau of Investigation assured Asher that nothing was amiss and went back to work, studying the material I had collected on the Nancy Morgan murder.

Several weeks before, I had met in Boone, North Carolina, with District Attorney Tom Rusher, who had prosecuted both Ed Walker and Richard Johnson. In the course of our two-hour interview, I revealed what I had learned about and from Richard Johnson. This was a clear departure from accepted journalistic practice. Had I been working on the story for a newspaper, I wouldn't have shared this information; I would have published first and let law enforcement pursue my findings later. But in a case this cold, I took a chance.

If the story of Nancy's life and death were a movie, a novel, or an episode in a television cop show, it would have ended soon after Richard Johnson's prison confessions. He would have pleaded guilty to some charge related to the VISTA worker's death and been sentenced for the crime, along with any surviving accomplices. But that didn't happen. This was real life, where truth can be complicated, messy, and elusive.

In general, journalists gather incriminating material and present it to the public, which includes authorities who may then act on it—or not. As an investigator, though, I was groping for concrete ways to determine if Johnson was telling the truth. The evidence, if it still existed, lay in the hands of the SBI, in the state medical examiner's archives, or with the FBI.

I located Charlie Chambers, the lead SBI investigator on the case in 1970, by now retired in Charlotte. At first, when I told him I had a confession and it wasn't from Ed Walker, he sounded relieved. "I knew it! I never liked Walker for it," he said, his testimony at the 1985 trial notwithstanding. "You don't know how much sleep has been lost over this case over the years. You wouldn't believe it." But his response to the news that the confession came from Richard Johnson was deflating. "Richard has lied to me so much," Chambers said. "He'd climb a tree backward before he'd tell the truth standing on the ground."

Chambers was amiable but resolute in declining to cooperate with me further without the approval of the SBI. Officials at the bureau's Raleigh headquarters refused to share any of their information on the murder case because they still considered it open. I also searched, initially without success, for the whereabouts of any of the surviving accomplices named by Johnson. Operating on my own, I felt I had taken the investigation as far as I could.

So when, at Rusher's suggestion, the two Asheville-based SBI agents, David Barnes and Bruce Jarvis, contacted me and asked if I would be willing to share my research on the case, I agreed. I offered them the opportunity to go through my material, including the FBI files I had acquired through the Freedom of Information Act, which they said they did not have. Ed Walker strongly disagreed with my decision; he thought I was wasting my time with Rusher and the SBI. "Proceed as you wish, but I think it is extremely counterproductive to share any information with them," he said.

I picked up Barnes and Jarvis at the private executive airport near downtown Orlando and drove them to my house. Oddly—to me— the agents seemed uninterested in the Richard Johnson scenario and remained focused on Ed Walker, despite his acquittal. I should have known better. After covering more than two dozen murder cases on both coasts, my experience strongly suggested that once law-enforcement officials settled on a suspect or a theory, they tended to refuse to be shaken from it.

The agents asked me nothing about Johnson's confessions but opined that they suspected the inmate had admitted to killing Nancy simply to elevate his status in prison from that of child murderer. Instead, they asked me questions about a green car with out-of-state license plates, apparently a reference to James Waldroup, Ed Walker's housemate in Bluff, who was absent at the time of the murder. Walker later confirmed that the car in question had been driven by James Waldroup, the Mars Hill College student, who had been in Georgia for a wedding that weekend.

I told Barnes and Jarvis that, in exchange for my cooperation, I hoped they would do some things that might prove or disprove Richard Johnson's story. Both Walker and I wanted the agents to find out if the fourteen sets of fingerprints taken from Nancy's car on the day her body was found were still on file with the SBI in Raleigh or the FBI in Washington. These could be compared with fingerprints on file for Richard Johnson and the four accomplices he had named, each of whom had an extensive arrest record.

I also asked the agents to determine once and for all if the physical evidence taken from Nancy's body was still being saved in Chapel Hill or Raleigh, as the current and former state medical examiners had told me. If so, I wanted them to make comparisons with Johnson's DNA and that of any of the surviving suspects they could locate and who would be willing to provide a sample. One court official who had attended Ed Walker's murder trial recalled medical testimony that the amount of semen recovered from Nancy's body suggested it had come from more than one man. For his part, Walker had told me several times he would be willing to provide a sample. Richard Johnson had offered to submit a DNA sample and to take a polygraph test as well.

Finally, I asked the agents to request from the FBI an unredacted version of the lengthy bureau file I had obtained through the Freedom of Information Act—normally a professional courtesy between law-enforcement agencies—and to share that information with me. They agreed to "consider" my requests, in the sympathetic but deceptively noncommittal way some law officers have. Again, my experience notwithstanding, I was naïve.

Barnes and Jarvis did pursue the investigation—for a while. Initial signs were promising. One of them told me they had visited Richard Johnson and had indeed administered a polygraph test. They found the results of both interview and polygraph ambiguous. But "we don't disbelieve him," Jarvis said in a telephone conversation. "At this point, it's a believable story."

In Virginia, the agents located one of the men Johnson had implicated. He agreed to take a polygraph test, which they said he passed. In their view, this cleared the suspect and cast serious doubt on Johnson's story. They gave me no word, however, regarding the fingerprints or the DNA. And instead of sending me an unexpurgated copy of the FBI file, which they could easily have requested from Washington, they sent me photocopies of news articles about the killing and the Walker trial, most of which I already had.

As time passed, the SBI agents apparently lost interest in the old case; in any event, they stopped responding to my inquiries. Ultimately, I figured they had decided not to pursue Johnson because they believed his confession to be false. They told me Johnson had once confessed to another murder—this one in eastern North Carolina—that they did not think was possible. In their view, he was an attention-seeking psychotic who cried wolf—or murder—too often. They remained convinced Ed Walker was the killer.

Walker was not surprised that the agents exerted little energy in following up Johnson's confession. He believed the SBI men had no real interest in solving the case. Their agendas, he said, were to protect themselves and to cover up the errors of the past. "It would be in their best interests to have Richard's story be completely discounted, and, as their track records clearly prove, they will not let truth or fact get in the way of their ambitions and agendas."

25

Looking back, if I hadn't been almost as impressed as my son by my visit from the SBI agents, my guard might have gone up immediately. From all the murder cases I had covered and read about, I should have remembered how resistant law-enforcement officials and prosecutors are to admitting they or their colleagues made a mistake. Instead, the SBI's brief surge of action on the Nancy Morgan case gave me hope. When the agents' interest wilted, I felt so disappointed and frustrated that for a while I considered giving up on the project.

But over the next few months, anger and determination replaced discouragement. I decided to go back over as much of the investigation as I could, challenging my own assumptions and, to the extent possible, forcing the authorities in North Carolina to do the same. Either they were wrong about who killed Nancy or I was. I intended to retrace my steps, go back to the central characters to probe their stories again, and try to track down witnesses and evidence that had so far eluded me.

First, with the help of Madison County's new young sheriff, John Ledford, I managed to locate Richard Johnson's pal Henry Sharpe, whom Johnson had implicated in the crime. Ledford knew all about Nancy's murder and was interested in anything that might at last break the case. He thought he knew where Sharpe was living, and he gave me the name of someone who might serve as a go-between in arranging an interview. It would be better, we agreed, for me rather than Ledford to talk to Sharpe, because I had no obligation to read the suspect his Miranda rights. But Ledford warned me that Sharpe's mental state was questionable. He had been shot several times in the head and was subject to strokes.

On the telephone, I told Sharpe's female companion I was researching a book about Hot Springs in the late 1960s and early 1970s—technically true—and Sharpe agreed to see me at his home in Woodfin, a town just outside Asheville. I found him, his partner, his grown son, and a friend from Hot Springs waiting for me on the wooden deck of Sharpe's manufactured house. After we moved inside, I joined Sharpe on a couch with a crocheted afghan draped over the back. Despite the stories I had heard about him, he seemed not at all threatening. Now in his sixties, he was dressed in a white T-shirt, khaki slacks, and a black cap, which he took off to show me one of the indentations in his forehead where he had been shot.

When I began asking Sharpe about his memories of Hot Springs and his friend Richard Johnson, he was initially wary but soon loosened up and shifted into storytelling mode. "Me and him ran together," Sharpe said. "We would stay out all night, running wild. We started setting buildings on fire there—nobody lived in them—just set them on fire." He told me that Johnson was "a mean fellow" who had been a bad influence on him. Describing himself as "a poor boy that had no money [and] stayed drunk all the time," he admitted, "I did stay in a lot of trouble. Whenever I got drunk, I was mean and just fought a lot."

It helped, he said, that his best friend's father could be depended on to pull strings. "Richard could do anything he wanted to do, and his daddy wouldn't bother him. Richard and I would do stuff, get in trouble, and Leroy, who was chief of police, would take us to Marshall, and Sheriff Ponder would drop the warrants on us." Remembering E. Y. as "a good feller," Sharpe said, "I would go down there to Marshall. He would put me in jail. Next morning, he would let me out, and I would catch a ride back to Hot Springs. Most of the time, he would have one of his deputies take me."

Gradually, I steered the conversation toward the murder of Nancy Morgan. On the day her body was discovered, Leroy Johnson was driving his son and Sharpe from the courthouse in Marshall, where they had appeared after their altercation with the VISTAS at the Hot Springs movie theater. Heading up the mountain, they noticed a law-enforcement vehicle on the shoulder and pulled in. Leroy went to see the body after telling the younger men to wait in the car.

I knew of no delicate way to ask Sharpe if he was involved in the murder. Richard Johnson, I told him, had admitted he had something to do with Nancy's death. Did he believe that?

"Sure don't, sure didn't," Sharpe said, although he acknowledged being in the group drinking beer that Sunday evening by the bridge at Hot Springs. "You see, now, Richard would lie a lot, but he didn't do nothing like that." Sharpe claimed the two men could have known nothing about the killing because they were running around together all that night. "He did not know she was dead when his daddy picked me and him up and drove us to the top of Hot Springs Mountain and seen this law sitting there. He pulled in, and we walked up there, and she was lying there dead."

Sharpe's vehement denial effectively ended the interview.

Later, I reminded myself that Sharpe could have been lying just as easily as Johnson. Not being in prison, perhaps he felt no similar compulsion to admit guilt. And even if it was true that he and Johnson were "running around together" at the time Nancy died and were ignorant of her death on the morning her body was found, it didn't mean the two hadn't taken part in her kidnapping and rape, along with the other men. Johnson's two confessions still struck me as genuine.

Keeping the momentum going, I launched another attempt to find the main witness against Ed Walker, Johnny Waldroup. This time, I contacted former sheriff Dedrick Brown, who told me I might find Waldroup in Cocke County, just across the Tennessee line—a place with a reputation for crime and corruption rivaling Madison County's. Twice, I visited the city hall, courthouse, and jail complex in the town of Newport, Tennessee, checking to see if Waldroup was incarcerated there. He wasn't. Twice, Sheriff Tunney Moore gave me the infamous witness's last known address. Each time, I found no one home.

On my third visit, in 1999, I met the new sheriff, D. C. Ramsey, who, in the relaxed way of law enforcement in the mountains, simply had Waldroup picked up from his home and brought to the sheriff's office to meet me.

Waldroup, in his late fifties, was by now a weathered man with heavily freckled arms and sparse red hair under his black cowboy hat. At first, he joshed with Ramsey, who admonished him to tell me the truth about Nancy's murder. Waldroup said he didn't want to talk in the office, so I drove him in my rented car back to his house for the interview. During the ride, he delivered a rambling monologue, complaining about his hearing and arthritis, his bad jobs and hard work. He spoke in a gravelly voice and had alcohol and tobacco on his breath.

When I pulled into the driveway, Waldroup said he wanted to do the interview in the car, not in his double-wide, tin-roofed mobile home along the river. Anxious and nervous, he looked away from me out the car's passenger-side window as he answered my questions. While we talked, he grew increasingly agitated, to the point that he was nearly

incoherent. He recalled well enough what had happened to him during
Joe Huff's cross-examination. "Made an ass out of me," he said bitterly.
"Said I'd sell my mother. And kindly fucked me up."

But the story he told of the killing was fundamentally different
from the account he had given on the witness stand at Ed Walker's
trial. I couldn't decide whether Waldroup had simply forgotten what
he originally told or whether he had come up with a more plausible account over the decades. In this version, too, he had spent Sunday night
at an Asheville motel. But now, he said he didn't return to Bluff until six
the next morning, when he saw Walker, soaking wet, sitting by himself
on his couch. The VISTA worker, Johnny said, had killed Nancy and
driven her alone in the government car to Tanyard Gap, stopping to fix
a flat tire and then leaving the body in the trunk, not on the backseat.
Then Walker returned on foot to Bluff in the rain and fog. Waldroup
said the VISTA worker threatened to kill him if he told what he had
seen and heard.

When I mentioned Richard Johnson and his Hot Springs friends
as possible suspects, it set Waldroup off. "That's wrong," he said hotly.
"That's bad wrong, dead wrong." The person responsible for Nancy
Morgan's death, he insisted, was Ed Walker. "That goddamn son of a
bitch is the one that killed her. That's all I know. . . . The murderer's
walking free, and it's Ed Walker." At that point, he stopped talking,
opened the car door, and stalked off.

By now, I had a group that claimed Ed Walker, not Richard Johnson, had killed Nancy Morgan, or at least that Johnson hadn't done it.
Johnny Waldroup insisted that Walker was the responsible party. Henry Sharpe was equally adamant that Johnson hadn't been involved. The
vehemence of Sharpe's and Waldroup's denials decidedly shook me.

Still, Walker's story of innocence and Johnson's of guilt seemed
plausible to me. Two members of the other camp, Sharpe and Waldroup, had a long history of being less than credible. But the other two

members, David Barnes and Bruce Jarvis, were respected SBI agents, even if I still chafed over what I saw as their failure to pursue all the evidence.

Unlike in a cold-case TV show, I couldn't script a definitive, plot-resolving flashback to reveal what actually happened to Nancy Morgan. Frustrated by the inconclusiveness of my interviews with Sharpe and Waldroup and troubled by the lingering doubts the SBI agents had raised, I began to weary of my trips to North Carolina. Every time I returned to Florida, I quickly became distracted by the exigencies of middle-class life. After 2000, I scaled back my week-long visits to Madison County from twice a year to once. I allowed myself to go slack on the case, weary of its twists and turns.

By 2009, approaching the fortieth anniversary of Nancy's death, I felt it was growing late for me to produce some resolution. I no longer saw her murder as a political assassination, but her thoughtless, sexually motivated killing demanded justice no less. I had to try one more time.

26

To finish the job of telling Nancy Morgan's story, I had to confront the SBI's skepticism and what I perceived as defensiveness on the part of law-enforcement officials in North Carolina. One failure in the investigation especially rankled: To my knowledge, no one at the SBI had ever asked for the DNA samples taken from the semen found in Nancy's body, in order to compare them with DNA from any of the suspects. Granted, DNA analysis in 1970 was in its infancy, but why hadn't anyone acted on this evidence either in 1984, when Ed Walker was arrested, or in 1999, after I reported Richard Johnson's confession? Did the samples still exist?

In 2009, I contacted North Carolina's state medical examiner, Dr. John Butts, who had helped me in the 1990s when I started the investigation in earnest. Butts, friendly and low-key, had been a year ahead of me at Duke. He had a sense of humor not uncommon among those in his line of work. When I met him at his office on the tenth floor of North Carolina Memorial Hospital in Chapel Hill, I noticed atop a filing cabinet a life-sized bronze skull wearing a blue and white Carolina baseball cap.

To my growing excitement, Butts confirmed that forensic material from Nancy's case had indeed been saved. Semen samples taken from vaginal and anal swabs had been placed on four slides preserved in white, translucent squares of paraffin. According to an evidence deposition form he showed me, the specimens had been turned over to the SBI on July 25, 2000—no doubt as a result of my persistent queries. Although the samples would never be available to me personally, I was reassured to know they still existed. But if the SBI had possessed the slides for the last nine years, why had it not performed tests to discover if any of the samples matched Richard Johnson's DNA? Or had it?

Next, I wanted to talk to Johnson again. I wondered if he would stand by his earlier confessions, and I hoped he might add some previously unmentioned detail that would at last confirm the truth of his story. But I feared he wouldn't talk to me at all. He might have decided that, having already served twenty-five years of his life sentence for killing his daughter, admitting involvement in the VISTA worker's death would extinguish any faint hope of his ever leaving prison.

My anxiety grew when two letters from Johnson arrived at my house after I left for North Carolina. My wife read them to me over the phone. Both were typically rambling. The inmate denied any involvement in the Nancy Morgan case and said he didn't want to meet with me.

I decided to ignore the letters and try to see him anyway. I located him in a secure facility outside Hickory, North Carolina, but before I could confirm a visit with him there, heart problems sent him to the medical unit at maximum-security Central Prison in Raleigh.

From Chapel Hill, I made the short drive to Raleigh, taking a chance on being able to see Johnson. By the time I arrived at the four-story prison, he was no longer in the medical-care unit but was housed in the diagnostic wing of the prison's hospital section. A guard there sent me to the first-floor visitors' entrance, where I requested a meeting. To my relief, Johnson's custodial officer called back to say that the inmate was on his way down.

Through the thick, scratched Plexiglas in the drab visitors' room, Johnson, wearing a brown prison uniform and a green baseball cap, looked dreadful. His weight had dropped from 250 pounds to 195, and his face looked drawn. Now sixty-one, he had four stents in his heart, he said, and was a candidate for open-heart surgery. Although he sometimes seemed vacant and distracted, he immediately began answering my questions about the abduction—to my surprise, without hesitation or any reference to the recent letters he had sent. He repeated the basic account he had given me twice before, and this time he did not object to my tape-recording the conversation, which was permitted at Central Prison.

Now, Johnson told me that one of the calls from E. Y. Ponder urging Nancy's return after the kidnapping had been to his father, Hot Springs police chief Leroy Johnson, who conveyed the message to Richard. "Fifteen times" over the years, he said, he had told E. Y. the true story of what happened, but Ponder "didn't want to believe it. He always wanted to believe that it happened at Walker's house."

Johnson still claimed he was not present when his friends drove Nancy's car to Tanyard Gap on Tuesday evening, but this time, he said, "I honestly believe they put her in the car alive." (In a subsequent letter, he explained that the last time he saw Nancy, she was alive, naked but unbound.) He was certain the others intended to leave her alive in the car, where she would soon be discovered. After all, he said, if they had wanted to cover up her death, they would have dressed her, put her behind the wheel of her car, and pushed it off some steep mountain shoulder, where it might never be found. If it was, people would have assumed she had fallen asleep at the wheel and driven over the edge.

None of the new details he offered added materially to the case against him—or so it seemed. But in fact, one apparent aside took on new significance by the end of my trip. Johnson mentioned that Donnie Gosnell, another of the men he said was involved in the assault, was never the same afterward. He drank, became morose, and finally shot himself to death while living in Jacksonville, Florida. I had heard earlier that Gosnell was dead, so I had made no effort to pursue further information about him. I would soon regret that I hadn't.

Toward the end of the interview, I asked Johnson what effect his confession might have on his prospects for being released from prison, especially since he had been turned down five times for parole. During his twenty-five years behind bars, he had accumulated seventy-eight infractions, for fighting, threats to officers, possession of weapons, and sexual offenses.

"All they could do is charge me," he said. "But I'm now doing life, and that's all I can do. So they can't give me no more time. It'd be a waste of the state's money."

Finally, I asked Johnson what he would say now to George Morgan, Nancy's brother, if he could speak to him.

He said his words would be, "I'm so sorry that it happened. Things just got out of hand. There ain't no good way to put it. It was all uncalled for. . . . Nancy Morgan does not leave my head and mind, and it is just like yesterday, and no way [of] calling it back or changing anything."

After getting up and walking away, he came back and asked me to say hello to Ed Walker.

Fortuitously, my interview with Johnson soon produced what I believed to be an important piece of corroborating information. It came after a short article appeared in the *Asheville Citizen-Times* on May 27, 2009, telling about my investigation of the Nancy Morgan case and mentioning my interest in an unnamed "Hot Springs man with a history of rape and arson" who was "in jail for having poisoned his daughter."

This was enough to prompt Richard Johnson's now-estranged son to contact me. Chris Johnson implicated his father in Nancy's sexual assault—and those of other women. "She wasn't the only one," the younger Johnson told me on the phone. "He raped another girl on Hot Springs Mountain" and was implicated in assaults on a number of other women in surrounding counties in North Carolina and Tennessee.

Chris Johnson said he had discovered this information while going through his grandmother's legal and personal papers after her death. He said he no longer had the documents, but he named one other woman he said had been hogtied and left on the mountainside.

Although the son believed the account of his father's involvement in Nancy's death, he said he could understand those who didn't: "He's the biggest liar in Madison County."

27

For me, the most persistent and troubling of all the loose ends in the case was the conclusion by SBI agents David Barnes and Bruce Jarvis that Richard Johnson's account of the abduction and rape was not credible. I wanted to confront them one more time, now that both men had retired after long and distinguished careers in law enforcement, and push for details about why they were so certain Ed Walker was responsible. I asked Sean Devereux, one of Asheville's most illustrious criminal defense attorneys, for help. Sean and I had been friends since meeting as Duke freshmen in the autumn of 1965. He agreed to arrange a meeting for me with the two agents, who still lived in the area.

That meeting took place around an oak conference table in Sean's office in his law firm's penthouse suite. Sean wore his usual lawyer's workday outfit—dark slacks, long-sleeved white shirt, tie, suit jacket hanging nearby. I wore the traditional journalist's uniform—twill slacks, blue button-down shirt, navy blazer. Barnes and Jarvis seemed dressed in character, too. Both retired men wore khaki slacks and knit polo shirts, Barnes's bearing the insignia of the FBI's national academy for law-enforcement training. The agents' white hair had thinned since they sat in my kitchen a decade before, and they remarked that I was noticeably grayer as well.

Barnes quickly took control of the interview, recounting the agents' efforts to pursue my leads in 1999 and 2000. He reiterated what he had told me in 2000—that the two had visited Johnson at the prison in Raleigh on April 11 that year. Johnson had repeated his confession for them, including the list of his alleged accomplices, and initialed a written statement that Jarvis took down.

Following their interview with Johnson, the agents said, they had located one of the men he named as an accomplice in the Nancy Morgan killing. Jackie Tweed, who was then living in Virginia, had a criminal history. On July 4, 1971, a year after Nancy's death, he and Hot Springs police chief Leroy Johnson, Richard's father, were involved in a celebrated shootout during a festival that brought three thousand people to the town. Tweed, in possession of a shotgun and having had too much to drink, became involved in an altercation with another man along the railroad tracks. In the course of breaking up the fight, Leroy Johnson gut-shot Tweed, who survived and received probation for his offense.

Accompanied by a Virginia State Police officer, Jarvis went to see Tweed at his home, but the man denied knowing anything about the killing. He willingly gave the two officers his fingerprints and three vials of blood for DNA testing. Neither the prints nor the DNA matched those in the SBI's possession, Barnes said. But to the best of Barnes's and my memories, it seemed that the agent's phone call to me in 2000 effectively ending the SBI's inquiry had come *before* the state medical examiner's office turned the forensic material over to the bureau that July. Therefore, Barnes could not be certain that the DNA samples from Nancy's body were ever compared with Tweed's. Jackie Tweed also submitted to a polygraph administered by a Virginia State Police examiner, and he passed, Jarvis said.

"When that part of [Richard Johnson's] story fell apart, we couldn't justify any further expense," Barnes told Sean and me. That included administering another polygraph to Johnson. Barnes said he had no doubt Johnson and his friends were hanging around the Hot Springs bridge the Sunday evening when Nancy drove to Ed Walker's. But that in itself proved nothing. Similarly, the agents insisted there was nothing in Johnson's account he could not have learned from reading newspaper accounts of the Walker trial or from Madison County jailhouse gossip.

Finally, the retired agents confirmed that much of the physical evidence from the case had been destroyed when the basement storage area of the SBI's old offices near the French Broad River had flooded sometime in the years before Ed Walker's trial.

I then shared with the SBI men a summary of my findings over the years, which I believed made the prosecution's case against Ed Walker implausible. My findings encompassed Johnny Waldroup's unreliability, the condition of Nancy's body, the persistent rumors of Richard Johnson's knowledge of the killing or involvement in it, Johnson's own confessions, and E. Y. Ponder's manipulation of the investigation.

Barnes and Jarvis responded by clinging to the Walker scenario, but their defense seemed pro forma. I wondered if they were just trying to protect the integrity of their SBI colleagues.

On at least one point, they agreed with me. Both agents were outspoken in their criticism of E. Y. Ponder. It was true, they said, that the late sheriff had made it almost impossible for outside investigators to operate in Madison County. "We didn't trust E. Y. as far as we could throw this building," Barnes said.

When they acknowledged in passing that they hadn't read the SBI's complete two-thousand-page case file on the murder, I looked at Sean. If my old Duke friend were a poker player, his "tell" would be a raised right eyebrow coupled with a sly smile, indicating extreme skepticism, if not downright disbelief. And there it was again.

After about two hours, the interview trailed off. We all rode the elevator to the lobby, where Sean and I said goodbye to the retired agents. The doors to the street had barely closed when Sean and I looked at each other for a silent moment. "Not much of an investigation," he said, echoing my own assessment of their work.

Barnes and Jarvis, too, must have come away from the meeting thinking they should have done more to follow up on the case. At nine the next morning, my cell phone rang at Elmer Hall's inn. Barnes wanted to explain some things and offer additional information gleaned from a subsequent review of the case file and from discussions in the car with Jarvis after the two left Sean's office.

First, he told me that—contrary to J. Edgar Hoover's marginal notes from 1970—between twenty and thirty Madison County men had been fingerprinted after Nancy's murder. But he would not say if the prints were still on file in Raleigh or with the FBI in Washington, D.C.

Those men fingerprinted included Richard Johnson and Henry Sharpe, and no matches were found with the prints taken from Nancy's car. Barnes cited this as further evidence that Johnson's account was false—rather than simply inconclusive. But he was unable to explain why, assuming Ed Walker was the killer, his prints weren't found on the steering wheel either, or anywhere inside the car. All he said was that generating usable latent prints could be difficult. (Johnson wrote me later that neither he nor Henry Sharpe nor Jackie Tweed was fingerprinted in the days after the murder. Months after Nancy's killing, he said, he had a perfunctory interview with an SBI agent, who accepted his story that he was home with his parents when the killing occurred. Without access to the SBI files, I had no way of determining which account was true.)

Barnes seemed most concerned that I thought he and Jarvis hadn't been interested in the material I showed them in 1999 and merely went through the motions. "We were interested," he insisted. Why else would two senior agents have used an SBI jet to come to Orlando, rather than asking a Florida investigator to do them a favor or sending a lower-level SBI agent on a commercial flight? "We didn't know who you were, or what your attitude was toward the police. We didn't trust you. We had to determine that you were not some kind of crank," he said. The agents had no vested interest, according to Barnes, in pinning responsibility for Nancy's murder on any particular suspect. "We really didn't care which way it went."

Later, during a phone call, I was stung when Barnes accused me of parsing the evidence in favor of Richard Johnson's account, just as I thought he and Jarvis were doing for Ed Walker. I wanted to show that I remained open to solid, evidence-based alternatives, that in the end I didn't care how the case unfolded. My client, insofar as I had one, was Nancy Morgan, not Ed Walker.

I asked Barnes if he would find out how many distinct semen samples were represented on the four slides held by the SBI lab for DNA testing. He e-mailed a response, saying, "Until the case is closed through a conviction, the SBI investigation will remain open. In that case, no information from the case or any evidence can be released." He added that Ed Walker was "no longer a suspect simply due to the fact that he was found not guilty by a jury."

Several months later, to my surprise, some action finally came through on the DNA samples—although not from the SBI. Following another article about the case in the Madison County weekly paper, the *News-Record and Sentinel*, Sheriff John Ledford and a local assistant district attorney, Gary Gavenus, revealed that they were reopening the case. They announced that the DNA samples—all of which, they said, came from a single individual—had been compared with Richard

Johnson's DNA but did not match. I was not terribly surprised. Forensic collection techniques were primitive in 1970, and forty years had passed since the samples were taken. Also, by Johnson's account, five men had taken part in the sexual assault over two days, so the absence of a match to just one of them did not, to my mind, rule him out as a suspect.

While the DNA result was disappointing, I didn't consider it definitive. In 2010, a scandal rocked the SBI's forensic lab, revealing faulty practices and questionable science dating back decades. This led to several resignations of top administrators.

My meeting with Barnes and Jarvis only deepened my skepticism about the SBI's investigation and its adherence to the Ed Walker theory. Bolstered by Chris Johnson's volunteered information about his father, I felt renewed confidence in the direction my investigation had taken—toward Richard Johnson—despite the lack of a DNA match. Now, the long-dead Donnie Gosnell was about to reenter the picture. He was the man Johnson had mentioned to me just weeks before at Central Prison as another of Nancy's abductors—the one who committed suicide.

The interview with the retired agents whetted Sean Devereux's interest in the case. A week later, he called me in Orlando to say he had located someone who had information to share, a man named Wade Edward "Eddie" Gosnell, a cousin of Donnie Gosnell's. Eddie Gosnell had grown up in Madison County and still lived there. Like Richard Johnson and Johnny Waldroup, he had frequently been in trouble with the law and just as frequently served as an informer for E. Y. Ponder.

I called Gosnell, who told me that the day Nancy's body was found, he had been visiting with the out-of-office sheriff. E. Y. drove with him to the crime scene, but because Gosnell was only sixteen, Ponder made him stay by the road while the lawman inspected the scene for about forty-five minutes.

More tantalizingly, Gosnell said that, the following year, he was drinking in a bar called Wolf Creek, across the Tennessee line, with two of his distant cousins, Blanche Gosnell and Donnie Gosnell, and Blanche's husband, Jackie Tweed. "We got to drinking, and Donnie said something about that girl getting killed in Hot Springs," Eddie Gosnell told me. "Donnie said something first, and then Jackie got to telling me about tying her up, that they didn't mean to kill her, that it was a sex thing." Over the years since then, Eddie said, "they told it more than once. I guess they trusted me back then."

I wanted Gosnell's story to be a conclusive piece of evidence that would wrap up the case. Yet caution dictated that I consider the source—a bar conversation related by a man with a shady past who had his own reputation for unreliability. Gosnell was currently a client of Sean's in a criminal case. Sean warned, "He might be telling you what you want to hear to keep me happy." He added that Gosnell had told him some "amazing stuff" over the preceding two years, some of which had turned out to be verifiably true and some of which remained murky. Although Gosnell had provided secondhand statements of Jackie Tweed's, Tweed himself denied involvement, passed a polygraph, and willingly gave fingerprints and blood samples that did not, in the mind of officials, tie him to the crime.

But even if it was not the bombshell I wanted, Gosnell's account came with no prior information or leading background from Sean or me that might have biased the telling. I could at least speculate, listening again to Richard Johnson's tape-recorded account, that Donnie Gosnell's guilt over the rape and murder had contributed to his eventual suicide.

28

By the middle of 2008, my family and friends persuaded me that fourteen years were long enough by any estimation to investigate Nancy Morgan's murder. So I pinned photographs of Nancy, maps of Madison County, and a Day-Glo orange "Elect E. Y. Ponder Sheriff" bumper sticker on the walls of my home office. I started listening to the music of Sheila Kay Adams, Bascom Lamar Lunsford, and other mountain singers on the CD player. And I began to write on weekends and on weeknights after work at the *Orlando Sentinel.* The process accelerated in July of that year, when I joined the masses of laid-off reporters in the "death-sizing" sweeping the newspaper industry.

Beginning to put Nancy's story into writing helped distill my unanswered questions and lingering doubts, prompting my final investigative trip to North Carolina in the spring of 2009. But even with the results of that trip, how was I to conclude this nonfiction tale when its loose ends and dangling clues marred a neat resolution? Excluding the possibility of a random act—say, a lone hitchhiker on the road at three in the morning who killed Nancy and simply walked home or out of the county—there remained two plausible but fundamentally different narratives of the murder: Richard Johnson's and E. Y. Ponder's, implicating Ed Walker.

A jury rejected the Ponder account in 1985, and nothing I had turned up since then made me think it was wrong. The prosecution's case was undermined by the unreliability of its chief witness, Johnny Waldroup. Equally important in the jurors' thinking was the condition of Nancy's body when it was found. It convinced them that she had died much later than early Monday morning, after her dinner with Walker, as the prosecutors and medical examiner argued. The later timing put Walker out of the frame.

I acknowledge that my research and my opinion might be colored by the fact that, although I have never thought of Ed Walker as a friend, we do share many of the values of our sixties generation. Given my cultural and economic background, he is someone I can identify with much more readily than I can with Richard Johnson, a man of the same generation but of a different class and culture and of vastly different values. But taking such possible bias into account and looking as objectively as possible at the evidence—or essentially the lack of persuasive evidence against Walker—I remain convinced of his innocence.

Rejecting the Ed Walker scenario propels me to Richard Johnson's version, or some variation of it. I have come to believe that Johnson and his friends, or at least people he knew, hijacked Nancy as she drove past Hot Springs on her way home early that Monday morning. The VISTA worker's death was the result of a rape that, like most such assaults in the United States, began as a crime of opportunity. It was carried out by local thugs, the sort of violence-prone young men, already petty criminals, who can disrupt otherwise decent communities anywhere—aimless drinkers with too much testosterone and no place to expend it. Nancy Morgan was not kidnapped, raped, and killed because she was liberal or loose, but because she was a vulnerable female. Any other young woman from outside Madison County—an Appalachian Trail hiker, a tourist—could have suffered a similar fate.

Early Monday morning, I believe, they drove Nancy around the county and perhaps into Tennessee. Later that day, they brought her to the old farm on Mill Ridge, where they took turns raping her. The men came and went for the next thirty-six hours, at least once feeding Nancy some kind of food that included the carrots later found in her stomach. At some point late on Tuesday or early Wednesday, they hogtied her with the nylon cord, without intending to kill her. Either on Mill Ridge or in the backseat of her Plymouth, she struggled, pulling the portion of the cord around her neck and cutting off the flow of oxygen until she died. Some or all of the men drove her the short distance from Mill Ridge to the old logging road in Tanyard Gap, where her body was discovered Wednesday morning by Jimmy Lewis.

This conclusion fits the physical and anecdotal evidence I have gathered and evaluated. Although doubts persist about Johnson's credibility, his confession is plausible. The three versions he gave to me, while differing in some particulars, were fundamentally consistent with each other, and their details were consistent with the crime-scene evidence and testimony about the case. That meshes with the preponderance of forensic interpretation—such as it is—of the condition of the body, as well as with the numerous accounts in which residents said they drove by the site earlier and did not see her car.

Eddie Gosnell's claim that his cousin Donnie Gosnell and Jackie Tweed admitted their involvement in the crime tends to corroborate this account—to my mind, strongly. So does Chris Johnson's report of having found papers of his late grandmother's that implicated his father in this and other crimes. And even Henry Sharpe's admission that he spent the day drinking with Richard Johnson—despite his denial of any involvement in the abduction and killing—places him in proximity.

Admittedly, a certain symmetry balances the two most likely narratives. Each relies on the word of a pathological liar, Johnny Waldroup in the first case and Richard Johnson in the second. Waldroup, it seems to me—just as it seemed to the jury in 1985—stood to gain by lying about Ed Walker's culpability. Johnson, on the other hand, had little to gain, apart from more prison time, by confessing falsely, notwithstanding the SBI agents' claim that it might earn him enhanced status in prison. Confessing truthfully, by contrast, might have eased a guilty conscience as he neared the end of his life.

The public may never know the truth of either man's words, especially if the DNA samples in the custody of the North Carolina State Bureau of Investigation are never tested against the prime suspects other than Richard Johnson, as I suspect they have not been and will not be. Although still deeply distrustful of the SBI, Ed Walker agreed after my prodding to be tested by an independent laboratory, and to let it compare the results to those held by state investigators. However, the SBI—despite the cloud by then hanging over its lab—declined to permit such a comparison. Walker says he does not want to involve himself in any additional life-disrupting investigation. And since he is no longer legally a suspect, he cannot be compelled to supply a DNA sample.

The inconsistencies in each of the two versions recall my days covering murder trials. Sometimes small, nagging bits of information, seemingly irreconcilable—like whether Nancy was wearing slacks or shorts when she drove to Walker's house—never do add up. And yet, missing pieces or no, a jury is asked to render a verdict—and usually does. If I were a juror, I would vote to convict Richard Johnson, at least of kidnapping and involuntary manslaughter. The evidence supports that Nancy's death came at the hands of more than one individual. But the additional living parties whose names have come to light—Henry Sharpe and Jackie Tweed—strongly deny involvement.

Will the case of Nancy Morgan ever be officially resolved? I doubt it. For fifteen years, the staff at SBI headquarters in Raleigh steadfastly refused to respond to my queries or to pursue the evidence I uncovered. Even as I was completing the manuscript for this book, an assistant director of the SBI returned my call and said he would look into the case—and then never called back. It is widely believed in North Carolina that the SBI has a tendency to release information that reflects favorably on its work and keeps the rest secret.

Whichever account of the killing is accurate, I believe a force larger than a single man, or even five men, must share the blame. Nancy Morgan's murder took place in a political culture in Madison County in which people in authority turned blind eyes to the actions of young men like Richard Johnson, who repeatedly got away with similar rapes, as well as theft, arson, assault, and other crimes. And yet it must be said that such crimes take place every day in America, north and south, rural, urban, and suburban. Political corruption can contaminate justice anywhere. Madison County is no more insular and violence-prone than lots of other places.

While I uncovered no grand conspiracy aimed at terrorizing VISTA workers because they might threaten the economic order of Madison County, Sheriff E. Y. Ponder's style of law enforcement, based on his network of informers, allowed men like Johnny Waldroup and Richard Johnson to intimidate and terrorize their neighbors with impunity. What made Nancy's murder different from opportunistic rapes and murders elsewhere was a so-called legal establishment that protected such men, a corrupt system that let Nancy's killers go unpunished.

Few people know more about Madison County and its ways than Richard Dillingham. The craggy, hardscrabble folklorist, who worked his way through Mars Hill College and then studied at the leftist Highlander Research and Education Center near Knoxville, Tennessee, is one of the county's wise men, a man with a weakness for quoting

Shakespeare. He has devoted his adult life to young people and to his belief that mountain dance, music, and song all serve as means of psychological survival. For years, he served as the director of the Rural Life Museum at Mars Hill College.

Even today, more than forty years since her body was found near where he was working in the sun, Dillingham is still angry about Nancy Morgan's death. He knows well the unintended damage that well-meaning outsiders can do. "Those who sent her to Madison County were naïve and stupid," he says, sitting in a rocking chair in the museum's Montague Building, dressed in one of his trademark flannel shirts. "Any fool would know that a bright and wonderful visionary coming from a different background and different value system and even a different class shouldn't have been sent into an area like this without enormous preparations." Nancy should have been taught "how you work with people, how you're good neighbors, how the local value systems are layered, and how to really help people." He considers her death "a horrible waste. I do not think that we did her justice on our side in helping to prepare her to render service in this area."

Happily, much has changed in Madison County since 1970, when Nancy died and the antipoverty workers departed, and even since 1985, when Ed Walker was acquitted of murder. The old insularity and hostility toward outsiders are largely gone. New and consolidated schools, staffed by teachers no longer beholden to political patronage, have raised educational standards. New roads, airline connections, satellite television, and the Internet link Madison County ever more readily with the rest of the country and the world, easing the sense of isolation. The county commission recently debated the cost of making Wi-Fi available throughout Madison. Although hunger, poverty, and unemployment still exist in the county, its three main towns—Mars Hill, Marshall, and Hot Springs—have undergone minor renaissances. Thanks to cheap rents, Marshall is becoming a mini-Asheville, drawing artists and craftspeople to previously vacant storefronts. Increased foot traffic on the Appalachian Trial, which runs down Hot Springs's main street, has provided economic stimulus, including a great store for hikers. The Hot Springs Visitors' Center, which once occupied a parked red caboose in the middle of town, now has a new permanent building on the site. A newly completed stretch of Interstate 26, which links Columbia, South Carolina, and Columbus, Ohio, passes along the edge of Mars Hill.

These days, when enough rain falls, the old flatboats on the French Broad are just a memory; the river is now a highway for rafts and kayaks. In season, almost as many of the rafters' yellow school buses are on the road as buses ferrying local students.

Innkeeper Elmer Hall and his progressive environmental allies put together a coalition that saved Bluff Mountain from clear-cutting. They hold a music festival every year to commemorate their victory. By the turn of the century, Elmer and Sunnybank Inn had become legendary among Appalachian Trail thru-hikers, so much so that he and his place made a cameo appearance—as "Brad Baird," quirky proprietor of the "Cosmic Possum Hikers Hostel"—in Sharyn McCrumb's 2002 mountain novel, *The Songcatcher*. Some scenes in the 2012 movie *The Hunger Games* were shot in Madison County five miles from Marshall at a site that stood in for the woods outside "District 12."

Best of all, the Ponder permissiveness in law enforcement is long gone, thanks to subsequent county sheriffs, from Republican Dedrick Brown to Democrat John Ledford. Sordid, meaningless crimes will no doubt continue to happen in Madison County as they do everywhere, but I like to think that a new regime of law enforcement—and the demands of local citizens—will not permit them, like Nancy Morgan's killing, to become unfinished business.

Fiction writers from Vicki Lane to Ron Rash to Wiley Cash continue to mine Madison County's rich, dark history and culture. Charles

Frazier's 2011 novel, *Nightwoods*, set in a town like Hot Springs, features a character who in some ways resembles Richard Johnson. Academics from Piedmont universities have begun buying and restoring second homes in the county. At least one has established a writers' retreat.

≡≡

Nancy Morgan's death continues to exert an effect on those whose lives she touched, like Mount Vernon High School classmate Donn Garvey Jr., who went on to become a public defender and insurance investigator. In early 2011, something triggered an anxiety episode regarding Nancy's death. "I don't know why, but I wanted to do something for Nancy. I thought about her every day." Garvey began calling local and state law-enforcement officials in the Madison County area to ask about the case, then traveled to North Carolina to contact people face to face. Ultimately, he felt he was being brushed off. He wasn't making any progress in solving the crime, despite his professional skills.

Finally, Garvey turned to his Catholic faith. "I arranged for a mass to be said for Nancy, and I wanted it to be on the anniversary of her death, June 17. I was there in St. Andrew the Apostle Church on June 17, 2011, in Mars Hill, where the priest said a mass for the dead for Nancy Morgan, and her name was loudly proclaimed amid those mountains. It was more emotional for me than I thought. . . . For reasons unknown to me, I think of Nancy a lot. I am happy to do so. It's not a haunting, more like an abiding friendship with someone far away."

Constant through all the economic and political changes in Madison County is the rugged grandeur of the mountains and the French Broad River. It impresses visitors and newcomers who continue to settle, just as it is a continuing source of love for those whose ancestors—Revolutionary War veterans walking south to claim their land grants—settled the hollers generations ago.

I am—as I was when I began the search for justice for Nancy Morgan decades ago, and as I will always be—an outsider, a flatlander, someone from "off" and "away." And yet, in my dark quest, I have come to love Madison County's land and its people.

Epilogue

In 2009, I had lunch with Ed Walker, whom I hadn't seen for years. We met at an Italian restaurant near my home, and I almost didn't recognize him. He was tanned, relaxed, and upbeat, his hair thinner but still mostly brown. Retired from his old job, he had a new one he liked, involving travel. Walker acknowledged that he had mellowed over the years and had largely put the murder trial behind him. He and his daughter had even held a ceremonial bonfire and destroyed all his files on the case. Smiling, he said that, were I approaching him for the first time that day, pressuring him to talk about the case, he would simply tell me to go fuck myself.

Nonetheless, he believed he had made the right decision in cooperating with me fifteen years earlier. He still felt a sense of being let down: "After all this effort, I don't feel like I won a thing. This will forever be a no-win situation for me." But he added, "I'm grateful I got on the train that was leaving, rather than standing in front of it."

He has now disappeared and no longer responds to my e-mails.

Joe Huff, Walker's defender, practiced law for another decade after the acquittal, until his family, friends, and colleagues, recognizing his increasing mental lapses, persuaded him to withdraw from practice. He died in 2002. A black-and-white portrait of him hangs on the wall at the front of the Madison County courtroom, to the left of the judge's bench.

Dropping by Mars Hill Baptist Church, which adjoins the college campus, I met the pastor who conducted Huff's funeral. He directed me to the attorney's grave, in the congregation's burial place on a hilltop, just across a small valley from the church. Huff lies beneath a large granite rectangle inscribed with the family name. The plot, among those of the Ponders, is in a grove of trees. As the preacher told me, the courtroom lion has the best view in the cemetery, bathed in breezes and looking directly across to the church. I stood for a few moments and silently apologized for taking so long to finish my work.

George Penland is gone, too, but his wonderful emporium remains, although his widow, Barbara, who sat on the Ed Walker jury, has consolidated the merchandise to mostly clothing. Customers pass no more produce in baskets outside the entrance.

E. Y. Ponder and his brother Zeno have died. Ironically, the Ponder clan in the new century has returned to high places in Madison County, though in a much transformed way. In 2009, two members of the new generation sat on the county commission, a third was mayor of Marshall, and a fourth was director of the county elections board. But none of these public figures was an offspring of Zeno or E. Y. The cohesive Ponder machine long ago disappeared. In the 2012 election, Republicans regained control of the county commission for the first time in many years, by a one-vote margin. The new chairman is none other than former judge James Baker, the assistant prosecutor in the Ed Walker case.

Over time, and sometimes as a composite, the Ponder brothers have migrated from local lore to popular culture. In Madison County mystery writer Vicki Lane's 2008 novel, *In a Dark Season*, they appear as the "Holcombes." One of her characters observes that "the 'Holcombe machine' wasn't all bad. . . . If you were a citizen with a legitimate gripe, you could take it to the Holcombes and get a fair deal—as long as you were registered to the right party. . . . The Holcombes weren't reckoned to be overly greedy. . . . They just liked the power for its own sake, being the big men in the county." In February 2012, the "Bloody Ferlin" episode of the snarky animated series *Archer* on the FX cable network featured a corrupt West Virginia sheriff named E. Z. Ponder.

Tom Rusher, who prosecuted both Walker and Richard Johnson, is still listed on the Web as a prosecutor.

In 2009, county sheriff John Ledford was tapped for a state law-enforcement job in Raleigh.

Jeffrey Hammer, VISTA supervisor for North Carolina, became a bearded Orthodox rabbi and changed his first name to Yaakov. He is preparing to move from Washington, D.C., to Israel.

Richard Johnson remains in the North Carolina prison system and has little chance of parole. Johnny Waldroup lives in Tennessee.

On February 13, 2009, at Roseland Memorial Cemetery outside Baton Rouge, I stood in silence under a gray sky with Nancy Morgan's brother George before a flat, polished gray stone engraved with Nancy's name and dates but no epitaph. Neither of us spoke; neither of us cried. I knelt to brush away a few small brown leaves on the square slab. I was tempted to observe the Jewish custom of leaving a small stone on the granite, signifying that a visitor had come, but I did not, thinking it was not my place to impose my culture on hers.

George, once a touring rock-and-roll musician and today a burly engineer with grown children, told me later that after his sister's death, "Nancy was never spoken of" in the family. "There were no memorials.

The arrest and the trial did not provoke any dialogue either. I know I didn't like to mention her for fear of setting my mother off crying."

As for his feelings more recently, George said, "I feel a bit more at peace, though I don't know why. I feel bad about Ed Walker, who, presumably innocent, is almost as much a victim as Nancy. He's been through a living hell that he can never fully escape. Richard Johnson's story fits well with what I have imagined to have happened for all of these years. I've long thought that those responsible must hold little value for life and freedom, be it theirs or others.'"

Now, as a former community organizer inhabits the White House, it seems Nancy Morgan's VISTA work has come full circle in Madison County. Duke University has established a student-staffed summer program for young people in the Spring Creek area. The project has had its challenges, some of which would be familiar to the VISTAs and all those who went before. But those students are doing good.

In my own children, I see the qualities that fired Nancy Morgan.

The case isn't much talked about in Madison County nowadays. The only physical trace of Nancy left there is a plaque on the wall inside the late Glendora Cutshall's mobile home in Hoot Owl Hollow, next to the VISTA worker's old cabin in Shelton Laurel. Originally hung when the cabin became a clinic after Nancy's death, it reads, "In loving memory of Nancy Dean Morgan, a dedicated VISTA worker who lost her life on June 18, 1970, while helping the people of the Laurel Community."

At the bottom is a quotation Glendora provided to sum up Nancy's short life, a fragment apparently paraphrased from Luke 7:47: "She loved so well."

Acknowledgments

The more complex the book, I have found, the more people I call on to help me—and the more I have the privilege of thanking. My greatest regret in this regard is that in the time it has taken to research, write, and rewrite this story, a number of those who helped make it possible did not live to see it in print, especially Joe Huff, Zeno and E. Y. Ponder, Glendora Cutshall, Page Hudson, Evelyn Underwood, and George Penland. As my evangelical friends like to say, sometimes things happen "in God's time."

A number of people helped me find my way in shaping the narrative: Jane Kepp, Peggy Payne, Laurel Goldman, and Rob Waters. And the two Steves, Kirk and Hoffius, together my late-innings Maxwell Perkins (if I may). Also at John F. Blair, Carolyn Sakowski, Trisina Dickerson, Debbie Hampton, and Angela Harwood. And Rob Gringle, who urged me to submit the manuscript to Blair.

My trusted circle of volunteer readers consisted of old hands—Rusty Wright, Clay Steinman, the Reverend Ernest Bennett—as well as some new ones—friends and neighbors Nancy Adler-Crowell, JoJo Dey, and Dr. Stan Sujka and enthusiastic supporters Marc and Jill Schwartz. I especially thank my great late-in-life friend and lunch companion, Dr. Norman Wall.

Former *Orlando Sentinel* colleagues Lorraine O'Connell (my old editor, who read several drafts), Barry Glenn (Internet wizard and editor again at *Orlando* magazine), Nancy Pate, and Greg Dawson also provided assistance and guidance. David Dobson, my longtime editor at Westminster John Knox, was generous in reading a manuscript that was destined for another publisher. Fergus Bordewich provided some much-needed editorial tough love. Sian Hunter was extremely encouraging at a critical moment. I also thank my longtime publicist, Kelly Hughes of DeChant-Hughes & Associates.

Nancy Morgan's family and friends, particularly George Morgan, Kristin Johnson, and Marty Tesoriero, were more than generous with their recollections.

Old Duke and Durham-area friends (and some new ones) were sources of both concrete help and emotional support. These included former Duke archivist Bill King; Bob Carney and B. Jeanne Davis, now in Baton Rouge; Georgeann Eubanks, for a perfect sentence in the perfect place, and a great critique; and Dale and Diane Pahl, who were gracious hosts in Durham. Others who aided my cause were Victor Strandberg, the late Reynolds Price, Sean Devereux, Ross Spears, Jake Phelps, Ann Bushyhead, John Valentine, Tom Campbell (shop at The Regulator Bookshop!), Bob Ashley, Alan Ray (my Duke roomie), Jean Cary, Karen Sindelar, Ross Spears, Jacquelyn Dowd Hall, and Elizabeth Tornquist (thanks for lunch; eat at Watts Grocery!).

In Stokes County, I thank my mentor and *New York Times* rabbi Wayne King and Paula Duggan, dear friends, generous hilltop hosts, and caregivers after my accident; in Weaverville, Yvette Wessel (for the great dinner); and in Winston-Salem, John Ehle (for the history lesson).

I am indebted to the research and library staff in Maitland, Florida, my home branch. In the libraries of Madison County, North Carolina, I thank the staff at the Hot Springs branch and Peggy Goforth and her colleagues at the Marshall branch. I also thank Holly MacKenzie at the *Asheville Citizen-Times*. Matt Bumgarner provided some excellent information on obscure points of North Carolina history. Thanks also go to my good friend across the water and fellow ink-stained wretch Stephen Bates (and his family). And to Phyllis Tickle at the Farm at Lucy, who has forgotten as much about the southern mountains as I will ever learn.

In Madison County, those who provided vital information included Richard Dillingham, Harley Jolley, Sheila Kay Adams, Jonathan Austin, Jerry Plemmons, Vicki Lane, former sheriff John Ledford, former sheriff Dedrick Brown, George Peery, Rob Neufeld, and Ann Ryder, who helped with Shelton family history, among other things. Particularly helpful was Pat Franklin, despite her misgivings about me and her affection and admiration for E. Y. Ponder.

Despite knowing that his handling of the Ed Walker trial was not the finest hour of his professional career, and that my portrayal of the proceedings would reflect that, Tom Rusher was extremely insightful and forthcoming—to a point. He hinted several times there was yet relevant material about the case that he could not share.

I am also indebted to Lisa Edmondson, who transcribed my interviews in two states and never gave up hope that I would finish, and to the helpful and friendly gang at the Winter Park Office Depot.

Frank Stasio, host of WUNC-FM's *The State of Things*, graciously supported this book and was kind enough to interview me at critical points in the process.

For nearly twenty years, my agent, Gail Hochman, listened patiently but with skepticism to my talk about Nancy Morgan's murder. She frequently reminded me that, while it seemed a good story in summary, "execution is everything." In the end, she kept her promise: "You write it, I'll read it."

And of course, my family has my gratitude: my wife, Sallie; son, Asher; daughter, Liza, who heroically saved my files when a tornado sent a huge oak tree crashing through my home office; and brother, Paul, who provided incisive and occasionally merciless suggestions. My mother-in-law, Charlotte Brown, has been steadfast in her support of all our family's endeavors, including this one.

Note on Sources and Methodology

Murder stories—in fact and in fiction—have exercised a durable hold on the American imagination. For at least seventy-five years, social scientists, reviewers, and mystery writers have struggled to explain the genre's enduring appeal. Psychiatrist Fredric Wertham, best known for his controversial theory that comic books lead to violent behavior, was more perceptive when he wrote that a murder case, especially if it comes to trial, can throw "a searchlight on the society in which it occurs, and we become aware of a fixed moment in social history." Decades later, Marilyn Stasio, longtime mystery reviewer for the *New York Times*, had a similar take. The goal of any true-crime writer, she observed, is "to use a murder investigation as a portal to a wider world," providing historical and political context.

Any study of Madison County begins with three books: *The French Broad* (Rinehart, 1955), by Wilma Dykeman; *The Kingdom of Madison: A Southern Mountain Fastness and Its People* (University of North

Carolina Press, 1973), by Manly Wade Wellman; and *Victims: A True Story of the Civil War* (University of Tennessee Press, 1981), by Phillip Shaw Paludan. Also valuable is *Bushwhackers: The Civil War in North Carolina—The Mountains* (John F. Blair, Publisher, 1988), by William R. Trotter.

In a larger sense, Harry Caudill's *Night Comes to the Cumberlands: A Biography of a Depressed Region* (Little Brown, 1963) and Horace Kephart's *Our Southern Highlanders: A Narrative of Adventure in the Southern Highlands and a Study of Life Among the Mountaineers* (University of Tennessee Press, 1976) remain the standards for understanding the southern Appalachians. Also worthwhile is the chapter on Zeno Ponder in *They Love a Man in the Country: Saints and Sinners in the South* (Peachtree Publishers, 1989), by Billy Bowles and Remer Tyson.

Fiction set along the western North Carolina–East Tennessee border—especially books by Thomas Wolfe, John Ehle, Sharyn McCrumb (the Ballad series in particular), Ron Rash, Vicki Lane, and the early Cormac McCarthy—fills in the gaps, capturing the atmosphere of the place and suggesting the motivations of the human hearts residing there.

After completing the first draft of this manuscript, I read other books that, given their parallels to my own, I found especially helpful in the editing and rewriting process. These were *Blood Done Sign My Name* (Three Rivers Press, 2004), by Timothy Tyson, and *American Taboo: A Murder in the Peace Corps* (HarperCollins, 2004), by Philip Weiss. Most recently, I profited from my reading of *Cemetery John: The Undiscovered Mastermind Behind the Lindbergh Kidnapping* (Overlook Hardcover, 2012), by Robert Zorn. I recommend them all.

On one research visit to Madison County, I listened in my car to a tape of James Elroy's *My Dark Places*, an account of his ultimately futile attempt to find his mother's killer. Elroy's intimidating, high-octane prose served as a reminder of how difficult and frustrating investigating an old murder can be.

I made ample use of the contemporaneous work of journalists who covered the murder of Nancy Morgan in 1970 and the trials of Richard Johnson in 1984 and Ed Walker in 1985. The reporting included stories from the *News-Record* of Madison County (Elizabeth Squire, Robert Koenig), the *Citizen and Times* of Asheville (Steve Morris, Jay Hensley, Lewis Green, Paul Clark), the *Charlotte Observer*, the Associated Press (Roger Jolley), United Press International, the *Baton Rouge Advocate* (Kenneth Dixon), the *Sarasota Herald Tribune* (Mary Williams), and especially stories by Kerry Gruson of the *News & Observer* of Raleigh. As often as possible, I tried to cite them in the text without disrupting the narrative.

I attempted to be as methodical and fair-minded as possible in my research. Over the course of twenty years, I conducted more than fifty interviews, most of them face to face but some on the telephone or via e-mail, in half a dozen cities outside Madison County and North Carolina. Despite the accepted conventions of true-crime writing, I resisted as much as possible attempts to reconstruct from my imagination any of the thoughts or events portrayed in this book. If I wrote that someone was thinking something, it was most often because that was what he or she told me.

Index